KU-248-912

NOTES ON A FOREIGN COUNTRY

Notes on a Foreign Country

Suzy Hansen

corsair

CORSAIR

First published in the US in 2017 by Farrar, Straus and Giroux
First published in Great Britain in 2018 by Corsair

Portions of this book originally appeared, in different form, in *The New York Times Magazine*, *The New Republic*, *The National*, *Bloomberg Businessweek*, *Bookforum*, *Newsweek*, the *London Review of Books*, *The New York Observer*, *The Baffler*, *The American Scholar*, and publications of the Institute of Current World Affairs.

1 3 5 7 9 10 8 6 4 2

Copyright © 2017 by Suzy Hansen

The moral right of the author has been asserted.

All rights reserved.
No part of this publication may be reproduced, stored in a
retrieval system, or transmitted, in any form or by any means, without
the prior permission in writing of the publisher, nor be otherwise circulated
in any form of binding or cover other than that in which it is published
and without a similar condition including this condition being
imposed on the subsequent purchaser.

A CIP catalogue record for this book
is available from the British Library.

Designed by Richard Oriolo

HB ISBN: 978-1-4721-5389-0

Printed and bound in Great Britain by
Clays Ltd, St Ives plc

Papers used by Corsair are from well-managed forests
and other responsible sources.

LONDON BOROUGH OF SUTTON LIBRARY SERVICE (SUT)	
30119 028 251 72 8	
Askews & Holts	Jan-2018
070.4332	

To my family,

who let me go,

and to P & M,

who told me to write

The pretensions of virtue are as offensive to God
as the pretensions of power.

—REINHOLD NIEBUHR

A woman—the statue of a woman
lifting in one hand a rag called liberty by
a document called history, and with the other
hand suffocating a child called Earth.

—ADONIS, "A GRAVE FOR NEW YORK" (1971), TRANSLATED BY
   SALMA KHADRA JAYYUSI

Some are guilty, while all are responsible.

—ABRAHAM JOSHUA HESCHEL

CONTENTS

CONTENTS

NOTES ON A FOREIGN COUNTRY

INTRODUCTION

It is still not clear if the United States—a country formed in great measure by those who have themselves escaped vast catastrophes, famines, dictatorships, persecution—it is far from certain that the men and women of this nation so full of hope and tolerance, will be able to feel that same empathy towards the other outcast members of our species.

—ARIEL DORFMAN

A FTER I HAD LIVED in Turkey for seven years, I visited a town called Soma, where two months earlier, a coal-mine fire had killed 301 men. Soma was located in western Turkey, slightly inland from the coastal city of Izmir, and to get there, my friend and I took a ferry from Istanbul to a town across the Sea of Marmara and rented a car. It was Ramadan then, and summer, and the townspeople, most of them observant and fasting for the holiday, moved slowly, as if they had been drugged. We stopped to eat cheese *pide* on benches by the seaside and watched shipping tankers as big and menacing as mountains glide too close to the shore. Women in head scarves strolled along the water, their children spinning away from and back to them like boomerangs skirting the pavement. I remembered how, when I first moved to the country, I had been surprised that someone wearing a head scarf would want to hang out at the beach. Everything surprised me then.

Turkey was a pleasant place to drive, its smooth roads lined with honey stands and olive oil kiosks and extremely tempting signs for Kangal puppy farms. (Kangals, native to Turkey, were sheep-guarding dogs that fought off wolves, so seeing them in innocent puppy form was like seeing a child before a lifetime of hard labor.) The Turkish highways, and the factories and depots that dominated them, always felt strangely like the East Coast of the United States. The entire country—even Istanbul—was not nearly as exotic as most people expected; it was not exotic anymore to me at all. By then I would also wonder whether the western Anatolian roads might have looked familiar because the Americans funded much of Turkey's postwar reconstruction with Marshall Plan money, everything from its roads to its schools to its military bases. As we drove, I had that disconcerting sense of déjà vu that I often had when traveling through foreign countries, as if I had been there before.

We were heading to Soma to research an article for a magazine, but the catastrophe disturbed me for reasons beyond journalistic curiosity. After the fire, the prime minister, Recep Tayyip Erdoğan, had visited Soma, and many townspeople protested in the streets because they blamed his government for the mine's dilapidated condition. One of the prime minister's men, wearing a dark, expensive suit, was photographed kicking a protestor on the ground. I remember thinking, *The government is kicking a citizen in the town where 301 men have just been killed and families are mourning.* The horror of Soma somehow seemed connected to the larger disintegration of the Middle East: the jihadists passing through Turkey on their way to Syria, the daily reports of terror, the disappearance of national borders. The question in my mind had stopped being how did it all fall apart, but when did it all begin.

Around that time, 2014, I noticed that both Western and Turkish friends had begun debating whether life had gotten better or worse. Terrorism, the refugee crisis, economic inequality, and climate change prompted these discussions, but sometimes the question came up around subjects more personal, such as the decision to have children. "Before, people had to worry about the bomb," a friend argued. "It was much worse fifty years ago." But I had the feeling now that our fears had become more personal, not of collective annihilation but of being torn limb from limb. Earlier that year, my friend, a photographer, offered me a print from her vast archive. There were photos of women in brightly printed dresses in Kenya, of teak trees in Bhutan, of a wedding couple dancing in India, and many were stunning, the sort of thing you might want on your wall. Yet I chose the stark, colorless desert photo of hundreds of tiny, faceless refugees sprawled across a hillside, crossing from Syria to Iraq, because in 2014, what other photo could you choose? It wasn't a time of dancing.

In Turkey, one of those still-modernizing, ascendant countries, life was supposed to have gotten better. The Soma accident—in which it became clear that human life in Turkey had been substantially devalued—was the moment, for me, when this myth of progress collapsed. *Is there life after Soma?* someone spray-painted on the sidewalk outside my apartment window. Like my photograph, the phrase captured the mood. I went to Soma because, like everyone, I wanted to understand how it happened. I was interested in all the gory technical aspects: the methane gases and the way coal burned and the standard safety rules for coal mining. I expected the reasons to be specific to Turkey, specific to that company and to that coal mine. I had in mind a scientific excavation, and instead, as seemed to be common in the years I lived abroad, the excavation I ended up with was historical.

WHEN WE ARRIVED, Soma was still heavy with tragedy. Signs hung from the buildings that said OUR PAIN IS IMMENSE. The hotel clerk at the Linyit Otel eyed us warily, frowning when we said we were journalists. He, like many shop owners and businessmen in Soma, didn't like the arrival of the foreigners, or the out-of-town activists, or the labor union radicals. "Don't get mixed up in this stuff," people would say to us, to one another. "Don't cause trouble."

My companion, Caner (pronounced Jahn-ehr), my oldest friend in

Turkey, made my coming to Soma much easier—not only because he was a man but because he was Turkish. Caner could also see things in Turkey that I could not; often he could see things about the world that I could not. After I wrote the story about Soma, for example, Caner helped with the fact-checking, which for this magazine, *The New York Times Magazine*, was especially rigorous, if not, at times, insane. (A fact-checker and I once spent a half hour debating the difference between *clubhouse* and *playhouse*.) Caner joked with some wonder about the zeal of American journalism and I explained that the obsessiveness was not only about legal issues but about maintaining a kind of objectivity. In other words, I said, the truth. He laughed at me: "But that attitude about your objectivity is political in and of itself."

Soma's main street looked like many Turkish towns: well maintained and orderly. Freshly tended flower beds flanked the roads, World War I memorials—good old Atatürk in bronze—shone as if newly polished, people scrubbed the pavement outside their shops. During the summer evenings in Soma, men, and sometimes women, gathered in one part of the central tea garden, and women and children, and sometimes men, gathered in the section called the family salon, and everyone would sit for hours smoking and gossiping past midnight. Soma wasn't a place where people went to bars, or rarely even out for dinner, but it had one fancy coffee shop with plush gray chairs, and one relatively expensive chain restaurant called Köfteci Ramiz. In these poor communities, there wasn't money for much else beyond the home, but Turkish families supported one another reflexively; a miner would work his whole life just to build two-room houses for his three sons. I was a thirty-six-year-old unmarried childless woman living thousands of miles away from her family, and had long subscribed to typical Western ideals of individualism. But with seven years of distance from New York I had come to believe that it was the Turkish family that held Turkey together, it was the strongest thing. Soma had a wholesome Mayberry quality to it, a sense of conservatism and distaste for provocation. All around the main square the watchful pillars of the community stood at the ready: the mosques, the men's teahouses, the mining company offices, the police, the ruling government's AK Party office, the mayor's hall, and, in the center of it all, in a large, black-reflector-windowed building, Türk-İş, the union that represented the coal miners of Soma.

We headed toward a narrow, pedestrianized street that was draped overhead with grapevines, which protected us from the miserable Aegean summer sun. A group of men gathered outside the office of DISK, a small, leftist labor union founded in the 1960s—one to which none of the miners belonged—that had set up shop in the aftermath of the disaster to teach the miners their rights. The union reps offered us plastic chairs, and some tea, and within minutes men began to sit down all around us, as if my appearance had been scheduled, which it had not.

Some of these men were the miners themselves. They had wizened faces, scrawny bodies as if undernourished, and bad teeth. I could tell which miners had been in the mine that day because they blinked constantly, as if unsure of where the next blow might come from. Turkey is a country where men are more important than women; sons more important than daughters; husbands more important than wives. In Turkey men were the warriors, the ones who had liberated the nation. It seemed suddenly that Turkey's men had been defeated, and if the state treated even the men this way, I thought, then everyone had been flayed of whatever had once protected them from the elements.

A MINER NAMED AHMET told me the story of what happened on May 13, 2014, the worst industrial accident in Turkey's ninety-year history. He and his wife, Tuğba, lived in a three-room stone house in a village of Soma called Kayrakaltı that was nestled amid cypress trees, fresh streams, and gentle, golden hills. Most of the 350 people of Kayrakaltı used to farm Turkey's famous Oriental tobacco, but around fifteen years ago, small farmers began to struggle, and so Ahmet went to work as a shearer-machine operator at a mine called Eynez, owned by Soma Holding.

When he arrived there that morning, Ahmet changed at his locker and put on his miner's coat and boots lined with iron, and then he and seven hundred men began their descent into the mine. *"Hadi! Hadi!"* (Come on! Come on!) the supervisors yelled, always with an eye to speed, to production. When the men changed shifts, they said to one another, *geçmiş olsun*, or get well soon, even *hakkını helal et*, which is a way Turks forgive one another, if they fear it is the last chance to do so. Ahmet's gallery was in one of the deepest parts of the mine, where the coal was extracted by a giant shearer machine manned by forty men. Ahmet worked all day, until suddenly, around 3:10 p.m., the shearer machine stopped working. The coal conveyor belts stopped working; the electricity stopped working; everything stopped working. The power had gone out. Only the lights on the miners' yellow helmets shone in the dark. Some electricians wearing gas masks arrived to tell them a cable exploded and a small fire had broken out. The miners in Ahmet's gallery figured it would take only half an hour before someone signaled it was safe to leave.

After the first hour passed, they began to worry. Why hadn't anyone come to talk to them? What was taking so long? Some of the men went to investigate what was happening, but they didn't come back. There were no safe rooms in the mine, so instead the miners began to pray. Black smoke was being pushed into their gallery, from both ends. All the miners had masks attached to their belts, but few had faith in them. The masks were old, and they were encrusted with coal dust. Some miners put them on and breathed in dirt. Some masks did not work at all.

The smoke began to burn the men's faces. Ahmet felt light-headed. Some knelt to the ground and stuck their faces in the mud, rubbing it over their skin, breathing it, slapping it into their mouths. They crouched and coughed, breathing that filthy coal-mine mud. Then men started to run, just to run anywhere. Ahmet saw Ibrahim, a portly engineer, sitting on the ground, his gas mask slung around his neck. He was breathing, but blood was coming out of his nose. A man named Ali sat under an old, useless conveyor belt. His body was cold. Ahmet realized what was happening: the miners were dying. He had no choice but to put on his mask and try to escape. As he passed, some of his friends turned toward him, arms stretched up, as if reaching for his hand.

When Ahmet climbed up a ladder to a second level, he saw bodies on a conveyer belt, as if the men had believed it would eventually carry them out. Other men lay on the ground. And near to them, also on the dirt floor, Ahmet saw dozens of rats that he knew were dead because their fangs were showing, their jaws open and stiff. *Here we are*, he thought, *the brotherhood of rats and men.*

Ahmet survived, eventually stumbling out of the mine into the klieg lights of rescue workers above. This was the image the country saw on television that day: thousands of families—fathers, mothers, wives, children, grandmothers—gendarmerie, state NGO rescue teams, police, and ambulance workers swarming around the entrances to the mine. People were screaming, pushing, crying, demanding answers. Every time a man emerged alive, coughing and black-faced, the crowd applauded. Every time a body was clumsily brought out on a stretcher, the great crowd wrenched and lurched forward, trying to see whether they could recognize anything at all: the cut of the hair, the curve of an eyebrow, the bend of a nose.

A MAN IN HIS SIXTIES named Tayfun, a representative from DISK, began telling the history of Soma. Most of the men had been tobacco farmers subsidized by and in service of the state-run company Tekel, which produced cigarettes popular among domestic consumers. For decades, Tekel sustained the farms of three million men and their families. Then, about forty years ago, the country opened its markets to foreign goods, including cigarettes. "We started to see on the streets your Parliaments there," said a miner, smirking and pointing at the Parliament in my hand.

In the 2000s, at the behest of the IMF, and in line with the ethos of privatization at the time, the Erdoğan government broke up Tekel, as they did so many state-run firms. The farmers lost their protection, and their jobs. "It happened step-by-step, it was slow," Tayfun said. "The farmers had hopes. They tried tomatoes. They tried cucumbers. But it wasn't enough. So the children of the farmers went into the mines."

In Soma, as in many places, the mines were run by a private company that sold all of its coal to the government for a low price. The government was also responsible for monitoring the mines' safety conditions. This codependent system made for zero accountability. The companies didn't care much when the ceilings of the mines had shoddy supports, or when the gas sensors, meant to detect methane and carbon monoxide, didn't work. Electric cables were old and hung haphazardly. There was no escape plan, or accident protocol, in the event of a fire.

The miners' working conditions were terrible, too. Their bosses punished them with enthusiasm, insulted them, yelled at them, even cursed their mothers and sisters. It was always those same words, *Hadi, hadi, hadi.* Come on, come on, come on. All day long, *hadi, hadi, hadi.* If a miner rested, he'd hear it again. If something went wrong, *hadi, hadi, hadi,* back to work. The bosses would do whatever it took to get the most production out of the miners, and production stopped for nothing.

"So the first two pillars of the tragedy were the state and the company," Tayfun continued, "and the triangle was completed with the union."

I was startled by this. "The union?"

Other men joined in enthusiastically.

"I bet they already know you are here!" one said.

"They have spies everywhere. If we talk to you, they will tell," said another.

"What do you mean they 'will tell'?" I asked. "Who will they tell?"

"They will tell the union."

"Not the company?"

"They are the same."

The miners' union with the black reflector windows, Türk-İş, had never advocated for better working conditions, or better pay, or even paid sick days for their miners. The miners were now convinced that everyone in the town was controlled by the union, which in turn meant the company, which in turn meant the government. The men called this thing the octopus.

"How did this union become this way?" I asked. "Was it always close to the state?"

"Of course," one man named Aydın said. Aydın had the manner of a historian. "It was an American-style union. It was founded in the early years of the Turkish Republic"—in the 1950s—"with the help of the United States." In other words, he suggested, this American influence, and America's own labor history, had helped to create a union that did not protect Turkish workers and whose negligence had led to the deaths of 301 men.

Aydın told me this and, later on that day, the entire history of the United States' and Turkey's workers, in a matter-of-fact tone. American influence usually was not invoked with particular venom or outrage, but merely as a fact of history. Most foreigners were not emotional about it. The only person suddenly emotional was the American, me, because of course for the American nothing about this was matter-of-fact. Americans are surprised by the direct relationship between their country and foreign ones because we don't acknowledge that America is an empire; it is impossible to understand a relationship if you are not aware you are in one. Those weeks in Soma, I heard about the way the United States had governed the world during the Cold War and after, and how its foreign policy shaped a course of history for Turkey that, even in small ways, led to the Soma tragedy. But of all the things I had discovered those days in that humble Turkish town, the resilience of my own innocence was the most terrifying.

As an adult I hadn't had a strong sense of what life should look like. I rarely imagined my wedding day, or the man I would marry, the house I would live in, my financial status, or whether I would have children. It wasn't always that way. My mother recently found piles of notebooks of mine from when I was a small child that were filled with plans for my future. I wrote out what I would do at every age—I was very ambitious: when I would get married and when I would have kids and when I would open a dance studio. This sort of planning stopped when I left my small hometown for college. The experience of going to a radically new place, as college was to me, completely upended my sense of the world and its possibilities, a transformation that happened again when I moved to New York, and again when I moved to Istanbul. All change is dramatic for provincial people. But the last move was the hardest. In Turkey, the upheaval was far more unsettling: after a while, I began to feel that the entire foundation of my consciousness was a lie.

For all their patriotism, Americans rarely think about how their national identities relate to their personal ones. This indifference is particular to the psychology of white Americans—who do not know that is what they are—and has a trajectory unique to the history of the United States. In recent years, however, this national identity has become more difficult to ignore. We can no longer travel in foreign countries without noticing the strange weight we carry with us, the unfamiliar contours of ourselves. After I moved to Istanbul, I bought a notebook, and unlike the confident child I wrote down not plans but a question: Who do we become if we don't become Americans, at least not in the way we always understood the word? I asked it because my years as an American abroad in the twenty-first century were not a joyous romp of self-discovery and romance, the kind we see in movies; mine were more of a shattering and a shame, and even now, I still don't know myself.

IN 2007, I won a writing fellowship that sent Americans abroad for two years at a time. I had applied for it on a whim. No part of me expected to win the thing. I never thought I would leave New York. I was almost thirty and my friends were coupling off and would soon be making loads of money to support their firstborn. Even as they wished me congratulations, I detected a look of concern on their faces, as if I was crazy to leave *all this*, as if twenty-nine was a little too late to be finding myself. I had never even been to Turkey before.

The fellowship had been created in the 1920s by Charles Crane, a Russophile and scion of a plumbing-parts fortune, whose company's in-house magazine, *Valve World*, published headlines such as "King Hussein of the Hejaz Enjoys the Crane Bathroom." After World War I, according to his biographer David Hapgood, Crane concluded that "Americans and especially American policy-makers were not well enough informed about the rest of the world," and began sending young men abroad for sometimes as long as ten years at a time as part of his Institute of Current World Affairs (ICWA). I suspected, given the nascent imperial era in which it was conceived, that the fellowship doubled as some sort of low-grade intelligence-gathering operation. After I moved to Turkey, and Turks began calling me a spy, an American friend suggested that maybe I was a postmodern spy—a spy who didn't know she was a spy. "Well, it's true in a way," he said drily. "Like all foreign correspondents, you're sending back information that, no matter how you intended it, will no doubt be used in the worst way imaginable."

The objective of Crane's fellowship in truth seems more benign. "Each man will be undertaking perhaps as difficult a task as there is, namely, that of interpreting a people, or a group, to itself and to others," one of ICWA's early prospectuses read in 1925. "Such a task requires . . . something beyond hard work and good intentions, something even beyond knowledge; sympathy, insight, the mellowness of time, the gift of expression are indispensable." In those years, the United States was not yet a superpower. Despite its occupations of the Philippines and Cuba, and its long history of slavery, its image for many abroad was still that of the anti-imperialist, rebel nation, a country that had, for the most part, resisted the worst temptations of colonialism and imperialism, instead preaching an unprecedented kind of liberation theology for the world. When President Woodrow Wilson famously argued in his Fourteen Points speech that all citizens deserved the right to determine their own political fates, he helped inspire leaders from all over the former Ottoman Empire—Eleftherios Venizelos of Greece, Sa'ad Zaghlul of Egypt, Mustafa Kemal Atatürk of Turkey—to fight for independence from foreign rule. In the 1910s, some perceived America as a messiah rescuing the world's peoples from the evils of Europe.

Yet these foreigners overestimated Wilson's knowledge of or interest in their part of the world. Wilson had no idea so many ethnicities and religions even existed. "You do not know and cannot appreciate the anxieties that I have experienced," he admitted, "as a result of many millions of people having their hopes raised by what I have said." Even forty years later, the Egyptian president and fervent nationalist Gamal Abdel Nasser would remind the United States that though the Americans had forgotten the principles of Woodrow Wilson, the Egyptians had not.

Charles Crane understood those hopes. After the war, in early 1919, President Wilson had dispatched Crane and a theologian named Henry Churchill King to travel throughout the former Ottoman Empire. In the spirit of self-determination, Wilson wanted to learn what form of governance these newly liberated peoples desired for themselves. Neither Crane nor King had spent much time in the region before. In those years, the entire army of the United States was one-twentieth the size of Germany's, and even smaller than Romania's or Bulgaria's, and it had no intelligence service in the Middle East, save for a single spy dispatched to Arabia during World War I as a Standard Oil speculator.

Crane and King interviewed thousands of people: Druze and Maronites, Turks and Armenians, Arabs and Jews. What they heard was that the people of the Middle East longed for independence, but they might accept the guardianship of the United States, a country about which they knew little except that it had not enslaved much of the world as had the British and the French. The great Turkish feminist Halide Edip Adıvar said to Mustafa Kemal (Atatürk) that the Americans were "the least harmful solution."

Many Arabs, Crane and King reported, even lauded America's "genuinely democratic spirit" and believed that "America had no territorial or colonial ambitions." Everywhere people told Crane they loved the American president and some even "knew the Fourteen Points by heart."

Crane's was the first survey of its kind. American government officials, however, ignored the findings of the King-Crane Commission, by then fully aware that the British and French had already hatched plans for carving up the region (known as the Sykes-Picot Agreement). Syria and Iraq became countries with haphazardly drawn lines running right through well-established communities, and French and British lackeys were installed as their rulers. President Wilson likely never read Crane's report.

The events that followed were catastrophic: the Greek-Turkish population exchange, the Israeli-Palestinian conflict, the dispossession of the Kurds and the Armenians, the subjugation of the Arabs, the rise of dictatorships, and more than a hundred years of turmoil that still lasts to this day. When the King-Crane report was later revealed in *Editor & Publisher*, the editors wrote that American policy makers' disregard for the report's findings was "an awesome spectacle . . . of how an uninformed democracy might precipitate the gravest consequences." They went on: "Wonderment has been expressed by Turk, Greek, Arab, Armenian, Jew, Syrian, and Druze, not to mention Europeans, as to what has become of the American Mission and its report, which they all dreamed would bring tranquility and a new order to the troubled Near East." Middle Easterners never understood what happened to this "Great Hope."

The exception was Turkey. Whereas Iraqis, Syrians, Palestinians, and Egyptians would still find themselves tethered to colonial rulers, the Turks won their independence from the Western powers and rebuilt their country themselves, an achievement about which they would never fail to remind me. Only one more world war later, Turkey, showered with funds by the nascent American empire, began to reconstruct its fragile identity in vague imitation of its benefactor. I learned about the Truman Doctrine and the Marshall Plan in college; I knew then that millions of dollars had gone to two countries called Greece and Turkey. But when I moved to Istanbul, at age twenty-nine, I had never questioned whether these funds had been anything other than some benevolent American act. In my mind, the scene played out like a rich man in town building a new school; the American president showed up with a sack of money and dropped it on a desk, no strings attached, and the townsfolk cheered with gratitude.

As Crane's organization had described, there is a difference between knowledge and that "beautiful place beyond it." But what would I learn by leaving America that was beyond good intentions, beyond sympathy, beyond the luxury of time? What else was there? I had hardly studied World War I. I had no idea that the people of the Middle East had been feeling betrayed by Americans for a hundred years. I had no idea that they had ever thought so highly of the United States in the first place.

A young Turkish artist who had just returned from a decade in New York once said to me, during a brief hopeful era in Turkey, "Western history is a farce and everyone knows it. Perhaps we can take the values that Americans have abused for material gain and do something better with them." I didn't tell him that most Americans would have no idea what he was talking about—that I, to some degree, also did not—but by then that feeling of newly recognized ignorance was one I knew well. You cannot grow up in the second half of the twentieth century in the United States of America and live abroad in the twenty-first and not feel it all the time. If I learned something about Turkey, I received it, as unsophisticated but curious people do, as a happy addition to my mind. But if I learned something about America in Turkey—or later in Egypt or Greece or Afghanistan or Iran—it felt like a disruption. My brain experienced the acquisition of such knowledge like a cavity filling: something drilled out, something shoved in, and afterward, a persistent, dull ache and a tooth that would never be the same.

IN THE WEEKS before my departure from New York, I spent hours explaining Turkey's international relevance to my bored loved ones, no doubt deploying the cliché that Istanbul was the bridge between East and West. At first, my family was not exactly thrilled for me; New York had been vile enough in their minds. My brother's reaction to the news that I had won this generous fellowship was something like "See? I told you she was going to get it," as if it had been a threat he'd been warning the home front about. My mother asked whether this meant I didn't want the pretty luggage she'd bought me for Christmas, imagining it wasn't fit for the Middle East, and like most women of her generation quietly hoorayed her daughter's adventure. My father, who feared that Islamic terrorists would soon bomb the entire Eastern Seaboard into the Atlantic, stayed up one night watching Pope Benedict's historic 2006 visit to Istanbul on CNN. I woke up to an e-mail time-stamped 3:00 a.m. that read: "Did you know that Turkey is 99 percent Muslim? Are you out of your mind?"

It is astonishing to me now, but I remember that I, the New Yorker who believed herself so different from her origins, replied calmly: "In Turkey, they restrain Islam. They make the women take their head scarves off and put them in a box before they are allowed to enter university campuses"— as if the women themselves did not mind this humiliating and inconvenient experience, as if I would ever deposit a precious piece of my wardrobe into some policeman's cardboard box. At that time, Western thinkers heralded Turkey as the one successful Muslim country, and its secularist founder, Atatürk, as the kind of dictator even a liberal could love. I wasn't just trying to reassure my father; apparently I feared Islam in those days, too. We had all lost our marbles after September 11.

I was inflicting myself on Turkey without good or sentimental reason. I had no connections to the country, but then again I had no connections to anywhere. I was American, two times removed from any European provenance or familial history. I once read that children who grow up hearing beloved family narratives have stronger senses of direction in life; for example, kids who know how their grandmother escaped the Holocaust with diamonds sewn into her jacket, or how their grandfather integrated the high school football team, find it easier to imagine their own life's purpose. Those without a narrative feel anxious and insecure. There is no cultural self to find, no spicy-smelling kitchen in which to rediscover distant cultural memories, no crimes or mistakes to learn from and redeem, no historical events to compare to current ones. My immigrant grandparents did what the United States of America told them to do: wipe the slate clean. The price of entrance was to forget the past. I was moving to Turkey in part because I had nowhere else to go.

Where I was from, few people chose to live abroad; many didn't even go on vacation. My town was located by the Jersey Shore, two hours from New York, in a county both working-class and filthy rich that would one day turn red for Donald Trump. My extended family operated an inexpensive public golf course; I worked there in summers as the hot dog girl; politics in my life were limited to small-businessman woes and prejudices: taxes and immigrants and not much else. My town, populated almost entirely by the descendants of white Christian Europeans, had few connections to the outside world, perhaps by choice, and so their resentments and fears festered with little reason to ever be expressed to anyone but one another. I don't remember much talk of foreign affairs, or of other countries, rarely even of New York, which loomed like a terrifying shadow above us, the place Americans went either to be mugged or to think they were better than everyone else. That was my sense of the outside world: where Americans went to be hurt or to hurt others. When I got into an elite college, I took this small-town defensiveness with me, but slowly discovered that the world was actually kaleidoscopic, full of possibilities.

So, of course, New York became the dream, the land of meaningful pursuits, a chance for absolution of my small-town sins. After college, I moved there and eventually got a job as a journalist at a weekly newspaper, *The New York Observer*, which was obsessed with New York. The newspaper was a formative journalistic experience, mainly because of its fatherly editor, Peter Kaplan, who wanted nothing more than for all of his kids to succeed. The month I started, in August 2004, the Republican Convention had come to New York. The Republicans' arrival felt like an insult to the city's liberals, those who had voted for Al Gore and were against the war in Iraq. As reporters, we crashed the parties and made fun of the rubes. But to me they didn't look much different from the New Yorkers. The Republicans were the world's warriors, another power elite. They had come to a city that not-so-secretly celebrated and worshipped the winners, no matter their deeds.

By then, New York had morphed, thanks to the Internet, into a cocaine-and-steroids version of itself. Working in the media offered a measure of civic responsibility and literary expression, but mostly, I discovered that for many it offered a somewhat respectable path to the new Internet-based celebrity. Young people at that time seemed desperate to be recognized by an external force, something beyond conventional notions of fame. The writer Alison Lurie compared this "celebrity complex" to the process by which totalitarian regimes render entire groups or ethnicities "nonpersons"; instead, in the "so-called advanced democratic societies," she wrote, people did this to themselves. Only a few years after September 11, we had in fact become *less* introspective. The compassionate efforts to understand our new, uncertain world were replaced by an ever more certain set of ways to manage it—money, marriage, brownstone, children, organic market, Pilates—all of it fueled by a sleazily exuberant stock market. During that Gilded Age—perhaps the last true Gilded Age—poor people mysteriously disappeared as if in some dirty war, banks replaced any normal shop or café or restaurant on every block, there was a weird obsession with food, which—we didn't know then—we would all soon be taking photos of and posting online. Social media didn't even exist, yet I already knew aspiring writers and ordinary folks who lived to be mentioned on one of several New York websites; it was so obvious already that appearing in the print newspaper didn't bring the same addictive thrill. Real life had taken on not only the speed and amnesia of the Internet, but the mania and madness of Wall Street, as the writer Frank Rich put it at the time. September 11 had been just another dip in the market. During the most catastrophic years of the wars in Iraq and Afghanistan, New York threw a giant party.

There was a terrible fissure between this surreal New York and the reality outside of it: the invasion of Iraq, this new terror war. The frantic scrambling to read books on the Taliban and Sayyid Qutb and Islam itself—which seemed to many not one of the world's three main monotheistic faiths but a newly discovered alien philosophy—didn't continue after the invasions of Afghanistan and Iraq. I don't remember a whole lot of people buying books about Iraq at all, except for the ones that made the case for invasion, like *Republic of Fear* and *The Threatening Storm*. By 2005, the wars disappeared from television. Had the media become so elitist, so dominated by Harvard and Yale graduates, that none of us knew the soldiers fighting, didn't feel impassioned by the wars? That very process I'd longed for when I moved to New York, the severing of my small-town identity, had only resulted in a new kind of ignorance, a disconnection from the rest of the country. To some sophisticates I met in New York, my apparent provinciality had been a kind of exoticism; I was a survivor of those horrible American places they glimpsed on Fox News. But New Yorkers were ignorant about them, too. And realizing this, suddenly, the New Yorkers I had so long admired and envied seemed to be the provincial ones—if they didn't understand their own country, I wasn't sure any of us could possibly understand the world.

The absence of genuine protest against the war in Iraq was explained away by the absence of a draft, as if our consciences would have been ignited if only someone else struck the match. What we didn't know to ask was how we would be feeling or acting if we knew Iraqis. Not "knew" them as in calling an Iraqi on the phone, but knew them as in their history, their experience, their history and experience with the United States. I do not remember having a sense of the Iraqi people, of an Iraqi family, of an Iraqi man, a normal Iraqi man—a doctor or a postman or a teacher, like someone you grew up with. Even if I did, I am simply not sure my brain would have known to test itself with the potential horrors that might befall that man: if this person was ripped apart by a cluster bomb, tortured in a prison, shot at an intersection while driving, his brains blown apart, his leg torn from his side, his wife and daughter and son screaming and crying in pain, all because of your country's military, your government, and because of you. Empathy was infrastructurally impossible. We couldn't imagine a real war, a war that encompassed our lives, a war occupying our favorite Brooklyn street of restaurants, a war that slung up barricades and checkpoints and manned the corners with scary men in armored suits dripping with weapons and screaming in a language we didn't understand. There simply was no way for the American mind, perhaps the *white* American mind, to imagine these things—not the horror, and not the responsibility—and so we did not.

For journalists this failure of imagination had larger repercussions, of course, because we informed the public, and because as the so-called liberal journalists we were extremely arrogant. We revered our supposedly unique American standards of objectivity, but we couldn't account for the fact—were not modest enough to know—that an objective American mind is first and foremost still an *American* mind. In being objective, we were actually leaving our judgment vulnerable to centuries of ingrained prejudices and black holes of knowledge. We failed to interrogate not only our sources but ourselves. I was surrounded by the most progressive-minded people in the country, and that wasn't enough. The problem wasn't politics.

To me, New York's beautiful diversity had been the best life America had to offer. But I knew there was something wrong with the way we were living. We walked around with this nagging sense that something had happened to us, but I didn't know what and didn't know why. That was one of the reasons I applied for the fellowship; I knew that my own confusion had to do with some central unawareness of the world, the kind that would only be reinforced, time and again, by the very thing I had once loved about New York, a sophistication built by an army of defense mechanisms. At the time, I never paid much attention to the history of Charles Crane, or why he had gone to Ottoman Turkey, or the significance of his King-Crane report, but I understood that I had been chosen for the fellowship for a reason somewhat in line with his philosophy—because the committee wanted to see what would happen if they dropped an ignorant person into a foreign place. I doubt that Charles Crane imagined that, in 2007, almost a hundred years after America's first world war, an American would be as ignorant as me.

I told everyone I chose Turkey because I wanted to learn about the Islamic world. The secret reason I wanted to go was that my favorite writer, James Baldwin, had lived in Istanbul in the 1960s on and off for ten years. I had seen a PBS documentary about Baldwin that said he felt more comfortable as a black, gay man in Istanbul than in Paris or New York. When I heard that, it made so little sense to me, sitting in my Brooklyn apartment, that a space opened in the universe. I couldn't believe that New York would be more illiberal than a place like Turkey, because I couldn't conceive of how prejudiced New York and Paris were in the 1950s, and because I thought that as you went east, life degraded into the past, the opposite of progress. The idea of Baldwin in Turkey somehow placed America's race problem, and America itself, in a mysterious and tantalizing international context. I took a chance that Istanbul might be the place where the secret workings of history would be revealed.

My interest in Baldwin had begun in part because he was the first person to explain who I was: a white American with a lot to learn. Americans have no sense of "tragedy," as he wrote in *Nobody Knows My Name*, and he must have been right because I had no idea what he meant. Sense of tragedy—what was that? And what would it mean if we *did* have a sense of tragedy? How would we live our lives? I couldn't change because I didn't know what was wrong with me in the first place. Baldwin had counseled a surprisingly simple and bewildering antidote to America's race problem, to white people's absence of tragedy and fear of death and irredeemable "innocence"—his remedy was love. The solution struck me as a facile punt, an admission that he had no solution, something, strangely, I thought was his duty to provide. The world's problems in 2001, when I first read Baldwin's books, seemed far too complex to be solved by an emotion. Love seemed too obvious, too easy, a conclusion that in and of itself was proof that the love Baldwin was talking about didn't come easily to me at all.

Maybe Baldwin knew white people would never understand him. But as Americans act out their despair in increasingly dangerous ways in the twenty-first century, Baldwin's observations from the twentieth began to sound more and more prophetic:

"This is the way people react to the loss of empire," he once wrote, "for the loss of an empire also implies a radical revision of the individual identity."

So, my question: Who do we become if we don't become Americans?

THIS IS A BOOK about an American living abroad in the era of American decline. When Baldwin, or Ernest Hemingway, or Henry James wrote from abroad, America had not yet achieved its full imperial status. The 1960s ushered in a golden era of global intellectual engagement—Robert Stone, Gore Vidal, Paul Theroux, Joan Didion, Mary McCarthy, among others—but even that would paradoxically fade in the age of globalization. As America, growing more powerful abroad, turned more inward-looking at home, so, too, did the going-abroad books, so many of them celebrating the transformation of one's self, and extolling a conception of the world as a meditation and wellness center for the spiritually challenged.

An American going abroad during the era of American decline encounters an entirely different set of circumstances. In these years after the wars in Iraq and Afghanistan, and the many more wars that followed, it has become more difficult to gallivant across the world, absorbing its wisdom and resources for one's own personal use. As an American abroad now, you do not have the same crazy, smiling confidence. You do not want to speak so loud. You feel always the vague risk of breaking something. In Turkey and elsewhere, in fact, I felt an almost physical sensation of intellectual and emotional discomfort, trying to grasp a reality for which I had no historical or cultural understanding. I would go, as a journalist, to write a story about Turkey or Greece or Egypt or Afghanistan, and inevitably someone would tell me some part of our shared history—theirs with America— of which I knew nothing. I would feel as though I could not write that story, just as I could not write the story of the coal miners, because when I asked "What happened?" I was more often than not met with a response that spanned sixty years. And if I didn't know this history, then what kind of story did I plan to tell?

In so many countries, I could not shake my own reflexive assumptions. No matter how well I knew the predatory aspects of capitalism, I still perceived Turkey's and Greece's economic advances as progress, a kind of maturation. No matter how deeply I understood America's manipulation of Egypt for its own foreign policy aims, I had never considered—could not grasp—how these policies may have affected individual lives beyond resentment and anti-Americanism. No matter how much I believed that no American was fit for nation-building, I saw Americans' good intentions in Afghanistan, even as a more cynical reality stared me in the face. Even when I disagreed with America's policies, I always believed in our inherent goodness, in my own. I would never have admitted it, or thought to say it, but looking back, I know that deep in my consciousness I thought that America was at the end of some evolutionary spectrum of civilization, and everyone else was trying to catch up.

In a sense my learning process abroad was threefold: I was learning about foreign countries; I was learning about America's role in the world; I was also slowly understanding my own psychology and temperament and prejudices—the very things that had made it so impossible to acquire worldly knowledge in the first place. American exceptionalism did not only define the United States as a special nation among lesser nations, it demanded that all Americans believe they, too, were born superior to others, a concept of goodness that requires the existence of evil for its own sustenance. How could I, as an American, understand a foreign people, when unconsciously I did not extend the most basic faith to other people that I extended to myself? This was a limitation that was beyond racism, beyond prejudice, and beyond ignorance. This was a kind of nationalism so insidious that I had not known to call it nationalism; this was a self-delusion so complete that I could not see where it began and ended, could not root it out, could not destroy it.

Yet we are living at a time when people are questioning—trying to question—their national identities in new ways. After the death of Margaret Thatcher, the actor Russell Brand (during his more serious years) published an essay about once catching a glimpse of the elderly Thatcher in some gardens along London's Strand. For Brand, as a young boy, Thatcher was the "headmistress of our country," the woman who taught her children that "there is no such thing as society" and that they should "ignore the suffering of others." Brand then did what in retrospect was the logical next step for a child of Thatcher: he considered her effect on his own mind. "What is more troubling," he writes, "is my inability to ascertain where my own selfishness ends and her neo-liberal inculcation begins." Part of the reason Brand felt compelled to question the Thatcher way of life was that so much of her economic philosophy had been recently upended by the financial crisis. But the remarkable thing was that the effect of the crisis on Brand's country had actually compelled him to question *himself.* He was not immune; he was not innocent, either.

Americans have in recent years been stumbling through the twilight of the American century, but largely without Brand's self-knowledge. Historians and pundits struggle to explain disturbing phenomena: Donald Trump, a flailing foreign policy, the rise of inequality, daily shootings, the tragic plea "Black lives matter." Incipient decline might account for the collective anxiety gripping the country, the fears and rages, what is, in the end, a desperate confusion. For the first time since World War II, the lives of American citizens, who have long been self-sufficient and individualistic—the masters of their own fates—have become entwined with the fate of their nation in a palpable way. It is also perhaps the first time Americans are confronting a powerlessness that the rest of the world has always felt, not only within their own borders but as pawns in a larger international game. Globalization, it turns out, has not meant the

Americanization of the world; it has made Americans, in some ways, more like everyone else.

In academia, there has been a call to internationalize history or, in the words of the historian Erez Manela, "to examine how the United States has been reflected in the world, in the histories of other societies," which suggests that entire nations—billions of lives—cannot be studied without considering the intervening history of the United States. A profound moral event has taken place, something bigger than what is cheerily reduced to McDonald's signs in Shanghai, or disparaged as mere anti-Americanism. Anti-Americanism is not some bitter mental disorder inflamed by conspiracy theories and misplaced furies and envy. It is a broken heart, a defensive crouch, a hundred-year-old relationship, bewilderment that an enormous force controls your life but does not know or love you.

Yet just as black American writers once desperately urged their white friends to come to terms with their violent but intimate relationship, foreigners have been constantly asking Americans to listen to them. The Pakistani author Mohsin Hamid and the American author Jay McInerney gave a talk in New York in 2012. During the question-and-answer period, an audience member joked that the best solution to the anti-American protests in Pakistan would be to give them all green cards to the United States. The audience member was very proud of this punch line. *Of course, most Americans believe that everyone in the world wants to live in the United States.* These were the sorts of things that seemed like obvious, factual truths to Americans. But then Hamid pointed out something that would be an obvious, factual truth to a Pakistani. He said: "There's an America that exists inside the borders of the United States, which is a very different entity from the America that projects its force outside the United States . . . There are kind of two Americas."

I kept encountering this idea of the two Americas. The Pakistani novelist Kamila Shamsie once wrote that the case of John Hersey's *Hiroshima* epitomized this divided existence. For Shamsie, there was one America, "which decides what price some other country's civilian population must pay for its victory," as well as another America, the one of John Hersey, "the America of looking at the destruction your nation has inflicted and telling it like it is." Shamsie wanted to know, however, where were all the John Herseys of today, the American writers or novelists making sense out of, say, the war on terror, the dirty wars in Latin America, or the oil-and-weapons obligations of the Middle East? She couldn't find many young novelists who even acknowledged American power in the world. Shamsie recounted an experience that I have heard time and time again from foreign friends: "I was startled to discover that when I said I was from Pakistan I was met with blankness—as if, in 1991, no one knew that through the 1980s Pakistan had been America's closest ally in its proxy war against the Soviets."

After September 11, Shamsie assumed that, of course, Americans "would now see its stories bound up with the stories of other places." But they didn't. Why was it that the people of the most powerful country in the world—powerful because of its influence *inside* so many foreign nations—did not feel or care to explore what that influence meant for even their *own* American identities? Where was this shared sense of fate that we had unilaterally imposed on Pakistanis, Iraqis, Afghans? Shamsie had grown up in Pakistan in the 1980s, always knowing, as she puts it, that thinking about her country's politics meant thinking about America's history and politics. "So in an America where fiction writers are so caught up in the idea of America in a way that perhaps has no parallel with any other national fiction, where the term Great American Novel weighs heavily on writers," she writes, "why is it that the fiction writers of my generation are so little concerned with the history of their own nation once that history exits the fifty states?" Her question echoed an experience I had in 2012 when I met an Iraqi man. Over the course of our conversation I asked him what Iraq was like in the 1980s and 1990s, when he was growing up. He smiled. "I am always amazed when Americans ask me this," he said. "How is it that you know nothing about us when you had so much to do with what became of our lives?"

The historian Jackson Lears wrote that Americans of the early twentieth century displayed a "dependence on empire for their prosperity, for their racial, social, and even moral identity as a people, and for the power that undergirded their dreams of personal and national regeneration." If the decline of the American empire may require, as Baldwin suggests, a radical revision of the individual identity, perhaps Americans have to more deeply understand what that imperial identity was in the first place. If America was an empire, was there even a difference between "home" and "abroad"?

Was it not all the same kingdom? Were we not locked in the same intimate relationship? Was not *their* pain very much *ours*? Might this relationship even be one, as Baldwin said, of love?

This book is by no means a comprehensive exploration of this subject, nor of all the countries I write about. Many historians and scholars and novelists—many more of them non-American—have chronicled the story of the American empire in far more expansive books. What follows are merely my reflections on going abroad in the twenty-first century and my attempts to see foreign countries clearly—ultimately, to see my own. Even though I use mostly foreigners' voices and writings in this book, I never asked them, essentially, "Why do you hate us?" They have been answering that question in complex and passionate ways for decades. The onus, I felt, was on me to catch up.

If I didn't, I would never be able to make sense of letters like this one publicly posted on Facebook on the anniversary of the Iraq War in 2013, by the Egyptian activist Alaa Abd El-Fattah, who, as of this writing, is still inside an Egyptian jail:

> To My American Friends:
>
> Ten years later and I still can't find the words to explain my anger to you, we talk about it a lot in Arabic, it is forever part of our context, the horror, the madness, the futility of it all, in fact it has become such a part of who we are that we need an anniversary to realize how epic in proportion it was. Ten years on and it still seems possible for you to debate and talk about it in polite or boring language. I'll never understand you and you'll never understand me.
>
> I know all of you (my friends) tried to stop it, I know millions more tried, I understand it wasn't done in your interests, you are not the state, you are not the war, you are not the corporations. But still I'm angry at each and every one of you, maybe it's irrational, maybe you as individuals hold no responsibility, maybe it's a reaction to all the cheesy manufactured soul searching forced down our throats in which the horror of it all is stripped down to the suffering of American soldiers and American families,

soldiers who died, soldiers who lost a limb, soldiers who were shocked at what they were capable of, soldiers who waited until they practiced the killing and torture themselves to realize that something was wrong. Murderers and pillagers who think the world owes them an apology, heroes even in the eyes of many of the millions who tried to stop the war. Maybe I include you, my friends, in my anger because you care, for what is the point of being angry at those who already made a commitment not to be human?

The scary part is I'm many steps removed from the war and its atrocities, I wonder at the anger felt by Iraqis who had to live every day of it? Until recently I wasn't just steps removed, I was an accomplice just like you, the battleships moving through the Suez Canal were enough to push us to revolution in just ten years. Ask any activist who experienced the 2003 antiwar protests in Tahrir and they'll tell you it started then, for you see we couldn't live with the thought that Iraqis would look at us with anger in their hearts. Our incomplete and much-abused revolutions are our gift to you, join it and revolt now, for nothing short of revolution will ever redeem you.

"I'll never understand you and you'll never understand me." Was that true? If we Americans admired the Egyptians for their revolutionary spirit from afar, if so many of us envied their passion and their commitment to a cause, then I wonder why we did not feel connected to Egyptians when clearly, in some way, they, like the rest of the world, felt inherently, inextricably, passionately connected to us.

That day I visited the Turkish coal miners, asking over and over those same American questions—"What happened here?" "How did this happen?" "What went wrong?" "How did your country fail to protect you?"—Ahmet, the survivor, interrupted me. A hush fell over the room, not because they thought him rude but because they all viewed me the same way: as a curiosity.

"But, ma'am, I have a question for you," he said. "Why didn't you come before the fire? Why didn't you think of us before?"

1.

FIRST TIME EAST: TURKEY

Never again could she think there was but one narrative and that this narrative belonged only to herself, that she might create her own tiny little happiness and live safely within it.

—KIRAN DESAI

OVER TIME I CAME TO REGARD the view of Istanbul from an airplane with a sense of claustrophobia. The red-roofed buildings sprawled across the entire visible landscape, as if created with digital magic for a sci-fi film. It was so incomprehensibly enormous, a planet city. I would search with rising panic for where this endless concrete would finally be broken by the natural earth: the Black Sea, the Marmara, the elegantly slithering Bosphorus, a patch of forest with its tree heads bowed against the siege. Istanbul was bigger than the country, as Turks liked to say; it ate everything in its path, and over time its appetite would grow monstrous. But that first day in 2007, I looked down at Istanbul with nothing but admiration, the gentle surprise of the Western tourist who hadn't suspected the world had gone on without her. From my seat, the tankers waiting to enter the Bosphorus strait looked as if they were waiting to be admitted to the center of the world.

The Istanbul airport was modern and efficient, European, and what struck me first was how foreign it did not feel, at least not in the way I expected, which was to somehow be older looking than the decrepit airport in New York I had just left. The metal walls gleamed, porters stood at the ready, there was a Starbucks. Sliding doors beyond the luggage carousels opened like a curtain to a stage where an audience of expectant faces, mostly men with dark facial hair, lunged forward, eager to snatch their waddling grandmothers and lead them safely from the crowds. The room felt almost hushed, an obedience to order that I didn't yet understand. It was the airport of a stable country.

My sleek taxi swept past buildings whose architectural style resembled some strange combination of Florida housing developments and European suburbs, shopping malls as familiar as those I frequented in New Jersey. I never had fantasies about an exotic Orient, but I had not expected globalization to have seeped like heavy liquid into every corner of the earth. The roads were immaculate, tulips lined the drive, and everywhere billboards proclaimed hopeful new construction as if in some 1950s American film reel: the next promised land! As the car merged off the highway, I glimpsed the Sea of Marmara, glinting around those huge shipping tankers. The road then curved around the edge of the old city peninsula, ahead of which I finally saw the miraculous geography of greater Istanbul—three separate pieces of multicolored cityscape emerging from the middle of a bright blue sea. A storybook stone tower stood above a huddle of buildings cascading down a hill to the Bosphorus, which had a delicately webbed bridge spun over it, leading to—Asia? The closeness of the two continents seemed improbable, hopeful, as if the world was not so big and estranged after all; old white ferries scuttled back and forth like beetles dutifully carrying messages between the two lands. Seagulls cawed overhead—to me, the soundtrack of my Atlantic Ocean imposed on an Asian metropolis—and swooped down on tiny rowboats pegged to the shore. I could not believe how beautiful it all was, how it was exactly what I had wished for.

The apartment I eventually moved into was more than a hundred years old and had no heat and broken windows, but it was located in what I had imagined an Istanbul neighborhood would be: decaying but beautiful turn-of-the-century buildings and narrow planked stone streets, men loitering in doorways and smoking. Galata was on the European side of the city, once populated by Jews and Armenians and Greeks and now home to squatting Kurdish families and foreigners, its grandeur corroded and gritty. In my apartment, the shower sprayed straight into the bathroom, the kitchen was covered in dust, and the lobby was terrifyingly dark, but from the small balcony I could see the Hagia Sophia framed perfectly between two buildings, so I thought I was the luckiest person in the world. My new home was called the Şükran Apartmanı, or the Gratitude Apartments.

I knew only one person in the city, an American woman who was writing a book about Armenian-Turkish relations. After I unloaded my luggage, I dazedly followed her to meet a Kurdish PhD student named Caner so we could eat *künefe* in a shop that sold only *künefe*. Istanbul, in some heavenly seeming economic phase between the old world and early capitalism, still had shops that only did one thing: sell eggs, bake *simit* (the Turkish bagel), or make *künefe*, a syrupy dessert Turks felt no guilt making with both melted butter and cheese. Sometimes these shops were nothing but an oven and a couple of tables on a concrete floor, but their employees stood around staring at their customers vigilantly, delivered their desserts with the pride and confidence of an artist. Turkish hospitality was not obsequious; to the contrary, they were the ones in control. It had the curious effect of making you feel beholden to them even as they catered to you, the illusion of a relationship formed. These daily interactions went a long way, and for a long time, toward allowing me to pretend I was not lonely.

Caner and my American friend were continuing some conversation they had begun days before, and I watched Caner with the carefulness of a scientist. He was soft-spoken and serious, and he could roll his cigarettes gracefully without his eyes leaving your face. Earlier that day, the military had raided a "liberal" magazine called *Nokta*, which he told us about in a solemn tone, because it published some classified documents concerning the possible plotting of a military coup. A military coup was too fantastical a concept for me to take seriously; instead, I wondered when he said the magazine was "liberal" whether he had actually meant "radical." I still had the reflex that the police only went after bad people. Caner said that the military wasn't able to finish photocopying everything in one day, so they decided to complete their raid later. He seemed angry. I realized, with no small measure of surprise, that if you were a leftist in Turkey, your enemy was the military, not Islam.

After a while, I drew up the courage to try to impress Caner with my scattered knowledge of Turkey's political situation. I asked him about the outgoing president's assertion, in so many words, that Turkey was danger-ously close to falling into the hands of radical Islam, which was the par-lance of the time. The Turkish president was your standard secular Middle Eastern politician, the kind constantly warning about Islam, it seemed, in order to scare people. The only thing that stood a chance against the ideo-logical purposefulness of Islamic political parties was the ideological pur-posefulness of being anti-Islam. The secularists talked about Islam more than anyone else.

"Do you think he actually believes that Turkey will fall into the hands of radical Islam?" I said, spitting out clichés with confidence. "Or is he just saying that to win votes for his party?"

Caner was looking at me as if I were insane. "Belief?" he said. "Belief is not about facts. Belief is about a political position." This seemed to both answer and not answer the question. Was he on to me? Could he tell what I was really asking was: *Is* Turkey falling into the hands of radical Islam? At the time, in 2007, this was all anyone wanted to know. Caner looked as if "radical Islam" was the last thing on his mind. I longed for him to say more, but I was quiet.

Caner was Kurdish, as well as Alevi, a branch of Islam considered he-retical by many members of the dominant Sunni sect in Turkey. It was great luck that he was the first person I met in Turkey, the prism through which I slowly tried to understand its politics, because as a member of two outcast minorities, he had no particular love for either the Islamists or sec-ularists, this party or that party. He thought everyone was terrible. He was able to see things more clearly, without passion, without ideology, and consequently without much hope. And bleak as that was, he was a constant reminder to try to think that way, to avoid the traps of one's own bias. I would find it very hard to do.

The following day, he took me to get a cheap secondhand cell phone and an illegitimate SIM card—to this day I am not sure why but the expedition added to my already exaggerated idea of Turkey as an early-stage capitalist country—and we walked across the Galata Bridge, the low-hanging expanse over the Golden Horn that connected European Beyoğlu, my neighborhood, to the old Ottoman city. I had heard that men fished off it—this being one of the most common romantic images of Istanbul—but that first day, it shocked me to see so many of them dangling rods and lethal hooks so close to what was a chaotic pedestrian walkway.

"Caner," I said. "Do they need a permit to fish off the bridge?"

"Permit?" He again looked at me as if I were insane. "Do . . . the fish have permits to swim?"

His question delighted me out of all proportion to its content. To look at the world from a new perspective is to feel as if the ropes holding you to the earth have been cut. Caner was going on, laughing, remembering how once a friend of his asked why we called fish "seafood," when that would make humans "landfood." "Don't confuse freedom with happiness," someone said to me in those years. But inside my mind I was reconstituting meanings the way Caner did with words. No one with the same set of constructs I had was watching me, and I had the space to look at everything so differently that I actually felt as if my brain were breathing. In fact, I felt like a child.

ORHAN PAMUK MADE Istanbul's *hüzün* famous—a fallen-empire melancholy and loss that suffused the city and its people—but Istanbul, at first, was far too beautiful for me to see evidence of rot. Those first days my leg muscles became sore from walking up and down Istanbul's steep hills over and over, trying to memorize it all for an impossible mental map. I was in love, as if I had been living in an upside-down world and suddenly someone had turned everything right-side up. Unlike New York, where buildings blocked the sky, Istanbul from the grand wide lens of its hilltops made you feel bigger, undiminished and uplifted. Down on the narrow streets, close-up, everything seemed to happen in miniature, like on a movie set, and therefore appeared incomparably more human-size: the peasant woman emerged from her shop sweeping; a man pulled his cart of old broken things; a tiny boy trailed after his father; at night a man peed into the doorway; ladies hobbled slowly, one foot, then the other, side to side; men smoked on stools outside hardware stores; antique furniture piled up outside rickety houses; a peddler sold eggs as if from a concession stand. Head scarves bobbed through the crowds like buoys. Rather than some Islamic menace, they seemed like turn-of-the-century Edith Wharton characters in souped-up bonnets. Covered women looked perfectly normal, here, where they lived, carrying grocery bags, walking to work, far away from the theoretical world in which I had imagined them. The impact of merely seeing foreign things with my own eyes was the equivalent of reading a thousand history books. I found that I was watching life more carefully, that every nerve was alive to my environment.

I didn't speak the language, so those first months I lived in a state of white noise and visual bliss. I was forced to look, and to see. In fact, the first time I would return to New York after a year in Istanbul, twelve months of gazing at the Bosphorus, I took a subway over the Manhattan Bridge and it was as if I saw the water in New York for the first time. It wasn't that I noticed its relative homeliness compared to the Bosphorus; it was that I had never actually looked at it. In Istanbul, I ran down every evening to a dusty parking lot where the attendants sipped tea and watched the sun slip behind the minarets and into the Golden Horn: Topkapı Palace, the Blue Mosque, the Galata Tower, the mouth of the Bosphorus. You could see everything from there, but it was just a parking lot, whose inhabitants were three attendants, a cat lady and her ten cats, and three stray dogs. "Come, sit down," the parking lot attendant would say, offering me tea. I stood and watched the sun disappear behind the old city, its red glare thrown across the Bosphorus, transforming the windows of the Asian side into a thousand copper fires. The stray dogs cuddled in the dirt together and howled when the mosque began its call to prayer. In New York such property would be worth millions of dollars and bought up for condos. I'd read somewhere that the Byzantines believed that everyone, rich and poor, deserved a home with a view of the Bosphorus, rather than that it was the exclusive property of a wealthy few. Everything in Turkey seemed antithetical to where I came from.

The real poor, whose ramshackle houses I could sometimes spot lodged into the hill crevices, had arrived in Istanbul during the great global migration to cities that began in the 1950s, by the village-load. Entire towns from Anatolia would claim a patch of land—whether at the open city edges or jammed in between the mansions—and quickly assemble their concrete and tin shelters so that they couldn't be evicted; they put facts on the ground. The slums of Istanbul were called *gecekondu*, which meant "built overnight," and Istanbul politicians, walking that peculiar line between wily and humane, hurried to promise their new potential constituents electricity and water, knowing that such amenities would win them votes. Regardless of intention, they let them stay. I rarely saw homeless people in Istanbul, and slums never looked nearly as bad as they did in photos of Rio or Nairobi, and even this seemed to me proof of the Turks' enduring humanity. I was the exact opposite of the Americans I'd met my first night in town, who complained about the food, the taxi drivers, the fact that no Turks spoke English. I loved everything, operating in a state of constant emotional genuflection before this secret society that had let me in.

Up the Bosphorus, in the northern villages, there were Ferrari dealerships and ice-cream-cone mansions stacked up steep hills. The Bosphorus looked like some celebrity vacation retreat, like Lake Como. It had the air of exclusivity and endless leisure. Women sat outside for hours at sidewalk tables, all exhausting shades of blond, their thin frames weighed down by Marc Jacobs or Gucci bags. Where did they get all this money? How did they make it? (I had only ever been as far east as Sarajevo.) I looked out the taxi window in Istanbul with a sudden sinking feeling I couldn't put my finger on until years later. Like many of my reactions in those days, this one was embarrassing: it was as if it had never occurred to me that Turkey could be so rich. I would not have thought it could look like this: *better than us.* I had been invested in an idea of the East's inferiority without even knowing it, and its comparative extraordinariness shook my own self-belief. This was perhaps, too, my first sense of America's decline, and I felt it take me down with it, as if America's shabbiness said something about myself or, worse, as if Turkey's *success* said something about myself. Was this the same sense of failure Americans had felt when but a handful of men breached American borders and brought the towers down, their power somehow stronger than ours? Was this where American rage came from?

My own rage, a petulant kind of shame-rage, would emerge in Turkish class. My first days of lessons were a disaster of soul-shattering proportions. I had been good at languages in school in that way Americans are—to prepare for tests but never to actually speak them—and had barely glanced at a Turkish textbook before my plane landed, a light perusal of which would have informed me that Turkish was the Ironman of languages, one that shared almost no words with English, and worse, whose sentence structure was the reverse of ours. Unlike an American's first experience of, say, Italian or Arabic, Turkish was not some liberation of the tongue. Turkish felt like a purposely designed obstacle course, all the *g*'s and *k*'s stuck in odd places, as if the founders of the Turkish Republic, who reformed Ottoman Turkish into a new language for a new nation, wanted foreigners to know their place. Well, I knew mine. I couldn't say the words. I couldn't even hear them. My mouth felt slow and stupid; my tongue a flabby, inflexible thing. When I left my language class the first day, I felt a surprising kind of pain, like when you are teased on the playground. I had been instantly rendered the hapless American of stereotype and scorn.

AT THAT TIME, American journalists moved to Iraq or Afghanistan, or at least Beirut or Cairo, but Turkey was a country rarely written about in the newspapers, and few people back home, I could tell, thought I had chosen Istanbul for reasons beyond the fact that it was a beautiful tourist destination. My explanation that I wanted to learn about Islam was somewhat true. After seven hundred years as an Islamic empire, Turkey had become a secular republic and, according to the standard history, dispatched Islam from public life. Atatürk had found a way to contain it. For the last eighty years, therefore, the Turks had been wrestling with this secularizing experiment perhaps with *lessons* for all of us. Wasn't Turkey the one Muslim country that, in those days, gave hope? Samuel Huntington's "clash of civilizations" seemed more intellectual than martial in Turkey, and I saw the country like some idea lab dreamed up for my benefit.

It's painful now to recall just how confused we all had been after September 11. *The Onion* headline two weeks later was "Holy Fucking Shit," which, I remember, in the magazine office where I worked had offered us a palpable sense of relief, because no one else knew what to do or how to react to September 11, as if emotions came from the memories of other emotional experiences, not from an organic place. The week before September 11, I had been reading David Halberstam's *War in a Time of Peace*, which was about the Clinton era—the period when we thought history was over. Halberstam quotes Clinton saying in 1992 to one of his Democrat colleagues: "'I've been traveling around our country for a year and no one cares about foreign policy other than about six journalists.'" The afternoon of the tragedy, my editor bosses—most of them impressively well-read and conscious of the downtrodden—dispatched me to go interview Palestinians because the sight of those towers falling down had made them first think of Israel, which I suppose was then the conflict Americans suspected Arabs might be angry with them about. I was twenty-four and did what I was told. I could only think of asking the people I thought might know Palestinians: the Egyptians who worked at my corner deli. I felt so ashamed of this entire expedition, racking my brain for confirmation that Palestinians and Egyptians had an affinity to each other, something I actually don't think I knew for sure at the time. The Egyptians said some Palestinians ran *another* deli down the street, and when I finally tracked them down to be interviewed, they were understandably bewildered. "Our fight is for Jerusalem, not New York," they said.

In that magazine office, I was surrounded by Berkeley liberals—my politics by then also had swung dramatically to the left—but September 11 made us unsure of ourselves, both disturbed and captivated by the exhortations of revenge emanating from our television sets. There were a few voices at the time counseling caution. One of them was the black writer John Edgar Wideman, who wrote an article in *Harper's Magazine* in opposition to the widely supported Afghan war, which he called phony "because it's being pitched to the world as righteous retaliation, as self-defense after a wicked, unwarranted sucker punch when in fact the terrible September 11 attack as well as the present military incursion into Afghanistan are episodes in a long-standing vicious competition." Wideman, as an "American of African descent," could not applaud his "president for doing unto foreign others what he's inflicted on me and mine." As an American of African descent, he was one of the few Americans who could after September 11 see anything clearly.

Later the American anthropologist Clifford Geertz, who had spent years living among Muslims in Islamic cultures as different as Indonesia and Morocco, would observe of that period in America something unprecedented: the construction of a new reality. Of all the "reality instructors" at the time, the Princeton historian Bernard Lewis was the most prominent; he would eventually come to advise President George W. Bush on the invasion of Iraq. The central message of Lewis's historical analysis was that a mysterious decay in the Muslim world had led to Muslim rage at their own impotence, and what had struck the United States in September was the beginning of a "war of the worlds" kind of showdown. Lewis's historical analysis was designed to match the emotional pitch of the public and political rhetoric, and, in Geertz's words, "to arouse the West, and most especially the United States, to armed response."

I did not support the wars, but ignorance is vulnerable to the atmosphere it is exposed to, and without realizing it, I absorbed the same fear of Islam and Muslims, not in a bigoted way, but in the more insidious manner of the well-intentioned liberal mediator. Many of us unconsciously settled for these softer versions of oppression, the kinds that fit easily into the American vision of its place in the world: as guardian and enforcer. I had believed that Islam was something to be tamed, that religious Turks were not to be trusted to choose their own way in life, that in fact all Turks, since most were Muslim, were people who must be restrained—from what exactly I don't know—and that "Islam" was a thing that I, an American abroad, should be thinking about solutions to, because that's what Americans always do.

. . .

I WAS IN THE RIGHT PLACE, because Turks had long been worried about Islam, and were especially worried the year that I arrived. An election was coming. The reigning prime minister, Recep Tayyip Erdoğan, was a religious man whose wife wore a head scarf. Now one of the candidates for president in the election, Abdullah Gül, was *also* a religious man whose wife wore a head scarf. This was new, and, apparently, traumatizing. The president's office had been created in the image of its founder, the secularist, modernist, *rakı*-drinking, womanizing, trailblazing, ballroom-dancing soldier-statesman Atatürk—a man who in the 1930s encouraged his adopted daughter, Sabiha Gökçen, to fly planes—and so the idea that that office would now be filled by a man who married his head-scarf-wearing wife when she was fifteen was for many akin to national-spiritual death. Political office, it seemed, was not just about politics but about Turkish identity. Erdoğan and Gül promised to preserve Turkey's secularist character, and instead used the language of democracy, liberalism, and human rights to argue for their own inclusion in political life. But the secularists in the country didn't trust them. Many of them flat-out hated them. The military, which the secularists (but not leftists like Caner) viewed as a necessary institution, and which had in the past overthrown the government four times in military coups, was threatening to intervene.

"Atatürk was a feminist? His daughter flew planes?" was a typical question I asked Caner. "They seem proud of that. It's kind of cool."

"Yes," he would deadpan. "She flew planes over Kurdish villages and dropped bombs on them and killed people."

He was referring to the Dersim Massacre of the 1930s, in which the Kurdish tribes of eastern Anatolia had revolted against the Turks, and rejected Atatürk's demands that their Kurdish region be Turkified. Atatürk, and his daughter, apparently, responded by killing some thirty to fifty thousand of them, thus depopulating the region of Kurds. Caner would not have forgotten about this, because his family was from Dersim. Istanbul's second airport, meanwhile, was named Sabiha Gökçen.

I would meet Caner often in those days at bars and cafés on İstiklal Caddesi, the city's main pedestrian artery, where one could find beer, lamb meatballs, bordellos, dance clubs, bookstores, movie theaters, and any number of pimps, thugs, and prostitutes. It was an irrepressibly energetic place, once the Grand Rue de Péra of Constantinople, the European district, now the domain of everyone and anyone, especially the young. I walked up and down it almost every day, trying to settle into some semblance of normal daily life in between Turkish classes and figuring out basic survival skills, like buying credits for my illegal cell phone. These were lazy, privileged days for a twenty-nine-year-old, and out of some guilt and genuine interest I engaged in my full-scale investigation of Turkey, trying desperately to understand everything in a few weeks.

It would be at least two years before I felt comfortable writing anything about it. Turkey's history was virtually impenetrable at first to an outsider; a double helix of twists and turns sharing few of the same twists and turns, phases and stages, revolutions and themes of other countries. Turkey was both empire and republic, Islamic and secular, democratic and fascistic. The "state" (the military and judiciary) was different from the "government" (Parliament, the prime minister, the local municipalities), which was different from the "Deep State" (a mysterious network of ex-military, intelligence, and thugs rumored to control the country behind the scenes), and each had its own pathologies and trajectories. Its political factions included, over the years, Republicans, Democrats, anti-imperialists, leftists, Maoists, Stalinists, Islamists, nationalists, leftist nationalists, Islamic nationalists, and some group called the Gray Wolves that made scary hand signals in the shape of wolf ears. New political party names seemed to crop up every year: the Republican People's Party and the Democrat Party, the Justice and Development Party and the Motherland Party, the National Salvation Party and the National Order Party and the National Development Party, the People's Labor Party and the People's Democracy Party, the Great Turkey Party and the New Turkey Party. The Communist Party still existed. The so-called Islamist political party embraced the West, and the secularist party did not. The Islamist party was capitalist, the secularist party was not. The country had been America's and Israel's staunchest ally, but the Turkish people liked neither very much. The head scarf was banned on university campuses and in government institutions, but you couldn't drink alcohol within one hundred feet of a mosque. Women had gotten the vote in 1930, you could buy the morning-after pill at the pharmacy, abortions were legal until the tenth week, but only 24 percent of women worked, and most girls seemed to call their boyfriends eighty-two times a day.

Caner patiently served as a human encyclopedia, explaining which newspapers were "nationalist" and which "religious," and which "liberal" and which "leftist"; what the difference was between a Marxist leftist and a Kemalist leftist; how gay Turks could evade military conscription by providing photos of themselves having sex—but only as a "bottom" because being a "top" didn't necessarily mean you were gay. As with Sabiha Gökçen, the adopted daughter of Atatürk, the world's first female fighter pilot, as well as the person who dropped bombs on thousands of Kurds who did not want to be Turkish, every time I learned some new factoid and parroted it back to Caner over coffee, he would return with the factoid's dark underbelly, as if there were two entirely distinct but parallel histories here, the official one and the real one. What was good in one was almost always bad in the other. I assumed this dual nature was particular to the troubled nation I had chosen, which I regarded with an unconscious but automatic parental concern. But each day my confidence as a journalist, as a person, as a thinker, declined.

Despite my confusion, it was an exciting time. On one of my first Saturdays in the country, thousands, maybe millions, of secularists took to the streets in Istanbul and Ankara and Izmir, waving red flags and protesting the presidency of Abdullah Gül. The protest was a bit like Mardi Gras, or the Fourth of July, without alcohol or beads or men sticking their hands down your pants. "Turkey is secular, and will remain secular!" they shouted. On a dreary highway in a northern Istanbul neighborhood, I watched a woman waving her huge flag, which fluttered violently in front of two women passing in head scarves, who had to flinch to avoid it. "We don't want an imam for president!" other women screamed. (Abdullah Gül was a businessman educated in London, but no matter.) A woman named Nur Serter, the vice president of the Atatürk Thought Association, told the crowd that the women were lining up "in front of the glorious Turkish army," according to reports. Türkan Saylan, president of the Association for Support of Contemporary Living, complained during those days that the government was transforming the presidential palace into "the palace of a religious order." Overwhelmingly, the angriest people were women, who believed an Islamic government might transform their lives. I was reading a book at the time by an academic whose mother went around wearing Atatürk pins and saying, "I have my Atatürk against their veils." That week, a female think tank writer observed, "If all Turkey's leaders come from the same Islamist background, they will—despite the progress they have made towards secularism—inevitably get pulled back to their roots."

The dreaded roots of which they spoke were the Ottoman Empire. During the nineteenth century, it was the Turks, not the Arabs, who constituted the world's imaginary Muslim menace. The Ottoman Empire was a vast multiethnic territory, one in which the intellectuals, the wealthy, and the artisans were largely Armenians, Greeks, Italians, and Jews. Its overlords, however, were the Turkish sultans, or the "Terrible Turks," and the Western world hated them. One editorial in an 1896 edition of *The New York Times*, for example, declared that the Turk being "driven out 'bag and baggage'" was, according to the newspaper, "the inner most desire of all of us." Americans primarily thought of Turks as Muslims who killed Christians, and when World War I broke out, their sympathies lay with the Christian Armenians and Greeks, whom the Turks were in the process of slaughtering. The Ottomans, who had sided with the Germans, lost the war, and the victorious Western powers eagerly parceled out Ottoman lands to France and Britain in the disastrous way that Charles Crane observed. The Turks, those people who had been stewards of one of the greatest empires in the world for seven hundred years, were offered nothing but a stump of land in Anatolia, surrounded by enemies, with no access to waterways, and without Constantinople, seat of its caliphate, urban jewel of the East. It was one of many grand humiliations.

In response, a group of young Turks—soldiers and intellectuals who had long wanted to overthrow the dyspeptic, antimodern sultans, eliminate the caliphate, and draw up a proper constitution—nursed a catastrophic sense of grievance. To Turks in Istanbul, the Western occupiers, as well as the besieged Christian locals, were acting like conquerors who had won the crusades. They believed that Greeks were mocking the muezzin and calling street dogs Mohammed; that British soldiers swatted at fezzes and tore off veils; that the fires in Istanbul's Muslim neighborhoods were acts of arson. Watching the dispossession of his people in disgust and fury, a

Turkish soldier named Mustafa Kemal boarded a ship to Samsun, launched the war for independence, ousted the Western powers, and established the Republic of Turkey.

The only people who hated the Ottoman Empire more than the West were Mustafa Kemal and his Kemalists. Atatürk believed, in part, that the backwardness of the Ottoman Empire had allowed for its defeat by the West. Their self-hatred inspired a renewal. Atatürk (which means "father of the Turks," a name he took in 1934) created not only a new state but a new "Turk," one with an identity, history, and philosophy of life strong enough to hold together a nation that did not exist. He drew on the ideas of an ideologue named Ziya Gökalp, who had been working on how to imagine the Ottoman religions, ethnicities, and cultures as one "nation"—"a community of individuals who have in common their language, religion, ethics, and aesthetics, acquired through a common education." This inclusive worldview would be subject to Atatürk's revisions. The "republic must be forced through by other means before the opposition had time to unite," Atatürk said. "A debate on it might be fatal." Gökalp had struggled to reconcile Islam, nationalism, and modernity, without racial undertones or religious authoritarianism. Atatürk opted for Turkism, a nationalism based on race, and laicism, a social system based on extreme secularism, for which Atatürk would be greatly admired by both Hitler and Mussolini.

The creation of the new Turk was a decidedly undemocratic process. Newspapers were closed, opposition members killed, history rewritten. Islam, Atatürk avowed, was the opposite of "modernity." It would have to be diminished, not destroyed. Atatürk recognized Islam's importance in fusing the new identity: they were Muslims after all, and the Christianity of the Greeks and Armenians was seen as a threat to the nascent nationalism. Above all, in communities long directed by their imams or their priests, the secular bureaucratic "state" would be privileged over religious leaders. So mosques were seized along with the properties belonging to churches. Sufi tekkes were shut down. Alevism was shunned. Drinking alcohol in public was permitted; buffalo-drawn carts were not. The script was changed from Arabic to roman, and the language dramatically altered to eliminate Persian and Arabic words, rendering millions of people illiterate overnight. Most famously, the veil was discouraged as retrograde, and the charismatic red fez was banned. For weeks, many men in Anatolia didn't even leave the house, so scandalized were they by the prospect of wearing a Western hat; others wrapped cloth around it and called it a turban; local politicians, upon seeing a fez-wearing rebel in the street, would immediately report him to the authorities. Atatürk deeply hated those conical hats:

"Gentlemen," Atatürk said in 1927, "it was necessary to abolish the fez, which sat on the heads of our nation as an emblem of ignorance, negligence, fanaticism and hatred of progress and civilization. [It was necessary] to accept in its place the hat, the headgear used by the whole civilized world; and in this way, to demonstrate that the Turkish nation, in its mentality as in other respects, in no way diverges from civilized social life."

The "Turk," meanwhile, was defined as modern, Muslim but specifically Sunni Muslim, and, most important, Turkic. The cosmopolitanism of Constantinople was deliberately destroyed. "Turkish schoolbooks taught new generations of students to see their distant ancestors as Turkic tribesmen, even if their grandfathers had actually been Salonican greengrocers or Sarajevan tailors," the historian Charles King writes. "Under the Ottomans, few of these families would have dreamed of using 'Turk' to describe themselves. That label was generally reserved for a country bumpkin more comfortable astride a donkey than in the sophisticated environs of Istanbul."

To further unify the new Turks, Atatürk posited something called the Sun Language Theory, which was, in the words of the anthropologist Ayşe Gül Altınay, "a racialized conception of *the history of all civilization* [italics mine] at the center of which lay the Turkish race, culture and language." Even groups like the Kurds, this new history argued, were in denial of their true Turkish identity. Atatürk demanded his people adopt a four-volume history called the Turkish History Thesis, which stated that their ancestors long ago descended from ancient peoples of Central Asia who had migrated to Anatolia, India, and China, where they disseminated their ancient culture. Among their descendants, in fact, were the Hittites of Anatolia, which conveniently allowed Atatürk to lay claim to a land then occupied by Greeks and Armenians and Kurds. Turkish, meanwhile, was declared a language from which many other languages had been derived, including Finnish and Hungarian, which happily connected Turks and Turkishness to the West. The Turks' most important chapter in history, therefore, was no longer its six hundred years as the Ottoman Empire; Atatürk elevated Central Asia's significance to marginalize Ottoman and Islamic influence. To make this point, Atatürk moved the capital from grand Constantinople to a terrible plain in Anatolia, closer to the Turks' Hittite roots. (The writer Christopher de Bellaigue called Ankara "a bare hillock on which to build a new cult.") Another of Atatürk's adopted daughters, Afet, set about proving scientifically that Turks—despite their newfound Central Asian origins—were not from the "yellow" race but the "white" one. Atatürk and his band of adopted daughters rewrote Turkish history, and invented a people.

An Ottoman aesthetic that had evolved over multiple centuries would be replaced with a Kemalist one dreamt up in only a few years. Even tulips became suspect. In 1933, scholars of Turkey's architectural revolution wrote, "Turkish architects today abandoned domes, floral ornaments and tile decoration. They are marching on a new and logical path." To these modernizers, this path meant mowing down all of the unique artistic techniques of the Ottoman past in order to embrace the bland, modern styles of everyone else in the present. "The temples that the Egyptians constructed for deities or the acropolis that the Greeks built for their Gods . . . or the fountains and mosques of the Turks," wrote Aptullah Ziya, an art critic, in 1932, "cannot be the source of art in the twentieth century, when airplanes are hovering in the skies and ocean liners are crossing the sea at phenomenal speeds."

During my own bewildering initiation days, I spent too much money on a beautiful book about the Kemalist era called *Modernism and Nation Building*. In it, I read that Le Corbusier, the master of modernism, lamented the disappearance of the Ottoman Empire, even as his own work was celebrated by the young Turks who destroyed it. Le Corbusier had genuinely admired the simplicity of the Ottomans' aesthetic, their "harmonious culture." Indeed, I was surprised when I first visited Topkapı Palace, the longtime environs of the sultans, to discover a modest sense of majesty, none of the jewels, brocades, excess, and curlicues of most kings and castles. All of its art and design—its painted miniatures and calligraphy, geometric rooftops and octagonal tiles, soft-domed mosques and proud minarets—struck me as careful and dignified, a civilization of endless busy work and love.

The Kemalists disparaged all of it. They instead built giant concrete slabs of buildings that seemed to squat possessively on the land. The ideology of high modernism, according to Sibel Bozdoğan, "appealed particularly to 'planners, engineers, architects, scientists and technicians' who 'wanted to use state power to bring about huge, utopian changes in people's work habits, living patterns, moral conduct and worldview.'" Many nations embraced high modernism—India, Brazil, Iran—but to the Turks, this modernism did not come with dangerous philosophies from the outside because modernity belonged as much to Turkey as to anyone. A Kemalist slogan at the time was "Being Western in spite of the West"—in other words, being postcolonial but modernizing. Turkey could manage such contortions better than the others because Turkey had never been colonized. For the Turkish Republicans, Bozdoğan writes, "contemporary civilization" was "the universal trajectory of progress that every nation had to follow—a teleological destiny that could not and should not be resisted."

This destiny meant a new lifestyle for the people as well. In cities such as Istanbul, the new Turkish citizen wore Western-style suits, and Western-cut dresses. Nuanced debates broke out in Parliament about whether to ban the *peçe*, or cloth that covers a woman's face; some local authorities simply wrenched off women's *çarşaflar*, or sheets, right in the street, "leaving them in their underpants." In 1931, a Turkish feminist named Nezihe Muhittin published a book called *The Turkish Woman* in which she wrote, "What was the woman of fifteen years ago but a 'monster' both in appearance and in personality?"

This violently transformative period was called the *inkilap*, or revolution. "What does the word 'modern' mean?" someone once asked Atatürk. "It means being a human being," he replied.

Atatürk was one of the world's first great modernizers, a word that to me, in 2007, had no historical meaning but a positive connotation that was as obvious as the word "happy." In Istanbul, Atatürk's photo was in every shop, every restaurant, sometimes looking like Dracula, other times like Kevin Kline. His statue rose in every square, and people stood still for a minute every November 10 at 9:05 a.m., at the time of his death—just stopped wherever they were and stared ahead like zombies, even if at a green light, even if in traffic, even if walking in the middle of the road. It all struck me as strange, obviously cultish, and depressingly old-fashioned. But after September 11, Bernard Lewis, the "reality creator" in America, the historian of Islam, celebrated Turkey as the model for the Middle East, the one Muslim country that had forged a modern, secularist state of relative stability out of the wreck of Islamic civilization. He proposed to George W. Bush that a contemporary iron-fisted Arab Atatürk could similarly create a secular, modern Iraq, with all new myths and infrastructure. This Turkey was the model for remaking the world in 1923; this Turkey was the model again in 2001.

The Kurds, who did not fit this model, who according to the new nationalist myths had always been Turkish, revolted. Thousands of people died in the war to subdue them, a task aided by Sabiha Gökçen, Atatürk's daughter—who herself may have been an Armenian orphan—the world's first female fighter pilot, a fact that much impressed the American newspaper that had once called for the demise of the Terrible Turks. "The advance in little more than a decade from the veil and harem to the air pilot's helmet and the battlefield," wrote *The New York Times*, "is a leap that makes even the Western imagination reel."

Turkish women had indeed made astounding strides. That their rights had been bestowed upon them by a man, one man in particular, would haunt Turkish feminism and Turkish democracy forever, as would all Turks' debt to their father-dictator, the man who had saved them from Western rapaciousness, Islamic torpor, even death itself. Atatürk's ideological descendants—the Kemalists—ruled the country for the next decades, until, it seemed, the very year I arrived. These Turks would also be the ones I would most often meet during my first months in Istanbul.

I MET THEM through random connections: friends of friends of friends, such as the Google colleague of my college roommate. Most of these people were very wealthy, transatlantic, English-speaking Turks with whom, our mutual acquaintances assumed, I would have the most in common. I would meet them at futuristic malls, eating burgers at French restaurants, where they spoke with almost perfect American accents. I experienced a kind of cognitive dissonance in these places, similar to when I went to American expat parties, of being among American people, speaking American English, laughing at American jokes, but not actually being in America, and thus feeling incomparably lost.

One woman invited me to a pool party in a *site*—which was a word for an upscale suburb with a gate—outside of Istanbul that to her was so prestigious she thought the cabdriver making three hundred dollars a month would know where it was. (He didn't.) The houses stood five stories tall, with bougainvillea bushes spilling over the gates, Ferraris in the drive, and pools in the back, around which girls sat reading *Us Weekly*. At dinnertime, Abdullah Gül appeared on television, and the crowd debated his "hidden agenda": Islamists talked a good game, they said, but harbored a secret mission to take over the world and install sharia law. I noticed, sitting in chairs in the corner, two enormous black-skinned dolls wearing aprons.

"Excuse me," I said. "But what are those?"

"I don't know," the owner of the house said. "They are my parents'."

"That's strange," I said. "Do you know what they are?"

They looked like mammy dolls.

"No," he said. Everyone shrugged. The woman who invited me looked as if she'd rather she hadn't.

"Do you know where they are from?" I asked. Perhaps these wealthy people had traveled to some African country in which such dolls were a local craft.

Finally, a young man said, "Maybe from New Orleans," referring to the catastrophic Hurricane Katrina only two years earlier. Everyone laughed.

To be fair, these Turks were callous in the way rich kids can be everywhere, but what I kept being told was that these people, who had spent time in New York or London, were more open-minded than their Islamic counterparts. I was often told that these so-called White Turks would be the ones most "like me." (And in the sense that they shared the racism of many white Americans, I suppose this was true.) They went to the best high schools and came from Westernized families and were not religious Muslims. They always asked me why I was in Turkey when I could have stayed in New York. "I want to understand the relationship between religion and politics in Turkey," I would say. They would respond that the Muslims "were ruining the country" or that they "wanted to turn the country into Iran." One woman told me that the "veil simply *is* oppression, and I'm sick of quasi-enlightened intellectuals in the West suggesting that it's a woman's choice to wear the veil or not—it's not a choice, they're coerced."

Many of them even developed a sign language for their agony, a political pantomime for the head scarf. In the midst of conversations they would drag their two hands around the sides of their face and under their chin. "Everything in Turkey is okay," they seemed to be saying, "but now we have this." And with that gesture I, especially me the Westerner, the foreigner, the uncovered free New York woman, was supposed to empathize with their despair.

Instead, I found these secular Westernized, so-called liberal people—my people—difficult to understand, so much so that I found I couldn't relate to many of their feminist principles, ones to which I ordinarily would have been sympathetic. Their contempt for their culture had a deathly air to it. They boiled with a kind of anger and prejudice that reminded me of the American South. I was reading Orhan Pamuk's *Snow* at the time, in which he wrote:

> No one who's even slightly Westernized can breathe free in this
> country unless they have a secular army protecting them, and
> no one needs this protection more than intellectuals who think
> they're better than everyone else and look down on other people—
> if it weren't for the army, the fanatics would be turning their rusty
> knives on the lot of them and their painted women, chopping
> them all into little pieces.

Such was the central paradox of Turkish culture—liberalism in service of an authoritarian national project. Even feminism at times could be used in service of immorality, violence, and nationalism, as if women had been empowered only so Turkey would be powerful. The irony was that sometimes when secularists or Kemalists talked about "modernity," they were talking about modernity as conceived by Atatürk seventy years earlier, during the formation of this Turkish Republican identity. To them, the rise of these religious politicians meant Turkey was going backward, back to the beginning, before Atatürk, before the "Turk." It was not just feminism or anti-religious fervor that compelled those women and men with flags to take to the streets, but their very identities as human beings. For these Turks, modernity was a religion in and of itself, and Atatürk their god. That was why girls had his signature tattooed on their arms. *The Turks have been brainwashed!* I thought. For a long time, I went on like this, believing two key fallacies: that this was my first brush with nationalist propaganda, and that the slavish devotion to "modernity" was something unique to the Turkish Republic, an abstract concept in which we Americans had never needed to engage.

IN MY FIRST WEEKS, I attended a conference on international press freedom at the Hilton hotel. The Hilton was in a zone of Istanbul seemingly designed precisely for conferences—spacious, monotonous, and full of travel agencies—halfway between Taksim Square, near where I lived, and Nişantaşı, an old, upper-class neighborhood where Spanish leather shoes cost five hundred dollars and Porsches regularly parked outside of cafés. The Hilton was by then one of Istanbul's oldest modern hotels, with gates strangely resembling a highway toll plaza, and a huge lawn that surrounded the hotel's modernist hulk of concrete, set far back from the road. The hotel had the shape of a giant 1960s television—a large screen on a small stand—and had the benevolent totalitarian aesthetic of the United Nations. As I drove in, I marveled at how much property it took up, as if it were one of the city's many military installations, or some other precious piece of state property. When I entered, I felt the strange experience of being home again, a feeling I assumed came from the corporate uniformity of all international brands. Spending time at the Hilton seemed to make it the sort of place that would keep me from understanding the real Turkey, which I would learn someday was the Hilton's point.

Journalists had come from all over the world to attend this conference on press freedom. I was new to Turkey, but even I knew that the Turkish journalists and thinkers on the panel largely supported the secularist point of view—there was the historian Andrew Mango, who had written a flattering biography of Atatürk; İlber Ortaylı, a historian known for denying the Armenian genocide; and Bassam Tibi, who wrote an article called "Turkey's Islamist Danger." The last of them was a man named Ertuğrul Özkök, the editor of one of Turkey's largest mainstream newspapers, *Hürriyet*, who spent most of the time insincerely wringing his hands over reader complaints that *Hürriyet* wasn't pro-secularist enough, although Caner had told me that *Hürriyet* was one of the most secularist newspapers in town.

"What can we do?" he said. "We get so many letters saying our paper does not enforce laicism enough. We have all these antigovernment columnists, but readers still complain!"

"Don't worry," Andrew Mango said at one point. "You share your problems with Europe, more evolved societies, rather than the Middle East."

"My generation had a strong republican education," Özkök said. "We thought the problem with Islam was over!"

"If Turkey has not had a civil war, it's because the military stopped it," said Mango.

I had been most disturbed that day by the American journalist who moderated the panel. He had reported from Turkey throughout the nineties, including for *The New York Times*. When the threat of military intervention came up, to the audience of Western journalists at the international press freedom conference, he intoned: "When I first moved to Turkey, I struggled to make sense of it. A friend told me a story, and it's a metaphor that I think will be helpful to all of you in understanding this place. My friend said, You have to think of Turkey as a bus. And the people riding the bus are the citizens. And the people driving the bus are the politicians. And any time the bus swerves a little this way or that way, the guardrails are there to keep it on course. The guardrails are the army."

I was surprised. This was not how American journalists—*New York Times* journalists—see democracy, I thought; Americans don't believe that a military, especially one threatening a coup, is a legitimate component of a democracy. I was only two weeks into the country, and thus knew nothing about foreign correspondents, male foreign correspondents, American male foreign correspondents, the history of *The New York Times*, the history of U.S.-Turkish relations, the history of the last hundred years. All I could see clearly at the time was a man spellbound by soldiers, and as I left the Hilton through its sad tollbooth, I assumed that this journalist was an exception to the rule.

ONE EVENING, after I had lived there for about six months, I took a ferry from European Istanbul to the Asian side to meet a Turkish woman for dinner. Those beetle-bug ferries were saturated in a 1970s aesthetic; all faded wood panels, sepia-toned lighting, and mustached men with nicotine-stained faces. Seagulls chased after us and Turks threw pieces of *simit* to their beaks. Men carried tea in tulip-shaped cups on trays, some sold strange, seemingly homemade, gadgets. Briefly, it felt as if everyone might know one another, or be related; after all, we'd all made the same decision to live in Istanbul. We were a breed, a club, a cult even. As we pulled farther away from the shore, the European side of the city expanded into a thousand new angles; something about the hills and curves and magnificence of the point of view meant that you always felt you were seeing the Old City for the first time. To this day, on those ferries, even in my darkest moments, I feel nothing but complete joy, as if immediately thrust into a state of meditation I cannot achieve on land, or on any other boat—an Istanbul-specific, ferry-bound peace.

Rana—that was her name—met me at the ferry terminal with a large smile and curly hair and an American accent. Her physical bearing was slightly tomboyish, not self-consciously feminine or rigid like that of many of the other Turkish women I saw, or thought I had seen at the time. Rana was open in many ways, and thankfully, since I had by then made few friends, she was open to me—perhaps if only because she had recently returned from New York herself, after a year doing a master of law, and missed it so much, she said, it felt as if her heart were broken. But she also loved Istanbul as much as I did—and she had a car. We embarked on a series of first dates: she took me to the boho coffee shop called Şimdi, where she'd met the love of her life, and to the independent record shop Lale Plak, where she had bought all her Nina Simone records; she showed me her favorite *meyhane* on the Asian side, where she taught me how to drink *rakı* the way the tough guys did. She drove me up the Bosphorus to the handsome Rumeli Hisarı, a fortress from which Mehmet the Conqueror had invaded Constantinople, and to a Polish village called Polonezköy slightly outside the city, where we grilled meat outdoors and lay on hammocks. Rana seemed to delight in my childish excitements as much as I did: I was still in the habit of finding everything in Istanbul beautiful or adorable. She took me to her office, an elegant campus overlooking the Bosphorus, where she worked as a corporate lawyer, and pointed out the famous jazz club under the Galata Tower where she had always dreamed she would sing. She introduced me to her two closest friends, men, both of whom were children of leftists, and who, like many of Rana's generation, had been raised after the 1980 coup to stay out of politics. Their generation was liberal-minded but apolitical, obeying the dictates of a new capitalist economy that demanded large salaries to survive.

Rana was cool and independent-minded and loving, and shared none of the prejudices of the White Turks I had met so far. But she, too, had emerged from an almost entirely secularist world: her mother came from a Kemalist, Westernized family, all of which I asked her about ceaselessly.

"The thing is, my mother tells me that when she grew up in a small town in Anatolia, in the fifties and sixties, girls rode bicycles in shorts and sleeveless shirts," Rana said. "And now she says, you know, you can't do that there. You can't do that anymore."

"But why? I mean, who says you can't?"

"You don't feel comfortable. You just wouldn't," she said. "You have to consider for a second that conservative religious people *are* different. Islam never experienced its renaissance, its enlightenment. And when it comes down to it religious people are not as liberal as we are, the way they live compared to the way we do."

What Rana was saying was not just the view of Turkish secularists, but the view of Americans as well: these ideas manifested in our discussions about 9/11 in more coded ways. For some reason it wasn't until I was in a foreign country, a Muslim country in which I passed religious people on the street every day, and where I often found myself agreeing with religious politicians, that I could sense something wasn't right about the Western view of the world. For Turks, for liberal-minded women like Rana, this debate brought with it much higher stakes, of course: her fear of an Islamicizing country was little different from the fear of a pious woman in a secularist one. Forced dress and behavior was normal in Turkish history. Somehow, though, because in Turkey the force that wanted to restrain Islam was the military, I could see that Westerners, too, were a people who wanted to change people's lives by force. What was the Enlightenment, what was liberalism?

Rana knew, too, better than I did, that something had gone wrong in Turkey's history.

"You know, I will have these moments," she said, looking distraught at the memory. "Where I will be driving, and I will see a covered woman, and of course I will stop and let her cross. And I wonder to myself whether that made her feel good that I did that, because women like me, uncovered women, aren't usually so kind. Another time, it was raining and a covered woman offered me her umbrella. I thanked her over and over because I was trying so hard to make that connection, to show that I appreciated what she did. And suddenly I felt like this must be what it was like in 1950s America, and she is black and I am white."

Some time later, we walked down Istiklal and passed a young woman in a fitted, sexy dress, and a tightly drawn head scarf. Rana scowled: "This is what I mean: If covering yourself to hide your sexuality is for Islam, then why is the dress so tight?" Somehow this mode of dress was acceptable to religious people, she explained, but if someone like Rana, a so-called secular woman, dressed in even a demonstrably unsexy way, a religious person might still condemn her for not wearing a head scarf.

Rana was angry about these complex Turkish social dynamics, but she didn't support the head scarf ban. My careless readings about Turkey's "head scarf issue"—my own reflex to control someone's religion, body, self—had been about something else. My logic was drawn from a fear that Islam was something dangerous, threatening, not a religion but a way of life chosen to resist the modern world the rest of us enlightened folks accepted, a religion that seemed to necessarily lead to violence and oppression, unlike Christianity or Judaism, which, I supposed, did not. Even liberals, even educated people, even New Yorkers—sometimes especially them—had come to believe something was wrong with *the religion* itself, which in turn could only mean the religion required external restraint, like the "guardrails" guiding a bus full of corrupt politicians. Where I had gotten the idea that Islam should be restrained seemed not difficult to pinpoint: I was influenced by the post–September 11 discourse of the time. *But where did I get this impulse to restrain anyone from anything in the first place?* I wondered, as if Rana's analogy to 1950s America had not just been made.

AT THE TIME, one of the White Turks' greatest fears had been of something called *mahalle baskısı*, or "neighborhood pressure." A prominent academic named Şerif Mardin, famous for a groundbreaking book on Islamic movements, had given an interview to a newspaper in which he mentioned the term, setting off a public panic. Secularists seized on Mardin's *mahalle baskısı*, described in the media as the steady pressure by religious people on secular people to be more Islamic, as scientific proof of their amorphous fears. In other words, even if Erdoğan did not force you to wear the head scarf, your neighbors will shame you into feeling like you have to. Many Turks interpreted the term, and his comments, to mean that Islam was a disease you could catch, that neighbors influenced one another to be more Islamic, and that people, often girls, felt pressure to conform to these beliefs. It was as if Islam had a unique conformist force to it, its own Jedi magic. Mardin had said:

> There is something called "neighborhood pressure" in Turkey.
> The "neighborhood pressure" is a phenomenon and an atmosphere
> very difficult for social scientists to describe. I believe this
> atmosphere exists in Turkey, independent of the AK Party.
> Therefore, if conditions are suitable for the development of such an
> atmosphere, the AK Party will also have to obey this atmosphere.

Mardin emphasized later that he did not mean that the AK Party was creating neighborhood pressure, but rather that the party would be likelier to submit to it. The secularists, not surprisingly, deduced that an Islamic party ruling the country would mean more Islam for everyone.

I went to visit Mardin, who lived in the kind of Turkish neighborhood where there would rarely be any pressure to be Islamic. It was another *site*, or gated community, in the wealthy northern hills above the seaside village of Bebek, where women might jog in half-shirts, and New York–style luxury apartment towers overshadowed mosque minarets. Mardin was old and wore a brace around his midsection. He had the modest wisdom of many aging academics.

"When I said that about neighborhood pressure, I had been responding to a man who was against the Orientalist elements in neighborhood life, against the people with loose trousers lounging in coffeehouses with their *nargile*," he said. "This man was speaking of the neighborhood as a place where 'backward' tendencies" were becoming more normal in reaction to modernity.

But when Mardin responded that there was such a thing as neighborhood pressure, he meant that it was "a state of mind, so to speak, of the people who, without being aware of it, promote a kind of life that is according to them an 'Islamic' kind of life. It's very difficult to apprehend because it's very evanescent. There is something that is both very cloudlike and at the same time real about it."

"So you are saying it is more than a religion?"

"Modern political science has always taken up religion as 'religion,' as a separate topos," he said. "But neither in the West nor in Islam is this the case. When you try to differentiate Islam from social life, that is a Western way of looking at it. Very recently Islam, society, and science were all things that were integrated in a way which we cannot really apprehend today. The weight of these former relations—that were very warm, very close, where people bonded around Islam—that bond was destroyed. Politics in its wider sense is also a way of making up for this bond which has been destroyed." What we were seeing now was a "translation of what is missing from society, into politics." Erdoğan, the AK Party, could be this translator.

The writer Pankaj Mishra once said that Islam was a civilization in a way Americans didn't understand, a way of life. Suddenly, I tried to imagine what those years of Kemalism, of modernization and nation-building, of secularization were like. It is difficult to find memoirs of postrevolutionary Turkey in English—memoirs that describe the sensation of being unable to read street signs, of seeing women unveiled, of losing one's identity and one's, as Mardin put it, atmosphere and way of social relations. *A Mind at Peace*, the 1949 novel by Ahmet Hamdi Tanpınar, is a rare glimpse of what it meant to experience both external and internal devastation: Istanbul ravaged by war and poverty; entire populations transferred out of the once cosmopolitan city; the loss of superpower status; the new Turkish Republican pressure to banish the rotting Ottoman past from their minds and to subordinate Islam.

"They're all orphans of a civilization collapse," one of his characters says. "What good does it do to destroy previous forms that have provided them with the strength to persevere? Great revolutions have long experimented with this, and they've served no purpose besides leaving the masses naked and exposed . . . What do you think we'll gain through such a refutation besides the loss of our very selves?"

Foreign observers at that time also expressed alarm over Atatürk's radical alterations. Exiled in Istanbul after fleeing Hitler, the German scholar Erich Auerbach lamented in letters to Walter Benjamin that Turkey had much in common with his own native land:

> Atatürk has had to force through everything he has done in a
> struggle against the European democracies on the one hand, and
> on the other against the old Muslim, pan-Islamist sultan economy,
> and the result is a fanatically, anti-traditional nationalism: a
> renunciation of all existing Islamic cultural tradition, a fastening
> onto a fantasy "ur-Turkey," technical modernization in the
> European sense in order to strike the hated and envied Europe
> with its own weapons. Hence the predisposition for European
> exiles as teachers, from whom one can learn without being afraid
> that they will spread foreign propaganda. The result: Nationalism
> in the superlative with the simultaneous destruction of the historic
> national character. This configuration, which in other countries
> such as Germany, Italy, and indeed also in Russia is not yet a
> certainty for everyone, steps forth here in complete nakedness.

Orhan Pamuk's idea of *hüzün*, or melancholy, had its roots in this period, too. "Ours was the guilt, loss, and jealousy felt at the sudden destruction of the last traces of a great culture and a great civilization that we were unfit or unprepared to inherit," he once wrote, "in our frenzy to turn Istanbul into a pale, poor, second-class imitation of a Western city."

But what Mardin was saying was more profound to me: that Islam had been the foundation of their human relations. Mardin, in fact, described this atmosphere with the Turkish word *hava*, which can mean "atmosphere" or "weather," but more commonly means "air," and in that beautiful Turkish phrasing I could see for the first time that Islam had been even more than a civilization. It had been the air they breathed.

We in the West still seemed to believe the old story of how a man transformed an Islamic empire into a secular republic: Atatürk came along, changed some rules, the people followed. Old Turkish textbooks didn't portray the suppression of Islam as anything other than a liberation. But I began to question for the first time what it was like to suddenly lose your language, your mode of dress, your idea of the world. My assumption had been that any social revolution that resulted in a country becoming more "modern," in the American sense, must have been a good thing. In Turkey, not only had this revolution been damaging, but it hadn't worked. It was strange, I was as critical of the United States as I thought one could be. But at that point, I still had no idea that with even those political views came an unassailable, perhaps unconscious faith in my country's inherent goodness, as well as in my country's Western way of living, and perhaps in my own inherent, God-given, Christian-American goodness as well.

ATATÜRK'S ERA of nation-building quickly mutated into a period of turbulence and fracture. The decades after Atatürk's revolution were like skipping records, beginning with an election and ending with a military coup, the country always having to start over and imagine itself again. Turks often explained military coups as a trauma, an erasure, leaving the society disjointed and incoherent. But as I had seen, even in 2007, Western journalists were still touting the military as the country's "guardrails," the guardian that kept Turkey on track to democracy. Westerners once believed this, during the Cold War, because of the fear of communism. Now, it was the fear of Islamism, and specifically the fear of Erdoğan.

In the 1960s, the country's vast population of poor, pious Muslims, long isolated in remote towns in the east, began flooding the cities, and Islamic brotherhoods urged their followers to find compromise with modernity. Reports from that period describe almost a small invasion of peasants, families from the Black Sea and Adana and Erzurum who squatted in the old beautiful buildings and erected shacks on spots of land. The new atmosphere gave birth to a new breed of politician, as many religious Turks devised ways to be both devout and, in Atatürk's phrase, "a human being." Out of that confident generation came Recep Tayyip Erdoğan, the man who was the leader of Turkey when I arrived and who is still as I write this sentence more popular than an Adele song.

Erdoğan grew up in Kasımpaşa, a blue-collar Istanbul neighborhood near the heart of the city. Like some cross between South Boston and old Italian Brooklyn, Kasımpaşa was a tribal, dangerous place, full of lower-class cowboy-immigrants from the Black Sea who may or may not have belonged to some mafia but definitely could beat you up. The men from Kasımpaşa—they were also called *kabadayı*, or tough guys—strutted up and down their hillside slope of the city with a particular macho swagger. "Walk behind the prime minister someday," a Kasımpaşa resident told me. "You'll see what it means to be Kasımpaşalı."

It was possible that this particular vanity, or pride, was very new. In the last fifty years—almost Tayyip Erdoğan's lifespan—the world of the average Turkish man had been dramatically transformed. He found decent work. He sent his children to college and bought his wife fancier clothes. He still didn't have some of the rights of his fellow citizens; if you were openly religious, or had a religious vocation, then you were explicitly banned from high-ranking officer positions within the military, for instance. (I once met an imam, who was also a muezzin, who was also the owner of a hostel by a pretty lake in the middle of the country, but what he really, really wanted to be was a commando. Such a thing was not possible in Turkey.) Nor was it possible for women who wore head scarves to serve in many state-run institutions, including Parliament. But more and more people in Turkey were middle-class and pious, and these Turks no longer felt snubbed by the Westernized elite, or by the West. They were spiritually redeemed and politically enfranchised by the rise of Kasımpaşa's native son, who would morph from a *simit* seller on the street to the most powerful and independent leader in the Middle East. Indeed, when I visited Kasımpaşa some years later, I discovered Erdoğan cell phone ringtones, Erdoğan shrines, six degrees of Erdoğan separation, and Erdoğan one-upmanship:

"Erdoğan and I were best friends. *Best* friends."

"My mother was midwife to Erdoğan's kids."

"I am two years older than Tayyip!"

In his twenties, Erdoğan joined an explicitly Islamist political party that had been led by Necmettin Erbakan since the late sixties, inspired in part by the Muslim Brotherhood of Egypt. Erbakan was an upper-class engineer who wore Versace ties, but his acolyte, Erdoğan, appealed to the working class. In 1994, at the age of forty, he was elected mayor of Istanbul, on a platform of clean hands, higher quality of life, and a devotion to municipal services. Even secularists gratefully recall that it was Erdoğan who got rid of the trash on the street corners, improved the water and the transportation systems, and planted the flowers. A journalist who interviewed Erdoğan in those years told me some people nicknamed him the Minister of Trees.

But Erdoğan terrified the elite by proclaiming himself the "imam of Istanbul" and banning alcohol in municipal buildings. In 1997, he read a poem at a public gathering: "The mosques are our barracks / the domes our helmets / the minarets our bayonets / and the believers our soldiers." Its author was none other than Ziya Gökalp, Turkey's founding nationalist intellectual, but Turkey's generals accused Erdoğan of using the poem as an Islamist rallying cry and sent him to prison. The military had just led a nonviolent coup against the rising so-called Islamists, dissolving the Welfare Party, closing religious schools, and banning the head scarf on university campuses. Thousands of young women would have to go to college abroad, including Erdoğan's daughter. His own brief time in prison wrought a marked change, if not in his political philosophy then in his political strategy: he became more acquiescent to his country's Western-looking foreign and economic policy, to European Union reforms, and, for a while anyway, to the military.

In 2001, he founded the AK Party, and allied with another group of canny, smooth-talking religious Muslims called the Gülenists, after its founder, Fethullah Gülen, a preacher who lives in Pennsylvania. They were a mysterious and powerful group. They advertised themselves as peace-loving and "moderate," a PR campaign that worked very well on Americans. Every month, Gülen representatives held seminars for foreign journalists in Istanbul, where they offered lectures related to the news of the day: the history of the AK Party, the compatibility of Islam with democracy. They introduced us to religious scholars and intellectuals, to young women pursuing PhDs who could confidently articulate their own reasons for wearing a head scarf. The Gülenists were aggressively helpful to foreigners. But many Turks, it seemed, feared their ubiquity; there was a sense that even the bread you bought at the local *fırın* might have been sponsored by the Gülen movement, that the bread itself could be "Gülen," as Turks put it.

The Gülenist newspaper, *Zaman*, one of the most popular in the country, also used Erdoğan's language of American liberalism and capitalism: "modernization," "human rights," "freedom," "pro-business," "privatization." Then I had not thought to even question these words, so dazzled was I that they—the *Islamists*—were using that language at all. The new AK Party spoke approvingly of the West, both as a model for the Turkish economy and as a beacon of religious liberty. Erdoğan advocated for a program of market liberalization once designed by the IMF. They were one of the only major parties—the formerly Islamist party—that fully supported joining Europe. In accordance with the EU's demands, the AK Party passed more than forty pieces of legislation to protect freedom of expression, improve the rights of women and children, and eliminate torture, and would eventually strengthen civilian control of the military, the last of which, of course, was the one most in Erdoğan's personal interest. For the first time in history, a civilian politician would be free to run Turkey how he chose. So enamored was I with this most important of steps toward real democracy—no more military in politics!—that I didn't consider how this newfound liberty might be corrosive even to a politician with the best possible intentions.

Both religious Turks and liberals were astonished at their "Tayyip's" ability to bring about real change. In 2004, *Time* had noted approvingly: "Western leaders have been scouring the Muslim world for moderate politicians who see their future in democracy and pluralism. Erdoğan may be the best find yet." Erdoğan and the AK Party appeared to be the sort of mild, moderate "good Muslims" who make Westerners feel better about the possibility of peace in the world, as well as the widespread appeal of Western-style democracy and market capitalism. And Erdoğan made me feel better, too. A friend from home said to me, "It feels utterly wrong that you would be more sympathetic to the Islamic party rather than the secular one." But Erdoğan and his party, who so ably used words like "freedom" and "democracy," appealed to me far more than the Turkish secularists who believed religious people were a threat to Atatürk's country, whose bloodlust could be aroused because of a poem. Like many of the journalists, I celebrated the fact that Erdoğan was "pro-business," because capitalism seemed like a Western antidote to the scary things about Islam. Many former leftists supported Erdoğan at that time—even the group of gay men I befriended in my neighborhood voted for him—and on some level, I supported Erdoğan, too. Could there be anyone more easily seduced by Erdoğan's up-by-the-bootstraps story than Americans who treasured that same myth about themselves? "For so long, the secularists imitated the West, and they were ashamed of where they came from," an artist told me. "Erdoğan doesn't have any of that shame, and you can tell." The AK Party won the election that year I arrived, and for the first time, Turkey had a prime minister, a president, and a ruling majority party in Parliament who were all former Islamists.

Rana had by then moved past any concern she had about Erdoğan and Gül's piousness. She was seven steps ahead of me already. Her concerns centered on potential corruption, the kind that might be especially tempting to a segment of society that never before had unfettered access to the state's economic and bureaucratic largesse. I admitted that few people in the foreign press at the time questioned the party's economic policies or finances.

"So for a lot of people this is about a question of money?" I asked.

I'm surprised she didn't kill me. "Obviously!" she nearly yelled. "Money, power, whatever. They're politicians! I mean, if you *Americans* aren't thinking about *money*, then who the hell will?"

Neither of us realized at the time that it was precisely because I was American that I did not think about *money*, not in this context anyway. I was consumed by this country's cultural revolution. I had never been somewhere, I thought, where national and personal identity had been so deliberately and methodically engineered, and here I was watching the whole thing fall apart. For me, everything was somehow representative of this what-it-meant-to-be-a-Turk question, and I took it as my duty to understand this strange virus—nationalism—to which I assumed the Turks had been uniquely prone.

AT THE TIME, I had three American friends working on books about the Armenian genocide, and when I applied for my fellowship, I, too, had wanted to investigate the Turkish-Armenian phenomenon, because for an American who knew nothing about Turkey, and who had read about the persecution of Orhan Pamuk for talking about the Armenians' suffering, the denial of genocide was the likeliest subject about which to be enraged. "How does a people go about forgetting the past?" I wrote in my application essay. One of these American friends invited me to Gallipoli, which had seen one of the most important battles in World War I, a giant victory for the flailing Turks, and from which Atatürk emerged as a brilliant hero. Our guide, Bülent, told us the National Ministry of Education made it mandatory for all Turkish students—every student in the country—to visit the peninsula "to build national consciousness." Thousands of kids ventured from all over Turkey to Gallipoli by the busload. In Turkey, courses in militarism begin early. One social studies textbook for fifth graders explained that "our duty is to eliminate all subversive and divisive threats directed to our country." Another read: "Turkish existence would come to an end if nationalism were abandoned." In high school, every Turkish student took a mandatory national security course, taught by military officers. "War and war-making are essential in our culture," one teacher explained. Turks learned that the military must stay strong to protect them from constant foreign and domestic threats. They were told the Kurds and Armenians inside Turkey tried to take Turkey from them. They were told Westerners outside Turkey tried to take away Turkey from them, too.

When, that October, six months after I arrived, Kurdish militants killed a dozen soldiers in an ambush in southeastern Turkey, my neighborhood turned into a strange fantasia of red flags. Even Caner couldn't hide that he was worried; the anger, the nationalism, the war cries, only one day old, already seemed as bad to him as it did in the nineties, when the Turkish state waged a vicious war against the Kurdistan Workers' Party, or the PKK, a Kurdish militant group, and by extension much of the Kurdish community. People marched down Istiklal Caddesi waving those enormous bloodred Turkish flags, the men sporting red bandannas like warriors, the women holding photos of Atatürk on sticks, the children clutching signs that read WE ARE ALL TURKS. Small vans decorated with photos of dead soldiers shuttled loads of people through the heart of the city and played 1930s-style anthems. Men sat out the windows of beat-up sedans wielding those man-size flags as if at the barricades; flag sellers stumbled beneath the weight of their wares on every block. Even Starbucks had a flag. At night, e-mails were dispatched urging people to march, to turn off their lights at nine thirty, to wear black. Flags were posted on Facebook, instead of personal photos. Black ribbons that had been worn on people's chests to commemorate the fallen littered the Metro. Even women were enlisting in the army—one was six months pregnant—along with the thousands of men who were volunteering to go back to it. Across Turkey men marched, armed with their young sons in one hand and guns in the other. Sometimes the young sons waved toy guns, too. The Beyoncé concert was canceled.

"Maybe we should buy a flag," Caner joked. "Just in case?"

By then, I had been often hanging out with Caner and his Kurdish friends, most of whom went to Boğaziçi University, the Harvard of Turkey. One evening, Caner was slowly drinking his four-lira vodka lemonade at one of the few cheap bars in the pleasant Istanbul neighborhood of Cihangir, where his parents, Orhan Pamuk, dog-owning expatriates, and Turkish soap opera actors shared a fancy Carrefour food store and stunning views of the Bosphorus. He told a joke:

> Once there were two Kurdish men and they really wanted to
> be Turks. So they went to a military commander and asked him,
> "How can we become Turkish?" And the military commander
> said, "Just go to the highest mountain and scream three times, 'I am
> a Turk, I am a Turk, I am a Turk!' And you will be a Turk." So the
> two Kurdish men went to the mountain and in order to get as high
> as possible the one stood on the other's back. He screamed, "I am

a Turk! I am a Turk! I am a Turk!" Then he stood there. When his friend below him said, "Hey, my turn," the Turk on top looked down at the Kurd and replied, "Shut up, bitch."

He told this joke with the typical irony and sly grin that he and his Kurdish friends employed regularly—when they teased one another about not really being Turks, when they called one another "peasant," when they derided ethnic music in favor of "modern" contemporary pop music, all as if pretending to suck up to an invisible Turkish minder. This humor protected as much as it might have isolated them.

At the time one of the only newspapers writing critically about the government's treatment of the Kurds, about the military, and about nationalism was a new one called *Taraf*. I went to visit the founder, the novelist and journalist Ahmet Altan. *Taraf*'s office was located on the Asian side of Istanbul, in a lively neighborhood called Kadıköy. Inside the office, I passed through two guards and a bag checkpoint. Very young people crouched over black laptops under fluorescent newsroom lights. It was carpeted, and felt like a bookstore. From the windows, I could see my neighborhood across the twinkling water.

Altan had been fired from newspapers and prosecuted for his columns many times. In Turkey, censorship served to bolster Turkish nationalism. Altan was once sentenced to a year and a half in jail for "inciting racial hatred." In 1999, he went to trial for insulting "the moral characteristic of the government and its armed and security forces." The year before, his crime was writing, according to one newspaper, "about government doctors who issued conflicting forensic examinations on a nine-year-old boy who had been molested." He had also been accused of collaborating with the PKK, and criticizing military generals.

Altan wanted to start *Taraf* because of the Kurdish issue. "Most Turks are very suspicious about the Kurds," he said. "The Turkish media likes to write 'our army, huge and powerful army'—a very chauvinistic approach."

Former lefties, or secular liberals like Altan, were at the time pushing this idea that it was actually the Westernized elite in Turkey, not the Erdoğan Islamists, who were responsible for Turkey's illiberalism.

"We learn a lot of lies, which is called history in Turkey," he said. "They worship Atatürk, he's a kind of superman. He cannot do anything wrong. Criticism about Atatürk is against the law. Some countries you can see only one man's statue. In Turkey, it's Atatürk. In Iraq, it was Saddam. In North Korea, it's Kim Jong. If there's only one kind of statue in a country, it means that country has a problem. The only goal of our education is to create obedient citizens who worship Atatürk and Kemalism."

Erdoğan didn't seem to believe in freedom of the press, either, I said, referring to some squabbles the prime minister had had lately with political cartoonists. Altan didn't come down hard on the AK Party.

"That's another enigma of Turkey," he said. "They are religious guys, conservative guys, but at the same time they are the most progressive party in Turkey right now. It's unbelievable: progressive conservatives! There is no such category in sociology or politics. But we have it. The media tries to say they will bring sharia to Turkey, which I do not believe. Turks are not those kinds of Muslims. We have our own style in religion."

"This is hard for many people in the West to understand," I said.

"I think they cannot understand Turkey," he said. "First of all, Turkey's a narcissistic society. One way we think we are the best, the other way we are very fragile. We can easily believe that we are humiliated. Yet we also have the arrogance of an empire. If you try to teach something to Turks, they reject it. You must praise them first: Turks, yes, you are the best." He paused, smoking. "For example, we learn that Atatürk said, 'One Turk is equal to the world.' We believe that."

He looked as if the conversation depressed him. Before I left his office, I asked: "Is it true your books sold a million copies in Turkey?"

"It was my essays," he said. "I like to write about emotions. Westerners do not like that. They like wisdom. I mean, Europe and the States—they adore intelligence and shallow literature. They don't like depth. I think they are afraid of emotions, maybe despise them, as if they cut some part of themselves, cut their souls out. I just say, Westerners, pity for them."

I looked at him quietly, reminded of something. He sounded like Baldwin, whose thoughts I believed were only thought by him, who I never imagined occupied the same reality as this Turkish stranger sitting across from me.

.   .   .

I HAD BEEN approaching Turkey like some specimen I could place under a microscope. This process is inherently hostile, but I did not know that at the time. I automatically sized up the country according to its successes and failures, delighting exaggeratedly over the former as if I had the lowest expectations, and feeling like an impatient teacher about the latter, one who believed her student just needed encouragement and guidance. Turkey was one of those "democratizing," "modernizing" countries, a condition that could be assessed through everything from its human rights to its national curriculum, its economy to its health care, its fashions to its urban transportation. To get around Istanbul, for example, you could buy something called an Akbil, a tiny button that attached to your key chain and was usable on buses, metros, and ferries. To me, the Akbil was brilliant, a stunning invention, and proof that the ruling religious government at the time must be as modern as—possibly more modern than—any American party.

But in Turkish nationalism, I saw Turkey's ugly, violent heart. It was necessarily exclusive, masculine, macho. Nationalism was a modern phenomenon, but Turkey's felt antimodern to me, stuck in the past, an antiquated force that compelled Turks to hate someone in order to maintain their love for themselves. Modernity, I believed at the time, and as I evidently believed about the United States, did not privilege the nation over the individual, did not worship myths conceived centuries ago. Turkey still needed to evolve, I thought, and nationalism, not Erdoğan, not Islam, was the impediment to its maturity. If there was anything that made Turks unique on earth, it was this brand of nationalism, and I wondered, innocently, how many years it would take for this young republic to mature. I felt proud of myself for feeling repelled by this nationalism as an observer, that because of my outsider neutrality, my unique objectivity, I could see this self-love for what it really was.

Here's the thing: no one ever tells Americans that when they move abroad, even if they are empathetic and sensitive humans—even if they come clean about their genetic inability to learn languages, even if they consider themselves leftist critics of their own government—that they will inevitably, and unconsciously, spend those first months in a foreign country feeling superior to everyone around them and to the nation in which they now have the privilege to live.

In one passage of the Nigerian novelist Chimamanda Ngozi Adichie's

Americanah, she describes her Nigerian narrator's encounter with a white American woman. They are discussing V. S. Naipaul's *A Bend in the River*, a novel about an Indian man living in Africa. The white woman says to the Nigerian woman that she had learned so much "about Africa" from it. The Nigerian woman

> did not think the novel was about Africa at all. It was about Europe, or the longing for Europe, about the battered self-image of an Indian man born in Africa, who felt so wounded, so diminished, by not having been born European, a member of a race which he had elevated for their ability to create, that he turned his imagined personal insufficiencies into an impatient contempt for Africa; in his knowing haughty attitude to the African, he could become, even if only fleetingly, a European.

To this, the white American woman responds huffily that she could understand *why an African person* would read the book that way. The white woman believed, Adichie writes, that she "was miraculously neutral in how she read books, while other people read emotionally." The white woman believes white people are neutral and everyone else is not.

I didn't live in Turkey in those days, I didn't live in the world. I lived in my zone of miraculous neutrality, an American neutrality, the most miraculous and neutral of all.

2.

FINDING ENGIN: TURKEY

Given our power and influence, which seem only to grow as disorder and misfortune afflict so many populations, it seems a sad failure that we have not done more to make the world intelligible to ourselves, and ourselves to the world. Shared history is certainly one basis for understanding.

—MARILYNNE ROBINSON

IN THOSE EARLY YEARS, Turkish women often asked me what I thought of Turkish men. "So are the men attacking you on the street?" they said, smiling. "No, of course not. They're all very kind," I replied. "But they must stare," they insisted. "No more in Istanbul than any man stares at any woman in any other city," I said, and we continued our dance. I wondered whether they were asking because Turkish men had been so oppressive, or because I was from the United States, where, in some fantasy, all women were free, and all men were well behaved.

In his book *Istanbul*, Orhan Pamuk quotes a newspaper column from 1974 that advised its readers, "When you see a beautiful woman in the street, don't look at her hatefully as if you're about to kill her and don't exhibit excessive longing either, just give her a little smile, avert your eyes and walk on." In *The Black Book*, Pamuk refers to these stares as "scowls." Shortly after I moved here, I decided the scowls were a test: *I am looking at you, will you treat me like a human being?* If I smiled at them, the men would relax, smile back, and respectfully look away. I detected something ugly in Turkish women's voices when they talked about men on the street—these weren't just men, but men from the East, members of the underclass. I reasoned that since the women were snobs, they couldn't be right.

My second year in Turkey, I moved to Cihangir, the neighborhood of Pamuk and my friend Caner. The stone-planked streets were lined with broad-leafed trees; elegant, four-story buildings—some nineteenth-century, others mid-twentieth—had all been painted in yellow and pink and blue pastels. A tiny green mosque doubled as a teahouse and chairs and tables spilled out into the main square, where people sat all day and night. Cats draped their slinky bodies across motorcycle seats, in windowsills, atop coffee bars; seemingly every corner or doorway had been christened with water bowls or bits of cat food; and in spring, it seemed as if you couldn't walk for stepping on kittens. Everywhere crumbling stairs descended down narrow, romantic passageways. The lucky tenants, those with apartments hanging from the hill, had the View, the Cihangir View, which spanned the Golden Horn, Asia, the Sea of Marmara as it meets the Bosphorus, and even the Princes' Islands in the distance. In Cihangir, everything was graceful, a troupe of ballerinas reincarnated as a city neighborhood.

And it was a *real* neighborhood, the way Jane Jacobs intended, the way of the Ottoman *mahalleler* of a hundred years ago, everyone keeping the organism alive: feeding, loving, protecting. I wanted to contribute to it. Every day, I took care to greet the pastry shop men, to wave at the grumpy parking lot attendants, to shop at the vegetable stand rather than the supermarket, sometimes buying tomatoes twice, as if paying some sort of Cihangir tax. The vegetable man smiled at me in a gentlemanly way, no matter whether he liked me or not.

Cihangir wasn't always so enchanting. In the 1950s, its mostly Greek inhabitants were chased out by Turkish mobs, their shop windows smashed; even this most cosmopolitan of old Istanbul neighborhoods saw the whitewash of Turkish nationalism. When the Greeks, Armenians, and Jews fled, rents plummeted and prostitutes planted roots in the gorgeous old buildings. Cihangir became a place you just didn't go to. I had friends whose mothers still forbade them from living in Cihangir, even as it is now, studded with wide glass storefronts selling IKEA-inspired lamps. Cihangir must have been really bad if, even wearing the conspicuous jewelry of global gentrification, it still scared Turkish moms. Cihangir, named for an Ottoman prince, had been reduced to a lady of ill repute. In Turkey, honor is more important than a good view of the Bosphorus.

The lessons of Istanbul often had to do with honor, but I had always missed that during my conversations with Turkish women about Turkish men. Then one night, for the first time in over a year, I gave in to my lazy New York ways and ordered in some food. (Okay, it wasn't food, it was two beers and a pack of cigarettes.) Two delivery boys arrived. They didn't have change for my fifty-lira bill, so I had to fish coins out of a bowl to pay them, and sheepishly I invited them in while they waited. One respectfully cast his eyes to the floor. The other grinned broadly, amused to be inside a foreign girl's home (I have red hair and freckles and am foreign-looking to Turks). In my mind, I was being neighborly; I almost offered them tea. I also felt stupid dumping all those coins in their hands, and so I over-compensated: "Please come back if I miscounted the change." Now I know—because my Turkish is better and I know how difficult that sentence actually is—that probably the only thing they understood was "please come back."

Two minutes after they'd left, the grinning delivery boy returned, claiming I had indeed left them a few coins short. I turned my back to him again to get his money. I had already acquired a kind of guilt being a foreigner in Turkey, as if all I did was cause Turks trouble. I am not sure where this came from. But as I was feeling ridiculous, the grinning boy came inside, shut the door behind him, and with one swift motion pushed himself against me and grabbed my ass.

I pulled away and he began to come toward me again until I ran for the open window and screamed at him, "I will scream!"

He looked at me, more surprised than I was, and left.

I called Rana, who was out to dinner. She rushed over in minutes. I noticed she was cracking her knuckles like some thug ready for a fight, and laughing.

"So what should we do?" I said. "Go to the police station?"

"No, what, are you kidding?" She laughed. "We don't go to the police station. We're going to tell the neighborhood. And they will beat him."

"What?"

"You'll see."

First, we talked to the guys at the *bakkal*, or market, in my building. Then the *bakkal* where the delivery boy had worked. Each time, the men seemed angry about the delivery boy, and perhaps even more intimidated by Rana's declaration, "I am a lawyer." As Rana had predicted, each guy we informed of the event immediately declared, hands shaking, that he would find the kid and break his face.

"I swear, I will beat him," one promised her.

"He will never be allowed in the neighborhood again," said another.

"Okay," said Rana after an hour or so of this extraordinary acquisition of pledges to violence. "So now you have three men who will beat him. That should be enough."

"For what? Enough for *what*?"

"So that he never does it again."

I had been robbed in Philadelphia and, worse, in New York. I would, in the years to come, go through far fewer moments of harassment, ass grabbing, and home following in Istanbul than I ever did in America. The neighborhood was indeed watching. But the particularly Turkish remedy of neighborhood justice unnerved me. "Why didn't you just call the police?" said one good-liberal, American male friend. "You just let these guys beat this kid up?" Yet when I told my friend who had grown up in India, he said: "Yeah. Sounds like the boy needs a slap."

The Turkish police, notoriously corrupt and violent themselves, had long ago faded from society as a proper regulating force, but neighborhood justice seemed to be more than mere punishment. This delivery boy had denigrated not only my honor but the whole neighborhood's—perhaps all of Turkey's—and so it was up to ordinary Turks to win it back. They would beat him not only because he was dangerous but also because he didn't know his place.

It was clear to me, as my neighbors listened to my story, that I hadn't known my place either. "These animals!" said a Turkish friend. "But why did you even open the door all the way? What were you thinking?" Caner shook his head. "I am telling you, you are too friendly, you smile too much. You cannot be this open." I had confused this young man with my friendliness. My self-conscious American class sensitivity had upset the order of things. But it was this kid who would be set straight, not me. When we told the owner of the deli where the kid worked about what happened, he said, "I am so sorry." Then he turned to Rana with shining eyes, looking as though he might dissolve from shame. "Sister, she is foreign, but I know her. She is a neighborhood girl."

Turks couldn't do anything about foreigners moving to their city, they couldn't do anything about the mysterious country folks moving there either. Instead, they exerted control over that which remained manageable—the boundaries between classes and sexes. My friends' point was: *While this class snobbery may offend your Western sensibilities, you, foreigner, are perhaps better off playing by the rules of this country, instead of your own.* If I was going to live in Turkey, I had to learn to think like a Turk. These were not my rules to break.

ONE DAY I WENT to Gebze at the end of Istanbul's commuter train line that runs along the Sea of Marmara. The thirty-mile trip took eighty minutes and passed through suburbs called Fenerbahçe, Suadiye, Bostancı, Kartal—the city couldn't be that big, could it?—but it wasn't until Gebze, an industrial village of cheap lime-green apartment buildings, metalworking plants, shipyards, and dreary, alien highways, that you felt you had really left Istanbul behind. Ask someone: "Where does Istanbul end?" They will say: "Gebze." Along the way I listened to a conversation between the man and woman sitting across from me, which was about the Italian peace activist who had been raped and killed in Gebze just two weeks before.

"Prison is not the solution," the woman said. The man glanced at me.

The mere presence of a foreigner might have re-aroused what had become a national, collective shame.

That March of 2008, Giuseppina Pasqualino di Marineo, or Pippa Bacca, a thirty-three-year-old Italian artist from Milan, had set out on a journey of performance art and peace activism. Following the lyrics of an Italian singer who prophesied that one day we would all come as brides to a world of peace, she and her friend Silvia Moro wore wedding dresses—frilly ones with cascades of lace—and began hitchhiking through Europe and the Middle East and Turkey, to show that all over the world, or, more specifically, in these maligned countries that border the eastern Mediterranean, human beings could be trusted. If these human beings saw two foreign women in wedding dresses standing on the side of the road, they would pick them up and help them travel to their next destination. The women believed that some sort of innate generosity needed to be proven in places like Bosnia, Turkey, and Israel. Their endeavor was called Brides on Tour. Its website proclaimed: "Hitchhiking is choosing to have faith in other human beings, and man, like a small god, rewards those who have faith in him."

For some reason, Pippa and Silvia decided to take two different routes in Istanbul and reunite in Beirut. Two days after Pippa left Istanbul, no one had heard from her, and her friends and family in Italy began to worry.

Over a week later, the police tracked down Pippa's phone. It led them to Murat Karataş, an unemployed man from Gebze. Karataş himself led the police to the woods where he'd stashed her naked body. He had also stolen Pippa's cash and camera; newspapers claimed there was a photo of Karataş on it, perhaps hours or minutes before he turned on her. Karataş had then used the camera at a relative's wedding, taken pictures of people dancing. Karataş told the police that he'd raped Pippa and then panicked, so he strangled her to death.

My previously scheduled trip to Gebze just after the murder of Pippa Bacca was a coincidence; I was going to visit a scholarship boarding school for poor kids. From the get-go, my Turkish friends frowned on the idea that I would go to Gebze, as if one foreigner's death would create a domino effect of embarrassing hate crimes. Heated conversations followed. Of all the weighty political issues in Turkey, the problems between men and women were the most elemental. They drove the debate about the head scarf, about modernity and secularism, the fears of the Islamic conservative ruling party. The reverse was also true: all those abstract questions dictated what happened in love, in the bedroom, and on the street.

To liberal Turkish women the harassment of women on the street was political. "I think this is what this pious government has done to Turkish society," said one thirty-year-old activist I spoke to. "By using women as a symbol in their political discourse, they have divided women into the pious and the bad. That's why the men stare so much, and make comments. Because they see me and they judge that they can treat me that way, as opposed to pious women who they'd never do that to. It used to be that they would see me, and see an educated woman, and so they would never treat me that way. But now it's different. It's worse in places like Istanbul or other cities where all these forces are thrown together. At least in the country they still have their strong families to keep the men in line."

Her criticisms of the government made as much sense as her class-based comments were unseemly, but when I expressed this feeling to Rana, she said:

"You don't get it. If you are alone on the street, and they attack you, they will think that is fine because, well, why were you alone on the street? And the police and the judges might think the same thing. You take too many risks walking around at night. I don't think you understand. It's not like the United States. I don't say this to you because I think Turkish men are all so terribly violent that there is a high chance of something happening; I say it because if you get unlucky, you are really, really unlucky."

Some months later, headlines came from the conservative Anatolian town of Yozgat. "The Second Pippa!" Two men on motorcycles had raped a Danish woman who'd been biking to Cappadocia. The Dane told the press that she didn't blame Turkey for her assault, that Denmark was just as bad. I, too, believed that you could probably sooner get raped at a Georgetown University house party than anywhere in Turkey. But there was something strange in this sort of reaction—to quickly dismiss the idea that personal violence had anything to do with nationality or ethnicity or religion, to jump up and shout, "Don't worry! We, too, have rapists!" This European—recently traumatized, her life forever changed—went out of her way to not cause offense. Those were tough days for Turkey and the European Union; it was the era of anti-Muslim cartoons, and the beginnings of a crisis in Paris *banlieues*. Pippa's Italian parents, too, had hastened to clarify that they did not blame the Turks for their daughter's death.

"It could have happened anywhere," said my American friend about the rape in Yozgat.

"It happens all the time." I shrugged.

But some people were angry and ashamed and not shrugging. Those people did blame Turkey and the Turks for these bad things, and those people were the Turks.

In Turkey, newspaper columnists are celebrities. There are seemingly hundreds of them. They take, and dictate, the country's intellectual and emotional pulse. These columns can be operatic, riddled with exclamation points and ellipses. But nothing had prepared me for the columnists' howling in response to Pippa Bacca's death, perhaps because that kind of self-flagellation would never occur in a country with a different understanding of individualism, or with a different sense of collective responsibility. One columnist, Semih İdiz, in a newspaper called *Milliyet*, was concerned that Pippa's death justified the Ottoman-era Italian expression "*Mamma li Turchi!*" (Mama, the Turks are coming!) He wrote: "There is such a great distance that we have to cover to reach the level of contemporary civilization that one is inevitably filled with pessimism while thinking how we will be able to cover it. Poor Pippa, I wish you had done your research without passing through our country."

"Pippa Bacca, why did you do such an unnecessary thing to send a message of peace to the world?" wrote another. "Wearing a wedding gown and touring the war-torn regions of the world and trying to prove that people are good in essence while hitchhiking. Why did you need to prove it? What purpose did this trip serve? We are ashamed, we are saddened, and we are trying to soothe ourselves by recalling the fact that the murderer was a former criminal."

Turks saw this devastating and public crime as an excuse to talk about the kind of behavior toward women that was apparently common in their society. In turn, they exposed the complexities of Turkish psychology—first and foremost, as Ahmet Altan had explained, their obsession with how the world saw them. "I wish somebody had warned her that people would start to degrade her death by calling it 'disappointing' because of the effect it would have on the promotion of Turkey," commented one writer. The dark joke was that even the murderer, at some point, exclaimed, "Oh no, this will be bad for the EU, won't it?" What psychological suffering these people have endured, I thought. First, the humiliation of World War I, and now the torture to get into the European Union, always this endless process of kissing the feet of their humiliators to join the Ring of the Civilized. In Turkey one man's disgrace was everyone's disgrace, just as one woman's sexual mishap ruined the whole family. The Turks, still at work in their laboratory of modern evolution, couldn't enjoy the luxury of American individualism. As an American friend put it: "Should we be feeling this kind of self-loathing every time an innocent person gets killed in Bedford-Stuyvesant?" Pippa's rape was the fault of the Turkish nation somehow, and one part of me wished they would give themselves a break.

But a growing part of me admired that the Turks still felt compelled to agonize about such things. The Western diagnosis of the murder—that Karataş was simply deranged—left me unsatisfied. A man who sees a woman on the street alone and because that is new to him, and because it suggests a certain kind of openness, decides that he should take her to the woods and force her to have sex with him—that's not derangement. That's decision making. And it's decision making by someone who doesn't perceive or care about the consequences related to his unfettered desires, perhaps because he's grown up in a world—whether that be his family, his village, or his country—where he truly believes that he'll get away with his crime. I couldn't help but see an unwelcome parallel between the Western diagnosis of derangement as the sole reason for rape and the Western artists' international art project; both were acts of erasure: "We were going to wash away the traces of war," Silvia told the press, "to cancel them." The inclination to suggest that a crime couldn't have a social cause, or could be so easily dismissed as an individual illness, seemed part of the same worldview that inspired Silvia and Pippa to set out in wedding dresses and wash the world free of memory.

· · ·

I STILL HAD NOT traveled east throughout the rest of the country, so when a photographer friend of mine set out to take photos of the former Armenian lands of Anatolia, I attached myself to her adventure. We planned to start in the northeastern corner of the country, in Erzurum, then drive to Erzincan, down the back roads through Kemaliye to Elazığ, up to Bingöl, beyond the dark green mountains of Lice, Ağaçlı, Kulp, and over to Muş and Bitlis. Tourist companies compared this drive to Route 66 in the States, but despite the natural beauty, there were very few tourists. The Turkish military fights a war with the Kurds in the east, and many Western Turks view the east as not only violent but behind.

"How did you find Internet in Bingöl?" Rana asked via e-mail from Istanbul.

"We're at a hotel and they have wireless," I replied.

"Oh my God."

At the Erzurum airport, we ate at the Snow City Airport Restaurant, which had broad windows and resembled a steel version of a ski lodge, with its high triangular ceiling and view of the mountains, its bad hot sandwiches and impatient children. The wireless connection worked upon our arrival and a week later did not. A large flat-screen TV was hooked up to the video game Tetris. A family of six watched a plane rev up on the runway, the tears steadily gathering in the women's eyes as the plane prepared for takeoff. They finally let themselves cry once the plane sped away, as if they hadn't believed that their relative would actually be leaving them until they saw the evidence themselves.

It was a spotless, proud airport complex, built to usher in more skiing-related tourism, aspiring to be a holiday destination, except that there were women moving slowly in black chadors and lots of *tesettür*, the belted, long coats and tightly drawn head scarves of current Turkish fashion. The women didn't look like skiers. There were *mescit* areas, tiny warrens for praying, and walls of windows facing the thick, jade-colored grasslands, and the gleaming, blinding, silver snowy peaks that cast their glare on us like the tips of light swords. The landscape looked as if it had been swept clean of unnecessary objects. Or maybe it was the opposite. Maybe the emptiness made the land seem vulnerable: to ugly condos, ski lodges, more Snow City Airport Restaurants, English-language signs stabbed into ancient grounds. The Euphrates begins there.

In his memoir *Blood-Dark Track*, the novelist Joseph O'Neill, who is of Turkish and Irish descent, writes of nothingness in a country that ought to be full of something. Everywhere you are conscious of the great absence discovered beyond yet another hill, mountain, ancient river, or contemporary man-made lake. The emptiness is a mirror. He writes:

> What I was really feeling, during these journeys, was the solipsistic anxiety that can result from being plunged among people with whom I stood in a relation of near-total mutual ignorance. To be among such strangers was a form of eradication; for which of them could bear witness to who I was? And the converse was also true: unable meaningfully to incorporate these Anatolians into my construction of the world, I lacked the ability to do them justice.

O'Neill's passage resonated with me because driving around eastern Turkey—my first time east—felt like confronting an enormous void. Although the landscape was beautiful, I often felt completely terrible, beset by a sense of menace that I couldn't shake for the rest of the trip.

I began to realize why I felt this way when we reached Kemah. The roads had been slow that day and it had gotten dark before we made it to a decent-size city. Kemah was a creepy place, I knew that before I even saw it. One hundred years ago, in June of 1915, the Turks had sent thousands of Armenians on a forced march and then shoved them off the cliffs overlooking the town. This, I found, was what happened so often to me in Turkey: You're learning about a country, you have read books, and so you know what bad things have happened, and where, and then you go to those places, and you can't help but feel haunted by your knowledge of the invisible past. You keep wanting to see it, though; to see those bad things playing out on the land before your eyes, to imagine that that big old tree was once *watered with blood*, to feel certain that the people who inhabited the town also carried with them if not the motives, then the memory of the crimes committed before their own births. Would the people of Kemah always bear a kinship to those thousands of Armenians pushed from the Kemah cliffs, or to the people who pushed them?

I kept seeing these connections—the dead Armenians, the Kurds, the ubiquitous Martyrs' Parks—connections I had never felt the moral compulsion to look for while traveling in, say, the Native American blood lands of Colorado or the old plantation fields of the American South. Suddenly, though, it was all I could think about—that I never made the same inquiries into my own country as I did here in Turkey. I judged the Turks; every time I read of another massacre, another disgrace, I somehow brought it to bear on the collective character of the people I was meeting, as if that history had formed them. But then what of mine, and what of me?

We drove into the village of Kemah along a river and across a bridge. On the right, there was a famous Selçuk *türbe*, or tomb, and then the road wound to the left and up a hill to the town. The mosque and teahouse sat at the center of the place and about ten men were sitting outside, drinking their tea. Most of the buildings seemed run-down, tables in front of restaurants turned over, unwelcoming. Two guys hung out of what passed for a sports car, their terrible techno music rattling the windows. There was a small hospital and one bank and three restaurants. The ever-faithful *jandarma*, or military police, stood guard at the bottom of the hill, right where the road began, as if it were a gate. At one point, I saw trucks of soldiers pass on the main road—a parade of camouflage unfolding forever, one after another, men's legs jangling together in the open-air back.

Turks in this part of the country often didn't allow women to stay in hotels alone, and in any case there wouldn't be any hotels in Kemah. We knew to ask for the *oğretmen evi*, or teachers' house, which was where civil servants stayed while traveling. It looked a bit like a high school, as if they wouldn't want their retired teachers or guests to ever feel displaced, and had the cold, tinny feeling of a psychiatric ward: no carpets, no cloth, no comfort, no niceties. In Turkey, I thought this was the aesthetic of an aggressive modernity: like the cold busts of Atatürk, his austere face and translucent eyes reminding his people of a vision of modernity now being wiped away by time.

Three little girls called to us soon after that: *"Abla! Abla!"* (Sister! Sister!) The three girls looked not at all like they might be from the same country. One, with fair, peachy skin and freckles and light brown hair, had nondescript features and a rangy athleticism. The second child looked drawn from an old Eastern European postcard: her face narrow, her nose large, her eyes the saddest and most stunning blue, her eyebrows thick as a brush, but her hair plain and straight brown. And the third girl didn't really look as if she were from Turkey at all. I assumed she was Kurdish, but even then she looked more like she was from Central Asia. Enormous almond eyes wrapped around the width of her head like sunglasses, her face tapered into a heart shape; her skin a perfect bronze, her hair stick-straight and black. My Turkish friend Aslı later told me that the reason all the girls looked different might have been because at least one of them was Armenian.

"Do you think you will ever leave here?" I asked one girl.

"No," she replied immediately, "we're of here."

We wondered whether everyone in the town knew one another, and they said that it was one big family, actually: Turks and Kurds.

We needed a restaurant, and asked the girls for advice. It was the night of the national soccer finals and yet everything was closed except for the *köfteci*, the man who made meatballs. It was empty and had about four tables, a pleasantly wooden place of the sort twee Brooklyn cafés tried to imitate. One man stood behind a counter, his back to an oven. We gingerly sat down, and the girls mistook our exhaustion for wariness. "Really, this is a very good restaurant," one girl said. "Promise." She looked so sad that the foreigners might be disappointed that I smiled with all my might.

The *köfte* was in fact very good. At some point, without even a good-bye, the girls had scattered, but later I saw them watching us from a balcony across the tiny street. The owner seemed pleased when we told him how good the *köfte* was, after he'd come around from the dusty counter to bring more bread to our table, swinging his stocky, strong body with the help of a crutch. He had only one leg.

Numerous men in Turkey had only one leg, and I realized I didn't know why. What could be the cause? Some outdated disease I wasn't familiar with? Some war I'd forgotten—the war with the Kurds, a stint in the army, an accident at work? This leglessness told me that there was something that I as an American, long isolated from the world's horrors, could not understand about a country like Turkey, maybe any country for that matter. This was a place where people lost their legs, and hobbled on crutches for the rest of their lives. They did not always have replacements fashioned on the knee, and they did not even bother to cover up the fact that they were legless. I watched the man's stump as he hopped back to his counter, and at that moment in the *köfte* restaurant in the middle of Anatolia, I realized I also had no idea how to meaningfully incorporate these people into my world, how to do them justice.

ONE EVENING, RANA invited me over to show me what she wryly called "a proper Turkish house." Her five-room apartment, which she shared with her mother, revealed little, if anything, "Turkish," save maybe the cabinet by the front door filled with slippers to wear after you removed your shoes. In Turkey, if you only moved between the Westernized homes and cafés— they didn't have to belong to wealthy people, just families who supported Atatürk's modernizing reforms—you wouldn't really feel as if you were in a foreign country at all. Even in those houses and cafés, however, there were things that reminded you that you were in a foreign country, like when, at some point in our conversation, Rana told me about a conversation she had with a Turkish man after September 11:

"I was horrified, of course," she said. "And I remember I spoke to a guy at a corner store that day who said something like *Finally, it's happened to them, too. We're not the only ones.*"

I had been telling her about a passage in one of Orhan Pamuk's essays, in which he said that what Americans didn't understand about Muslim men around the world was their sense of "humiliation" by the West. "The real challenge is to understand the spiritual lives of the poor, humiliated, discredited people who have been excluded from its fellowship," he wrote. What drives men "is not Islam or this idiocy people call the war between East and West, nor is it poverty; it is the impotence born of a constant humiliation, of a failure to make oneself understood, to have one's voice heard." I was impressed but confused as to why Pamuk had come up with this idea, because I thought that someone like Pamuk, a rich White Turk, had probably never been humiliated in his life.

Now here was Rana saying more or less the same thing about this male Turkish store clerk. It wasn't that I was surprised by these thoughts in general, but I was surprised by these thoughts coming from a Turk. *What had "happened" to them?* I wondered. Clearly something else was going on, some deeper emotional response to September 11.

Rana had once told me how as a child she felt she had to choose between the Soviet Union and America—she had to choose sides. She chose America because she liked the cartoons.

"Come on!" she had said. "Can't you see that for my whole life so much has been defined by America?"

I could not. But then, I hadn't known anything about Turkey at all. For someone like Rana, America defined her life in the broadest terms; it was an American world, with American-made international laws, American wars on her borders, American military bases on her country's soil, American movies in her movie theaters, American songs on the radio, American monetary exchange rates, American economic policies, American-style marriage proposals, and four whole pages devoted to American news in the Turkish newspapers. As we spoke, I could see that foreigners grew up without the very thing that Americans cherished so much about their American selves—their self-made story. In America, we believed we shaped every bit of our own history. Much of the rest of the world felt at least in part pushed along by an unseen force. We had good-and-evil narratives, and pop anthems of renewal. Turkey's music was all about despair and longing and loss. While I drew conclusions about Turks from their music, I had never applied such analysis to myself; I didn't stop to think that the way I was looking at Rana, at Turkey, at the world, was born of this particular place that I came from. I also had not been conscious at all of what my country had done to get to that place of dominance, while for Turks, for Turkey, that dominance meant so much.

That same year, Mohsin Hamid's novel *The Reluctant Fundamentalist*, one of the first great novels since September 11 to address the war on terror, had provoked some controversy because its protagonist smiles as he watches the Twin Towers fall on television. The character, Changez, is a Pakistani Princeton graduate and wealthy consultant living in New York. "Yes, despicable as it may sound, my initial reaction was to be remarkably pleased," Changez says. "I was caught up in the *symbolism* of it all, the fact that someone had so visibly brought America to her knees." Hamid's character is telling this story to an American, in fact, and so as to extend his empathy, the

Pakistani says that he is sure the American has such feelings, too. "Do you feel no joy at the video clips—so prevalent these days—of American munitions laying waste the structures of your enemies?" Hamid seems to know both that Americans have those thoughts and that they do not see the parallel.

Was Changez's smile not also the recognition that America was finally vulnerable like everyone else? Perhaps in some way, their reactions expressed the hope that Americans might now empathize differently with the suffering and death of others. "No country inflicts death so readily upon the inhabitants of other countries," Hamid writes, "frightens so many people so far away, as America." If when our mortal enemies, the Iranians, sat vigil for us after the attacks, was it also because they understood the pain we might be experiencing? The Iranians might have felt sympathy for us because they *knew* us. Americans were human to them, real things, real people. Which, for us, Turks, Iranians, Iraqis had never been.

In his novel, Hamid describes the post-9/11 New York that I had lived in throughout my twenties. "There was something undeniably retro about the flags and uniforms, about generals addressing cameras in war rooms and newspaper headlines featuring such words as *duty* and *honor*," he writes. "I had always thought of America as a nation that looked forward; for the first time I was struck by its determination to look *back*." Hamid was unquestionably correct about those days. But what shook me as I sat in Istanbul reading these words was how much this description of America reminded me of the Turkish nationalism I despised.

I GREW UP without a sense that the patriotism that saturated my life was somehow different from the nationalism of any other country, mainly because I hadn't known of those countries' existence. I grew up in a town in New Jersey called Wall, a Shore town that did not have its own beach. There were wealthy areas along the river, and winding avenues of white-fenced and red-barned horse farms, and poorer parts closer to the railroad tracks and the high school. Much of it was a landscape of pavement, plastic signs and Dunkin' Donuts, metal-framed shopping carts in vast parking lots. There was no center, no Main Street, as there was in most of the pleasant and plentiful beach towns, no tiny old movie theater or architecture that bespoke some sort of history or memory. On the timeline of suburban and exurban development, Wall felt stuck somehow.

During my childhood, I wasn't very conscious of anyone's professional life, but most of my friends' parents were teachers, nurses, cops, and electricians, except for the rare father who worked in "the City," and a handful of Italian families who did less legal things. My parents were descendants of working-class Danish and Italian and Irish immigrants who had little memory of their European origins, and my extended family ran a small public golf course (eighteen dollars a round), where I worked as a hot dog girl in the summers. Like many families, we owned guns; I am not sure I was ever exposed to the "liberal" argument about gun control, but I also never saw anyone shoot their gun. I felt, though, an undercurrent of violence in the town. I knew girls who had abusive boyfriends; the one gay kid in the school was pushed into garbage cans in the cafeteria. *Kick your ass. Get your ass kicked. He beat the shit out of that guy.* Every year, it seemed, someone died in a car accident, usually from drunk driving; one time, the high school displayed the smashed-up car on the school lawn.

We were all patriotic, but I can't even conceive of what else we would've been, because our entire experience was domestic, interior, American. We went to church on Sundays until church time was usurped by soccer games. I do not remember a strong sense of civic engagement; not with the community, or for the environment, or for poor people. I had the feeling, rather, that people could take things from you if you didn't stay vigilant. Our goals remained local: homecoming queen, state champs, a scholarship to Trenton State, cookouts in the backyard. The lone Chinese kid studied hard and went to Berkeley; the Indian went to Yale. Black people never came to Wall. The world was white, Christian; the world was us.

My father didn't fight in Vietnam, so the world did not come to me through those stories. "Only ten percent of the country were hippies," my father said once. "It's misrepresented in movies." "Did you protest the war?" I asked. Oh, of course, my mother would say, everyone did. My father didn't answer. Why did the war happen? Money, he replied. My parents hated "Washington," so sometimes they sounded like Ralph Nader and sometimes like Ronald Reagan; and they complained about Wall Street, New York, lawyers, Ivy League snobs, and Bill Clinton, who they seemed to believe had been elected president just to torture them.

In school, we did not study world maps, because international geography, as a subject, had been long ago phased out of state curriculums. America was the world; there was no sense of America being one country on a planet of many countries. Even the Soviet Union seemed something more like the Death Star, flying overhead and ready to laser us to smithereens, than a country with people in it. I have television memories of world events; even in my mind they appear on a screen: Oliver North testifying in the Iran-Contra hearings, the scarred, evil-seeming face of Manuel Noriega, Gorbachev and the maplike purple mark on his bald head; the movie-like quality, all flashes of light, of the bombing of Baghdad during the first Gulf War. Mostly what I remember of this war in Iraq was singing on the school bus—I was thirteen—wearing little yellow ribbons and becoming teary-eyed as I remembered the MTV video of the song.

And I'm proud to be an American
Where at least I know I'm free

That "at least" is funny. We were free, at the very least we were that. Everyone else was a chump, because they didn't even have that obvious thing—whatever it was, it didn't matter, it was the thing that we had, and no one else did, and we were proud and special. Even more, it would always be there, since of course I had no knowledge of why or how we had gotten that freedom, or what it meant. We were born with it. It was our God-given gift, our superpower.

By high school, I knew that communism had gone away, but never learned what communism had actually been ("bad" was enough). I read *Invisible Man*, but the only black people I knew were the ones on TV shows, or, again, on the news—like Yusef Salaam, one of the accused boys in the Central Park jogger case, his beautiful face instantly looking guilty to a stupid white girl because he dared to be proud. I am not sure I had any idea whatsoever what Islam was. Yusef Salaam was just a funny black name to me. Religion, politics, race—they washed over me like fuzzy things, troubled things that obviously meant something to someone somewhere but that had no relationship to me, to Wall, to America. I certainly had no idea that most people in the world felt those connections deeply.

Racism, anti-Semitism, prejudice—those things, however, on some unconscious level, I must have known. Those things were expressed in the fear of Asbury Park, which was black; in the resentment of the towns of Marlboro and Deal, which were known as Jewish; in the way Hispanics seemed exotic. Much of the Jersey Shore was segregated as if it were still the 1950s, and so prejudice was expressed through fear of anything outside of Wall, anything outside of the tiny white world in which we lived; people who live in such towns can go their whole lives without knowing about anyone different from them, aside from the racist, prejudiced, exotic representations they see on TV. If there was something that saved us from being outwardly racist, it was that in small towns like Wall, especially for girls, it was important to be *nice*, or *good*, and so this pressure tempered tendencies toward overt cruelty when we were young.

I was in high school for the Rwandan genocide and the war in Bosnia, but I was conscious of none of it at the time. During my senior year, I learned twentieth-century American history through the lyrics of Billy Joel's "We Didn't Start the Fire." The song lists the world's horrors and accomplishments—*Joe McCarthy, Richard Nixon, Studebaker, Television*—and then, in a way, exonerates Americans of all of it. *We didn't start the fire / No we didn't light it / But we tried to fight it.* Many years later, I unearthed a research project I made about the song. It looked depressingly like an elementary school art project. No doubt I'd used an encyclopedia to discover the events related to the lyrics: *1967, the Israeli-Palestinian war; 1968, the My Lai massacre.* The stranger thing to me, however, at that time, was not even how bare-bones my description of each of these massive events had been—two lines for the H-bomb—but rather that I'd ever known about them at all. History, America's history, the world's history, would slip in and out of my consciousness with no resonance whatsoever.

I was lucky that I had a mother who nourished my early-onset book addiction, an older brother with mysteriously acquired progressive politics, and a father who spent his evenings studying obscure golf antiques, lost in the pleasures of the past. In these days of the One Percent, I am nostalgic for Wall's middle-class modesty and its sea-salt Jersey Shore air. But as a teenager I knew that the only thing that could rescue me from the Wall of fear and Billy Joel was a good college. I wish I had paid more attention to that history lesson, though. At least then I would have known what "Nasser" meant before I went off to college, which was in the Ivy League.

I went to the University of Pennsylvania. The lack of interest in the world that I'd known in Wall found its reflection in Penn, although here the children were wealthy, highly educated, and apolitical. During orientation, the Wharton School told its students they were "the smartest people in the country," or so I had heard. (Donald Trump Jr. was there then, too.) At Penn, in 1999, everyone wanted to be an investment banker, and many would go on to bring down the world economy a decade later. But they were more educated than I was; in American literature class, they had even heard of William Faulkner. When my best friend from Wall revealed one night that she hadn't heard of John McEnroe or Jerry Garcia, some boys on the dormitory hall called us ignorant, and white trash, and chastised us for not reading magazines. We were hurt, and surprised; white trash was something we said about other people at the Jersey Shore. My boyfriend from Wall accused me of going to Penn solely to find a boyfriend who drove a Ferrari, and the boys at Penn made fun of the Camaros we drove in high school. Class in America was not something easily delineated by large categories, certainly not ones most of us had any structural or intellectual understanding of; class was a constellation of a million little materialistic cultural signifiers, and the insult, loss, or acquisition of any of them could transform one's future entirely. In the end, I chose to pursue the new life Penn offered me. The kids I met had parents who were doctors or academics; many of them had already even been to Europe! Penn, for all its superficiality, felt one step closer to a larger world.

Still, I cannot remember any of us being conscious of foreign events during my four years of college (1995 to 1999), except the first months of freshman year, when Yitzhak Rabin was assassinated. I hadn't known who he was. There were wars in Eritrea and Nepal; Afghanistan, Kosovo, East Timor, Kargil. Embassies in Nairobi and Dar es Salaam were bombed.

Panama, Nicaragua—I couldn't keep Latin American countries straight—
Osama bin Laden, Clinton bombing Iraq—nope. Maybe I knew "Saddam
Hussein," which had the same evil resonance of "communism." I remember *Wag the Dog*, a satire of how Americans started a fake war with
"terrorists"—a word I never paused to question—to distract from domestic scandals, which at the time was what many would accuse Clinton of
doing in Afghanistan during the Monica Lewinsky affair. I never thought
about Afghanistan. What country was in *Wag the Dog*? Albania. There
was a typical American callousness in our reaction to the country they
chose for the movie, an indifference that said, *Some bumblefuck country,
it doesn't matter which one they choose.*

I became an adult in the go-go 1990s, the decade when, according to
America's foremost intellectuals, "history" ended, America triumphant,
the Cold War won by a landslide. The historian David Schmitz writes that
by that time, the idea that America won because of "its values and steadfast
adherence to the promotion of liberalism and democracy" was dominating
"op-ed pages, popular magazines, and the best-seller lists." These ideas were
the ambient noise, the elevator music, the echoes of my most formative
years. But for me there was also an intervention—a chance experience in
the basement of Penn's library.

I came across a line in a book, in which the historian was arguing that
long ago, during the slavery era, black people and white people had defined
their identities in opposition to each other's, and the revelation to me, of
course, was not that black people had conceived of their identities in response to ours, but that our white identities had been composed in conscious objection to *theirs*. I'd had no idea that we'd ever had to define our
identities at all, because to me, white Americans were born fully formed,
completely detached from any sort of complicated past. Even now, I can
remember that shiver of recognition that only comes when you learn something that expands, just a tiny bit, your sense of reality. What made me
angry was that this revelation was something about who I *was*—how much
more did I not know about myself?

It was because of this text that I decided to study civil rights history,
and partially why, after graduation, I picked up the books of James Baldwin, the first of which was *No Name in the Street*. Baldwin gave me the

sense of meeting someone who knew me better, and with a far more sophisticated critical arsenal than I had myself. There was this line:

> But I have always been struck, in America, by an emotional
> poverty so bottomless, and a terror of human life, of human touch,
> so deep, that virtually no American appears able to achieve any
> viable, organic connection between his public stance and his
> private life.

And this one:

> All of the Western nations have been caught in a lie, the lie of their
> pretended humanism; this means that their history has no moral
> justification, and that the West has no moral authority.

And this one:

> White Americans are probably the sickest and certainly the
> most dangerous people, of any color, to be found in the world
> today.

I know why this came as a shock to me then, at twenty-two, and it
wasn't necessarily because he said I was sick, though that was part of it.
It was because he kept calling me that thing: "white American." In my
reaction I justified his accusation. I knew I was white, and I knew I was
American, but it was not what I understood to be my identity; for me,
self-definition was about gender, personality, religion, education, dreams. I
only thought about finding myself, becoming myself, discovering myself,
which, I hadn't known, was the most white American thing of all. I still
did not think about my place in the larger world, or that perhaps an entire
history—the history of white Americans—had something to do with who
I was. My lack of consciousness was dangerous because it exonerated me of
responsibility, of history, of a role—it allowed me to believe I was innocent,
or that white American was not an identity like Muslim or Turk. About
this indifference, Baldwin writes:

White children, in the main, and whether they are rich or
poor, grow up with a grasp of reality so feeble that they can very
accurately be described as deluded—about themselves and the
world they live in. White people have managed to get through
entire lifetimes in this euphoric state . . . People who cling to their
delusions find it difficult, if not impossible, to learn anything
worth learning.

Young white Americans of course go through pain, insecurity, heartache. But it is very, very rare that young white Americans come across someone who tells them in harsh, unforgiving terms that *they* might be merely the easy winners of an ugly game, and indeed because of their ignorance and misused power, they might actually be the losers within a greater moral universe. My reaction to this was far different from the normal pain of rejection—it was the pain of suddenly sensing one's inherent hopelessness, the exact opposite of the endless promise on which a white American life depends. Had not America's terrible race history already determined my fate? The "Western party is over, and the white man's sun has set," was one of the last lines of Baldwin's book.

In Istanbul—in a somewhat desperate attempt to connect America and the world through James Baldwin—I focused my efforts on finding Engin Cezzar, the Turkish actor who first invited Baldwin to Turkey. I still didn't understand everything Baldwin wrote, I knew there was something that as a white American I was missing, and thus I knew that my ability to understand Turkey and the world around me would be inherently compromised. Baldwin's books had an effect on my psyche, if only the beginnings of one. The philosopher Jonathan Lear has written that certain books can provoke an ethical transformation in their readers, and in his essay on the subject, he describes the types of people who might be in need of such an ethical transformation as those who live in "unjust societies":

Unjust societies tend to cloud the minds of those who live within
them. Such societies hold themselves together not by force alone
but by powerful imaginative structures that instill fear and
complacency in the population. Those who, at least on the surface,

profit from injustice tend to be brought up in ways that encourage insensitivity to the suffering on which their advantaged life depends. *If we are inhabitants of an unjust social order, it is likely that our own possibilities for thought will be tainted by the injustice we are trying to understand.* [italics mine]

If people produced by an unjust society wanted to understand the world, they had to accept that they might not be ethical people, that there was something about how their minds worked that was fundamentally unethical. The levers and pulleys worked in an unethical way. The machine had been built by an unethical system, and eroded over time in an unethical environment, and only if people learned to anticipate the grinding of the gears would they be able to confront a world they had spent most of their lives disregarding.

BACK THEN, MY DAYS in Istanbul dissolved into the nights, a formless kind of existence. I had no office to go to, no job to keep, and I was thirty years old, an age at which people either choose to grow up or remain stuck in the exploratory and idle phase of late-late youth. Starting all over again in a foreign country—making friends, learning a new language, trying to find your way through a city—meant almost certainly choosing the latter. I spent many nights out until the wee hours—like the evening I drank beer with a young Turkish man named Emre, who had attended college with a friend of mine from the States.

We sat outside in a passageway in Tünel, a neighborhood where the streets were packed with tiny tables, which young Turks filled every night, smoking and drinking beer and having tea. The din rattled off the old buildings until it built into a roar. A friend had told me that Emre was one of the most brilliant people he'd ever met. I was gaining a lot from his analysis of Turkish politics, especially when I asked him whether he voted for the AK Party, and he spat back, outraged, "Did you vote for George W. Bush?" until which point I had not realized the two might be equivalent. Then, three beers in, Emre mentioned that the United States had planned the September 11 attacks.

I had heard this before. Conspiracy theories, as I thought of them, were common in Turkey; for example, when the military claimed the PKK, the Kurdish militant group, had attacked a police station, some Turks believed the military had done it; they believed it even in cases where Turkish civilians had died. In other words, right-wing forces, like the military, bombed neutral targets, or even right-wing targets, so they could then blame it on the left-wing groups, like the PKK. To Turks, bombing one's own country seemed like a real possibility.

"Come on, you don't believe that," I said.

"Why not?" he snapped. "I do."

"But it's a conspiracy theory."

He laughed. "You Americans always dismiss these things as conspiracy theories. It's the rest of us in the world who have been the victims of *your* conspiracies."

I ignored him. "I guess I have faith in American journalism," I said. "Someone else would have figured this out if it were true."

He smiled. "I'm sorry, there's no way they didn't have something to do with it, and now this war?" he said, referring to the war in Iraq. "It's impossible that the United States couldn't stop such a thing, and impossible that the Muslims could pull it off."

Around that time a bomb went off in the Istanbul neighborhood of Güngören. When I went there the following day, old and young men were repairing the shattered windows of a clothing shop under the blank, watchful eyes of naked mannequins, and a handful of policemen clutched riot shields opposite tiny pink girls jumping around in empty fountains. Huge red Turkish flags hung from balconies where families drank tea; one woman had stretched a flag across the frame from which the glass of her window had been blown out by the bombs. The terrorists had targeted a pedestrian street in a middle-class neighborhood of no significant political or religious character. There were no Byzantine treasures or European corporate headquarters there, either. Just a civilian cross section of working, living, breathing Istanbul, shopping before bedtime. The second bomb exploded out of a garbage bin after 10:00 p.m., killing 17 people and injuring 150, thanks to a tactic the Iraq War had made cruelly familiar: set off one bomb, draw hundreds of concerned citizens to the scene, then set off the other. One witness caught an image of the second bomb exploding, on his cell phone.

"Who does everyone think did this?" I asked my young cabdriver, who'd lived in Istanbul his whole life. "Maybe al-Qaida?"

"Could be," he said.

"Not the PKK?"

"Could be," he replied again.

"This is the problem when something like this happens now," a friend said later. "You think: It could be the PKK, it could be DHKP/C [a radical leftist group], it could be al-Qaida, it could be the 'Deep State'—it could be anyone!"

The Deep State, or mafialike paramilitary organizations operating outside of the law, sometimes at the behest of the official military, was another story. Turks explained that the Deep State had been formed during the Cold War, as a way of countering communism, and then mutated into a force for destroying all threats to the Turkish state. At the time, prosecutors had launched what would become known as the Ergenekon trial, which alleged that a group of ultrasecularists and nationalists, including military officers and journalists, had been behind the majority of Turkish crimes in the last few decades. (The Ergenekon mafia apparently had been named for a Turkish myth in which the Turks are descended from wolves.) Many believed it had killed the Armenian writer Hrant Dink, threatened the life of Orhan Pamuk, and had been involved in hundreds of extrajudicial killings of Kurds since the 1990s. Could one group possibly be responsible for all these acts? It strained credulity. But the point was that Turks had been living for years with the idea that some secret force controlled the fate of their nation.

In fact, elements of the Deep State were rumored to have had ties to the CIA during the Cold War, and though that, too, smacked of a conspiracy theory, this was the reality Turks, and Emre, lived in. The sheer number of international interventions the Americans launched in those decades is astonishing, especially those during years when American power was considered comparatively innocent. There were the successful assassinations: Lumumba in 1961, Trujillo in 1961, Diem in 1963, Allende in 1973. There were the unsuccessful assassinations: Castro, Castro, and Castro. There were the much-hoped-for assassinations: Nasser, Nasser, Nasser. And, of course, U.S.-sponsored, -supported, or -staged regime change: Iran, Guatemala, Iraq, Congo, Syria, Dominican Republic, South Vietnam, Indonesia, Brazil, Chile, Bolivia, Uruguay, and Argentina. The Americans trained or supported secret police forces everywhere from Cambodia to Colombia, the Philippines to Peru, Iran to Vietnam. Many Turks believed that the United States at least encouraged the 1971 and 1980 military coups in Turkey, though I could find little about these events in any conventional histories anywhere.

But what I could see was that the effects of such meddling were comparable to those of September 11—just as huge, as life changing, as disruptive to the country and to people's lives. The reason Emre may not have believed that September 11 was a straightforward affair of evidence and proof was that his experience, his reality, told him that very rarely were any of these surreally monumental events easily explainable. After all, was there much difference between a foreigner's paranoia that the Americans planned September 11 and the Americans' paranoia that the whole world should pay for September 11 with an endless global war on terror?

In the midcentury, the CIA's misdeeds were often executed by right-wing groups who attacked neutral targets, and then blamed leftist groups or Communists to justify even more violence, or regime change. Just as the Turks so often believed about terror in Turkey. The CIA's ultimate goal was often what Emre suspected about the World Trade Center attacks: an excuse for wider war.

THE NEXT TIME a Turk, a young student at Istanbul's Boğaziçi University, told me she believed America had bombed itself on September 11—I heard this with some regularity—I repeated my claim about believing in the integrity of American journalism. She replied, a bit sheepishly, "Well, right, we can't trust our journalism. We can't take that for granted." The words "take that for granted" gave me pause. Having lived in Turkey for over a year, witnessing how their own nationalistic propaganda had inspired their views of the world and of themselves, their newspapers and their school curriculums, I wondered from where the belief in our objectivity and rigor in journalism came. Why would Americans be objective and everyone else subjective? From where did we get this special power? I thought that because Turkey had poorly functioning institutions—they didn't have a reliable justice system, as compared to an American system I believed to be functional—it often felt as if there was no truth; for example, a man would be murdered and no one would ever be able to prove who did it. Turks were always skeptical of official histories, and blithely dismissive of the government's line. But was it rather that the Turks, with their beautiful skepticism, were actually just less nationalist than me?

American exceptionalism had declared our country unique in the world, the one truly free and modern country, and instead of ever considering that that exceptionalism was no different from any other country's nationalistic propaganda, I had internalized this belief as the basis of my reality. Wasn't that indeed what successful propaganda was supposed to do? I had not questioned the institution of American journalism *outside* of the standards it set for itself, which, after all, was the only way I would discern its flaws and prejudices; instead, I accepted those standards as the best standards any country could possibly have. Likewise, if I had long ago succumbed to the pathology of American nationalism, I wouldn't know it—*even* if I understood the history of injustice in America, *even* if I was furious about the invasion of Iraq. I was a white American. I still had this fundamental faith in my country in a way that suddenly, in comparison to the Turks, made me feel immature and naïve.

I had come to notice that a community of activists and intellectuals in Turkey—the liberal ones—were indeed questioning what "Turkishness" meant in new ways. Many of them had been brainwashed in their schools about their own history, about Atatürk, about the supposed evil of the Armenians and the Kurds and the Arabs, about the fragility of their borders and the rapaciousness of all outsiders, about the historic and eternal goodness of the Turkish Republic.

"It is different in the United States," I once said, not entirely realizing what I was saying until the words came out. I had never been called upon to explain this. "We are told it is the greatest country on earth. The thing is, we will never reconsider that narrative the way you are doing just now. Because to us, that isn't propaganda, that is truth. And to us, that isn't nationalism, it's patriotism. And the thing is, we will never question any of it because at the same time, all we are being told is how freethinking we are, that we are free. So we don't know there is anything wrong in believing our country is the greatest on earth. The whole thing sort of convinces you that a collective consciousness in the world came to that very conclusion."

"Wow," a friend once replied. "How strange. That is a very quiet kind of fascism, isn't it?"

It was a quiet kind of fascism that would mean I would always see Turkey as beneath the country I came from, and also that would mean I believed my uniquely benevolent country to have uniquely benevolent intentions toward the peoples of the world. That night of conspiracy theories, Emre had alleged that I was a spy. "That information is being used for something," Emre said. "You are a spy." As an American emissary in the wider world, writing about foreigners, governments, economies partaking in some larger system and scheme of things, I was an agent somehow. Emre lived in the American world as a foreigner, as someone less powerful, as someone who believed that one mere newspaper article could mean war, that one misplaced opinion could mean an intervention by the IMF, that my attitude, my prejudice, my lack of generosity could be entirely false, inaccurate, damaging, but that it would be taken for truth by the powerful newspapers and magazines I wrote for, thus shaping perceptions of Turkey forever. Years later, a journalist told me he loved working for a major newspaper because the White House read it, because he could "influence policy." Emre had told me how likely it was I would screw this up; he was saying to me: First, spy, do no harm.

ONCE YOU REALIZE that the way you have looked at the world—the way you viewed your country, your history, your life—has been muddled, you begin a process of shedding layers of skin. It's a slow process, you break down, you open up, but you also resist, much like how the body can begin to heal, only to fall back into its sicker state. I became so conscious of my assumptions that a new reflex began to emerge. Baldwin said the end of the empire necessitated the radical revision of identity. If the Turkish identity was so bound up in its relationship to the state, wasn't ours? What was that state and what was that history?

I began to read the newspaper differently. I could see how alienating it was to foreigners, the way articles spoke always from a position of American power, treating foreign countries as if they were America's misbehaving children. I listened to my compatriots with critical ears: the way our discussion of foreign policy had become infused since September 11 with these officious, official words, bureaucratic corporate military language: collateral damage, imminent threat, freedom, freedom, freedom. I read history differently, too. That year Drew Gilpin Faust published a book called *This Republic of Suffering*, whose central argument is that Americans during the Civil War were barbaric. I realized that American pundits often described the Middle East as some foreign, chaotic, unraveling, atavistic, violent, inhuman place but were oblivious to their own extraordinarily barbaric history: the Indian wars, the tree-strung lynchings, the My Lai massacre. And the American Civil War, which, as Faust writes, "produced carnage that has often been thought reserved for the combination of technological proficiency and inhumanity characteristic of a later time."

When the financial crisis struck, I could see from Turkey all the countries that were being felled by this distant mother ship, this strange empire that wasn't. I thought of all the Wharton School investment-banker kids I went to college with in the 1990s, we being the earliest beneficiaries of the delusions of globalization, we who lived and thrived in this fantasy world that preyed not only on our own American people but on the people we never thought about very far away. I found myself ranting in bars at night about my classmates. "Those people know nothing about the rest of the world!" I said. "They have no idea that what they do affects the global economy! What their stupid games could mean for a farmer in Ukraine!" Maybe I said Turkey, maybe Egypt, maybe Guam. Who knows. I was so angry, I had so much contempt for them, and for Americans, and for myself, who also had no idea how that global economy, how anything, worked.

AFTER FIFTEEN MONTHS in Istanbul, I finally met Engin Cezzar on a raw winter's day, when the clouds turned the Bosphorus a milky pewter and the air filled with the smell of burning coal. Around the same time a

Polish scholar named Magdalena J. Zaborowska had released a book called *James Baldwin's Turkish Decade*, and an Istanbul bookstore had showcased a new collection of letters between Cezzar and Baldwin. The book's Turkish publisher gave me Cezzar's phone number. It turned out he lived near me, in a neighborhood called Gümüşsuyu. The prospect of this New York–Istanbul connection was thrilling—and comforting. I showed up at Cezzar's door expecting this Turkish theater actor to tell me the meaning of life, and dutifully carrying the newly published book of letters in my hand. When Cezzar opened the door, he looked at the book.

"Well, don't read Jimmy Baldwin in Turkish, for Christ's sake," he said. "Welcome."

Cezzar was about seventy-five, but spry and playful. A black-and-white photo of him I had found revealed a brooding dark face in which all its magnificent curves—his nostrils, his lips, his eyebrows, even the waves in his hair—seemed as if they had been composed in perfect union. Much of that unity had dissolved with age, but his voice, that piercingly clear stage voice, sounded like it hadn't changed since his youth. He spoke in an old-school dramatic accent, as if prepared to launch into Shakespeare. Cezzar was a famous man, although I still didn't understand enough about Turkey to know how "famous" a famous *theater* actor could possibly be in Turkey. His was also a mysterious generation—the Atatürk generation—born at the founding of the Republic but that experienced the intellectual freedom and social chaos of the 1960s. His huge windows looked out onto the Golden Horn, the mouth of the Bosphorus where it meets the Sea of Marmara; all these old *Istanbullus*, I thought, had procured the View long ago, apartments with windows as seemingly expansive as an aquarium. Gümüşsuyu's position on the hill was so steep it felt as if you could slide into the water. Close to us, enormous, voracious seagulls crashed and cawed around two mosque minarets, threatening with open beaks to break through Cezzar's vulnerable window glass.

"The night before you called me I had a long, long dream and Jimmy was in the dream," he said. "Jimmy was the lead! The place was huge and crowded, a big big big party. At least a thousand people, and I was there and I saw Jimmy, and Jimmy had a tray in his hands, like the ones the cigarette girls carry. I watched him for a little bit, and then he came near and then

I showed myself. My God, what a meeting that was! Jimmy had risen from the dead. But he was in such good shape, so well dressed, so unbelievable, he was laughing—he laughed you know three mouthfuls when he laughed. So we had this beautiful reunion. And the next morning you called."

He looked at me meaningfully for a long time.

"That's really nice," I said. I was nervous. "You met Baldwin first in New York, right? Not here."

He began to tell the story of how he came to the fabled Actors Studio in New York in the 1950s, after a chance encounter with the Greek-Turkish-American director Elia Kazan, whose films included *America America*, based on Kazan's own book about immigrating to New York. I felt plunged into a time when "America" meant something else entirely: an object of desperate yearning for Turkish actors and Greek directors, as if they, too, had merely been provincials from New Jersey who wanted to make it big in New York.

"I went to the Actors Studio. Kazan said, 'You're a long way from home.' And I said, 'You're a long way from home, too, baby; much longer—you're from Kayseri and I'm from Istanbul.'" He laughed and continued: "And by then Jimmy had become Kazan's assistant. To learn about the theater."

"Why do you think you and Baldwin hit it off?"

"Very simple," he said. "To begin with we were both strangers. I was more of a stranger, but he was a 'nigger,' for crissakes. And it was not a very good time for 'niggers.' Actually the worst time, perhaps. There was no other black boy, and I was the only—what?—stranger. I mean, I don't know if you can call Italians foreigners? You can call Marlon Polish, he was there. Eli Wallach, he's Italian. And Fonda, she's straight American. Anyway, so Jimmy and I held on to each other—a very strange unspoken sympathy."

"And when did Baldwin come to Istanbul?"

"Baldwin arrived three years after he promised he was coming," he said. "'Baby, I'm broke, I'm sick, I need your help,' he said. I'd become very famous—even in Shakespeare's time no one actor played Hamlet that long, which was two hundred consecutive shows—and so I had money and a house and wanted him to come. He knew me, loved me, trusted me. Then he became accustomed to Istanbul. People loved him. I introduced him to the Robert College crowd"—the American school—"all the professors there who were very good and very gay. Robert College is famous for that. Very well-read, very intellectual. I took him to Taksim bars, Pera, Beyoğlu—several others, Asmalımescit, taught him how to drink *rakı*. Then the shit hit the fan, *Another Country* came out and it was a big hit and everyone was after him. And he was being called back to New York to the marketplace. And he had to go."

"Had he been one of the few black people around in Istanbul?" I asked. "I read that people didn't refer to him as black, but as *Arap*."

"No, not one of the only black people around," Cezzar said. "Turkey's very used to black people from the days of the empire, there were lots of black slaves brought into Turkey, they had become heads of the harem, the eunuchs, poor things. There are a lot of cotton pickers in the south of Turkey who came from Sudan. So people were used to it, it wasn't a shock."

"So he didn't feel racism here?"

"Not at all."

"Was it hard being gay?"

"Of course people knew he was gay," he said. "He wasn't hiding it. Jimmy never acted gay, but people came to know. He felt more comfortable as a gay man because men are affectionate here. Americans see it and say, 'Look, it's a Muslim country and they're openly gay!'"

There it was, the reason I had come to Istanbul in the first place, the words I heard on that documentary—*more comfortable as a black, gay man there than Paris or New York*—that made me apply for the fellowship and move to Turkey because I couldn't imagine how complex Istanbul could be. I now knew almost all of my perceptions of the "East" had been muddled not only by ignorance but by deeply buried, unconscious assumptions over which I once had no control. A feeling of melancholy fell over me, as if I had only moved to Turkey for a silly reason.

"When he first got here, we were walking in front of the Marmara Hotel and in front of us were two soldiers, very ordinary soldiers, and they had linked pinkies—it's very famous," Cezzar continued. "It's not like holding hands, it's more an Anatolian tradition. Jimmy saw this and said, 'My

God, look at the way they are walking! They are holding hands! Oh, oh, what a beautiful country.' Anatolian soldiers always walk like this when they come to Istanbul because they are afraid of getting lost in the big city. That was very typical in the sixties. But the whole of the Ottoman Empire was gay. It's true. You know that?"

Those giant seagulls, the size of vultures, banged on the window with their beaks. Cezzar went to the kitchen to get some food and dutifully tossed it in the air.

"Were the sixties an exciting time for theater here?" I asked.

"For everything, baby!" He said "baby" like Baldwin did. "In 1960, there was this coup on the seventh of May and it was a very democratic coup. Very idealistic young officers, very well-read and cultured, they took down the party and my God they hung the prime minister, which is not funny at all, and then they made a new constitution—very liberal and open-minded. Very little censorship. So after the coup the Turkish theater took a great leap because the writers began to write freely and well and unafraid."

"So could you do those same plays you did in the sixties today?"

"Are you kidding? That play we did in 1967—*Fortune*—if I put it on today, they would hang me. Or they would make me a suspect in the Ergenekon trial."

The Ergenekon trial was the one the government had been conducting against the Deep State, military officers, and secularist notables. Many Turks by then suspected it was corrupt, a way for the AK Party government to ruin the opposition once and for all. Cezzar continued—"I'm not kidding! If I did *Hair* today, they would shoot me. It's awful!"—suddenly veering in a direction I hadn't expected:

"I'm very sorry but this awful American policy is killing us. They want Turkey to be a mild Islamic republic. Horrific! If we can survive this, this Holocaust—there's going to be a Holocaust—we'll be all right. Secularism is our only weapon in the Middle East. We're the only secular republic in the Middle East! But we're always under the dollars of the American state. But to be secular is something else. Look at these other places in the Middle East—you can't come around the table and shake each other's hand. This is what America's policies . . ."

He walked away and went into the back of the house, talking to a cat

that had been meowing like crazy. He spoke to him in Turkish. "*Gel!*
Nemo! *Gel!*" I didn't say anything in response to his American tangent
because it sounded like the irrational rantings of a hard-core Kemalist who
remains so convinced of his country's destiny to be secular that he con-
cludes the only reason many Turks are religious is that—of all things—the
Americans were pushing them toward a more Islamic future. This seemed
to me paranoia at its worst.

"Istanbul in the sixties was much different," he continued. "Much more
civilized, more human. Baby, the population of Istanbul was less than one
million. Almost everybody knew everybody else. It was beautiful, it was
Byzantium, it was the empire. Istanbul was not a commercial or political or
touristic center, but it was intense. Very few people but very intense happen-
ings. Jimmy became such good friends with Yaşar Kemal"—one of Turkey's
greatest writers, a Kurd, and a committed leftist—"you wouldn't believe
it. They understood each other perfectly and they didn't speak a word of
each other's language—talking about Dostoyevsky and Faulkner. They
were singing blues. Yaşar's a real mountain Kurd. They were singing Kurdish
songs and drinking *rakı*.

"Nineteen twenty-three to 1973—those were all Republican eras.
We are the only group that's feverishly holding on to secularism and the
Republic. Then America started with NATO, other international treaties,
and slowly but surely Turkey became a strategic partner—the most dangerous thing in the world to me. And dollars came in. Commerce."

"How did Baldwin talk about this?"

"He always had this rage, this unbelievable rage against America. He
already had this hatred from his Harlem days of the white American. The
white American. He used to say there is no Negro problem in America,
there is a white problem. After the assassinations, he lost all hope. Two things
I would have loved to have seen Jimmy react to—one, 9/11, and two,
Barack. I certainly don't think Baldwin would have believed in 9/11. Most
of the world thinks it was a plot by the CIA. Now it looks like a plot,
because the American Middle Eastern policy went crazy. The most unjust
war is what happened in Iraq."

"Wouldn't the America of today be an America Baldwin would like to
come home to?" I asked, because he had mentioned Obama.

"That's bullshit, that's really ridiculous, sorry. It's that simple, is it?"

. . .

WHEN BALDWIN ARRIVED on Cezzar's doorstep in Istanbul in 1961, the fact that Turkey was a Muslim country had nothing to do with his decision, "except, perhaps, that it's a relief to deal with people who, whatever they are pretending, are not pretending to be Christians," as Baldwin said. Martin Luther King Jr. led a Christian civil rights movement, but many African Americans at the time predicated their resistance on the rejection of Christianity and the embrace of Islam—not only an alternative religion but a rejection of the white Christian West and all of its imperialisms. "In the realm of power," Baldwin wrote in the 1960s, "Christianity has operated with an unmitigated arrogance and cruelty." *The Fire Next Time*, the book that Baldwin would partly write in Istanbul, today reads like a foreshadowing of September 11:

> In order to deal with the untapped and dormant force of the previously subjugated, in order to survive as a human, moving moral weight in the world, America and all the Western nations will be forced to reexamine themselves and release themselves from many things that are now taken to be sacred, and to discard nearly all the assumptions that have been used to justify their lives and their anguish and their crimes so long.

Muslim Istanbul became Baldwin's refuge. At the time, the Ottoman Empire's exhausted former capital was a no-man's-land among Europe and the Soviet Union and the Arab Middle East. This lack of definition heightened the city's appeal. "I feel free in Turkey," Baldwin told Yaşar Kemal, who replied: "Jimmy, that's because you're an American." He spent his years in Istanbul combing through the *sahaflar*, or secondhand book stalls near the Grand Bazaar, having tea in Sultanahmet, socializing heartily with Turks and foreigners alike—Marlon Brando paid a visit—and finishing his novel *Another Country*. He also put on plays with Cezzar, including John Herbert's *Fortune and Men's Eyes*, which is about gay men in a correctional facility. To Baldwin, the Turkish theater scene of the 1960s was more radical than America's.

Baldwin lived for a time in a grand old house on the Bosphorus called the Paşa's Library, named for the nineteenth-century intellectual Ahmet Vefik Paşa. It hung from a cliff over Rumeli Hisarı, from where Mehmet the Conqueror launched his attack on Byzantium, and near Robert College, which had been established by American missionaries a hundred years before. In a black-and-white film made by the Turkish director Sedat Pakay, Baldwin sits at his desk in front of the window with the view of the Bosphorus, a glass of whiskey by the typewriter and a cigarette in hand, watching the U.S. Navy ships skulk through the water. "The American power follows one everywhere," he said. America "has dragged itself, and may well have dragged the world, onto the very edge of a kind of unimaginable conflict, which could be the end of all of us, and has done it out of a really weird determination to protect something called the American way of life, which used to be called manifest destiny." While Istanbul was an escape from the horrors of the sixties at home, according to Zaborowska, Turkey sharpened Baldwin's sense of America's "imperial presence" abroad. For him, it was "a revelation" to see the functioning of "power politics and foreign aid . . . in that sort of theatre." Those were the early days of the Turks' waning love affair with America. They still saw America as a benevolent safe port, a delusion Baldwin sought to cure.

What was the nature of this "imperial presence" that he was noticing in Turkey in the 1960s, a country that had seemed to me in the scope of America's history abroad so much less important than Vietnam or Central America? He described the country as a "satellite on the Russian border" where one learned about "brutality and the power of the Western world" by "living with people whom nobody cares about, who are bounced like a tennis ball between the great powers," very much reminding me of what Rana had said about the cartoons. Baldwin's observations from long ago felt like time capsules. Turkey had mostly avoided any direct military confrontations with America, and so, in the era of Iraq and Afghanistan, I had not been much interested in their relationship. But if Baldwin recognized it, something must have been happening there, a different kind of influence.

It began, Cezzar would tell me, in 1946, when the USS *Missouri* sailed up the Bosphorus and docked in front of Dolmabahçe Palace, ostensibly to deliver the remains of the Turkish ambassador to the United States, Münir Ertegün (father of Atlantic Records cofounder Ahmet). The visit was widely received as a declaration of American support for Turkey against the Soviets. In preparation for the event Turks washed their cars, repainted their shops, and inspected their brothels. The word WELCOME was strung between the minarets of mosques. "When the ship anchored," writes the academic Aylin Yalçın, "applause, shouts and songs of the crowd revealed their enthusiasm and joy." That week, President Harry Truman's special envoy met with then president İsmet İnönü, to establish their commitment "to democratize Turkey."

Cezzar remembered that day the sailors came ashore, too.

"In the forties, the Americans made a big gesture. The Turkish ambassador to Washington died, and they put his body on the biggest, most powerful war machine of the time, the *Missouri*. Huge, beautiful, right there, we used to go to school down there—in Karaköy." He was pointing out the window, down below to the shores of the Golden Horn. "And they took us on board—everyone could go. The American sailors who we'd only seen on film—in their beautiful white uniforms—gave us chocolates and sweets. It was the beginning of some sort of treaty—when they started giving money to Turkey. The soldiers gave the children chewing gum.

"And then the next day the whole class was sick. We all had diarrhea. The teacher had to send us all home. Nobody knew what had happened to us. We had not seen chewing gum before. We thought it was chocolate. They gave us so much. We all swallowed the chewing gum.

"And that was the beginning of the American influence in Turkey!"

THE *MISSOURI* LEFT BEHIND a people infatuated with America. In those first years, the Turks drank Coke and 7Up, ate American foods, played with American toys, and listened to American music. Turkish kids read *Little Women* and *Pollyanna*, and comic books about American frontier history that, according to Yalçın, taught "Turkish children to love the white Americans and hate the Indians," a love affair that would not last long. They would soon have the experience Baldwin had as a child, of watching American Westerns and realizing he was not John Wayne or

Gary Cooper, but that the Indians were *him*. Some twenty years earlier, Baldwin had warned that if America was not "able, and quickly, to face and begin to eliminate the sources of this discontent in our own country, we will never be able to do it on the great stage of the world." By the time he had gotten to Istanbul, the Americans had already laid claim to Turkey. I was slowly discerning through Baldwin and Cezzar a connection between the way Americans had defined their identity as white people against the identity of black people, and the country's relationship with the rest of the world.

My own love for Turkey, for Istanbul, had been in some ways shallow. I was infatuated with the way the architecture and smoking salons resisted modernity, the persistence of horse-drawn carts and traveling knife sharpeners and *boza* sellers calling out their wares. What I loved were the ways in which Turkey was different from America. But the similarities between Turkey and America were ones I never expected. The United States had been a tabula rasa, and so had the modern Turkish Republic. Denial and forgetting were crucial to the patriotism that held the idea of the Turkish nation together, and to its nationalism. They had been crucial to America's nationalism, too.

One of those many pieces of my own history I had forgotten, or had not known, was that the United States had had a relationship with Turkey, a kind of long-distance imperial relationship. Was I not of the place that had exerted power over them? Would not that assertion of power necessarily come with prejudice? For a year and a half, I realized, I had not been seeing Turkey plain. In 2006, before I left America, I had written about the Turks and the Armenian genocide: *How does a people go about forgetting the past?* Now I asked myself, *How did I*, and worse: *What else did I not know?*

Before I left Engin Cezzar's home for the last time, I asked: "When you went to the United States, where did they think you were from?"

"Turkey. But no one knew about the place."

3.

A COLD WAR MIND:
AMERICA AND THE WORLD

MAFIA BOSS: You're the guys that scare me. You're the people
that make big wars. Let me ask you something. We Italians,
we got our families and we got the church. The Irish, they have
the homeland. The Jews, their traditions. Even the n——, they
got their music. What about you people, Mr. Carlson, what do
you have?

CIA OFFICER: The United States of America. The rest of you are
just visiting.

—*THE GOOD SHEPHERD* (FILM)

WITHOUT BALDWIN I MAY NEVER have begun to see America
in Istanbul, or Turkey itself. What Baldwin's books illuminated and
then stripped of its white readers was an unconscious certitude in their
own cognitive abilities, even or especially among the well educated. He
made me doubt my assumptions. Rana and I often discussed the meaning
of ignorance. Whenever I learned something new in Turkey—no doubt
wildly annoying to Rana—I would say, "See, no American knows that."
"No American knows we have our nuclear weapons in Turkey." "No

American knows James Baldwin lived in Turkey." "No American knows Turkish kids once chose between American and Russian cartoons." To me, Americans knowing every shard of historical detail might have meant a humbler American monolith and a less violent world. Rana would reply that Turks were ignorant, too; they didn't know about the countries around them, about twentieth-century history, about their own Eastern Kurdish cities. Why did I think Americans should be different?

In the 1960s, Baldwin had a similar conversation with a Turkish film-maker. "American ignorance is a new phenomenon," he said.

> It's not the ignorance of your peasant in Anatolia, or any peasant anywhere . . . If you are dealing with people who do not know how to read and know they don't know how to read, it is at least conceivable that you can teach them how to read. If an African peasant doesn't know how to drive a tractor, or how to irrigate a barren field, he can be taught those things. But I don't know what you do with the people who are ignorant in the way Americans are ignorant. Who believe they can read, and who read their *Reader's Digest*, *Time* magazine, the *Daily News*, who think that's reading, who think they know something about the world because they are told that they do.

Baldwin was making the distinction between a lack of education and the ignorance of the complacently powerful, those who had faith that their esteemed institutions would teach them what they needed to know about the world. "You can't expect people to know about countries they have never been to," Rana said. But what if their own *country* had, in a way, been to that foreign country? If America had extended itself over the world, had even in spirit occupied many foreign countries, had not Americans in some way been there themselves? Had not a connection been made?

The more I realized how little I knew about Turkey, the more it seemed that the American claim to exceptionalism necessarily obscured something about America itself. My problem was that not only had I not known much about the Middle East, but what I *did* know, and how I *did* think, had been an obstacle to original and accurate and moral thinking.

This could only mean that in order to see a foreign country clearly, I would first have to excavate my mind. I would have to take apart the myths about America—as I had with Turkey—one by one. The American empire, for American citizens, was difficult to locate, I would discover, because it had long ago developed ways of preventing its own citizens from knowing the contours of its existence.

THE BRITISH HISTORIAN Tony Judt once observed that Americans have a strange allergy to the word "empire." Thomas Jefferson referred to the U.S. as an "empire for liberty," the state of New York is called the "Empire State," but still the word sounds reactionary to Americans, like a leftist harangue, perhaps even just too old-fashioned and out-of-date for a modern superpower. Non-Americans, like Judt, use the words "empire" and "imperial" casually. In Hamid's *The Reluctant Fundamentalist*, a Chilean man accuses Changez, who is Pakistani and works on Wall Street, of working for an "adopted empire" as a "modern day janissary." I once saw an Egyptian man post on Facebook, "I am going to the Empire today," in regard to an upcoming trip to New York City.

But Americans, I noticed, only began using the word with relative comfort after the financial crisis, when the "empire," whatever it meant, appeared to be on the verge of precipitous decline. Only then, with the balm of self-pity and perhaps their own American brand of *hüzün*, did it become easier to accept that they, the onetime anti-imperial revolutionaries, the world's foremost lovers of freedom and independence, might be little different from the British suppressing an Indian revolt, or the French colonizing Algeria, or the Belgians divesting Congo of its resources. Rejecting the word "empire" had long been a way for Americans to avoid taking responsibility for acting like one, which was a habit embedded into the American character from the moment of its birth.

Americans learn a folksy, even dorky version of American history; I remember the Puritans in their funny clothes, Plymouth Rock, drawings of the Pilgrims breaking corn with the Indians, George Washington sitting on a boat in some river. Those are a child's memories, but the takeaway was a romantic notion of struggle and discovery. From a distance, this history looks far different. The German political sociologist Claus Offe argues that taming a land covered in wilderness meant for the settlers a return to a premodern state; to survive, the early Americans had to reenact, in double time, the phases of European civilization: first as hunters and gatherers, then as farmers, and, finally, as industrialists. Thus, from the nation's first colonial settlement, the American people enjoyed an unprecedented opportunity for rebirth, which came with a nearly ritualistic form of amnesia. Becoming an American demanded that they forget their history—it made them forever innocent.

The Americans could replicate this process over and over through westward expansion, the ultimate free-for-all for white people. From abroad, bitter-sounding observers noted something odd about this obsession with freedom; D. H. Lawrence warned that the shout of freedom "is a rattling of chains, always was." But for Americans, going west—in essence, as the writer and Protestant clergyman Josiah Strong said in 1885, "creating of more and higher wants"—was the very meaning of true civilization. What that meant was that the Americans' sense of freedom was always tied not only to the acquisition of new lands but to the subjugation of new peoples, what an epigraph in a Herman Melville story calls "the empire of necessity."

With the closing of the western frontier, Americans turned outward. Most of this early phase of imperial history is portrayed in schools as an unfortunate turn of events. At the turn of the century, revolts in sugar-rich Cuba against the Spanish gave the Americans an excuse to intervene, thereby acquiring their first economic satellite, for which they would often tolerate the brutality of local rulers. During this Spanish-American War period, the Americans also established a foothold in Asia, in the Philippines. This distant imperial endeavor inspired a rabid debate at home; intellectuals at the time worried what kind of country their nation was becoming. The philosopher William James argued that all humans suffer from a blindness toward those who are different from them; it would forever be impossible for man, he warned, to fully sympathize with the "Other." But the Americans, as they had from the beginning, had reason to believe in their own unique abilities to bring civilization to the uncivilized. As Christians they possessed a messianic faith in the purpose of their Promised Land to guide the rest of the world to heaven.

Of course, it wasn't only religious fervor that led the Americans to seek resources in foreign lands. In his influential 1959 book *The Tragedy of American Diplomacy*, William Appleman Williams argued—for which he was excoriated by Kennedy acolytes such as Arthur Schlesinger Jr. for being pro-Communist—that the United States, from the beginning, needed to expand its borders to keep the economy growing. Unless the nation tapped into new markets in which to acquire natural resources, as well as to sell American goods, American factories would close, jobs would be lost, people would riot, and civil unrest would ensue. Peace and prosperity, the twin promises of American life, would wither without expansion. Williams was one of the first figures urging Americans to look more honestly at their foreign policy, and to accept what it was becoming—a different kind of empire, one that asserted itself first through economic means, not necessarily full-scale physical appropriation of territory (although often that, too). The book was popular at the time of its publishing, even receiving endorsements from newspapers such as *The New York Times*. The historian Greg Grandin believes such prescient warnings disappeared into the fervor of America's post–Cold War self-congratulation; surely, there was no longer any reason to worry about empire now that the United States had proven its own political system's superiority over the rest.

But back then, even an alleged critic of American empire like Williams had been gentle in his assessment of American ideals, writing that, for example, the Americans had been "sincere" in their *intentions* to transform Cuba into a mini-America. They believed they could "ultimately create a Cuba that would be responsibly self-governed, economically prosperous, and socially stable and happy," he writes. "All, of course, in the image of America." His usage of the word "sincere" was the sort of thing that Americans, eager for affirmation, likely took the wrong way.

The idea of good intentions would obscure the racism that enabled expansion. In a more sophisticated formulation of my college-girl realization that black and white identities were defined in relation to each other, Grandin explains that the ideal of a "rational man who stood at the center of an enlightened world," that is, the white man, was conceived against "its fantasized opposite: a slave, bonded as much to his appetites as he was to his master." Presidents McKinley, Taft, and Roosevelt alternately referred to their new foreign subjects as *little brown men*, savages, and bandits, and our supposed idealist crusader Woodrow Wilson argued that while the European subjects of former empires didn't require American tutelage, brown subjects in the Middle East certainly did. Once racist ideology seeped into the rationale for American diplomacy, it would be difficult to ever snuff it out. Among the highest levels of government, racism hid behind innocuous words of charity and imperialist actions that no one dared call by their name.

I grew up with little sense of this history, and didn't incorporate it into my assessment of American foreign policy, or myself. The born-again experience that characterized the very founding of America would later be reenacted by millions of immigrants like me, whose freedom also meant severing from their past. In Turkey, when I would bring up the Armenian genocide, the foundational slaughter of a Christian minority that allowed for the creation of the Turkish state, Turks would often remind me of the elimination of the Native Americans. This was a defensive rhetorical trick on their part, but my reflex, even if only in my mind, was to reply that "that was many hundreds of years ago," which was how I actually felt. Technically, it was true: my family didn't own slaves either. About the appropriation of land, the plundering of resources, the taming of rivers, the enslavement of people, and the destruction of plains and mountains—all of which contributed to making my country the wealthiest and most powerful on earth, and myself a beneficiary of it—I could say, "I had nothing to do with that and it is not a part of me."

The suppression of the Native Americans, the insistence on slavery in a constitution that otherwise proclaimed the liberation of a people, and the economic necessity of territorial expansion would forever connect America's racial history to its foreign policy, its African American communities to Cubans and Filipinos, James Baldwin to Turkey. As early as 1959, Williams went as far as to say that America needed a kind of truth and reconciliation commission about the history of twentieth-century American foreign policy and the relationship between that foreign policy and the domestic economy, a reckoning with the fact that America's much vaunted prosperity and peace at home would simply not have been possible without its violence at home—and abroad. If Americans didn't face such realities, Williams warned, they would continue to believe that "world power was thrust upon" them, and that "a unique combination of economic power, intellectual and practical genius, and moral rigor" enables America "to build a better world—without erecting an empire in the process." The Americans were in active denial of their empire even as they laid its foundations. They saw themselves as helpless and ingenuous first responders to fate, a feeling that would deepen with the siren call of World War II.

IN THE YEARS after September 11 and the financial crisis, and after the moral and military failures in Iraq and Afghanistan, I noticed that writers and pundits had become increasingly nostalgic for World War II—what they called America's "good war." To them, World War II wasn't a war of military and economic dominance, a bid for power, but a seamlessly executed rescue operation for which the Americans won the world's fealty and gratitude. We still saw ourselves as friendly GIs handing out Hershey bars, someone giving stuff out to a crowd of delighted supplicants. In recent years, there was a sense that America had somehow gotten "worse" at the business of warfare, which suggested that the Americans had ever been good at it in the first place. I, too, caught myself sometimes thinking that in contrast to the gloomy present day, the Americans once held the admiration of the world, especially in the 1940s. This kind of language, aquired no doubt from countless history lessons in school, or on the nightly news, or from my parents, had hardened into truth. Our victory in World War II is more crucial to Americans' ideas of themselves than they may even realize, but I wanted to understand what this self-image left out. Among many omissions were two glaring realities: that the vanquished populations of the Axis powers did not much enjoy the humiliation of American occupation, and that during World War II, the supposed "good war," the Americans dropped the nuclear bomb.

That the American liberators behaved badly after World War II has been well established: from Paris to Cairo, American soldiers were allowed to run riot through the streets and prey on the women. But rarely do Americans read foreign testimonies of how American occupation was experienced by its victims, nor are they exposed to the Japanese, German, or Italian versions of this history, as in Curzio Malaparte's satrirical novel *The Skin*.

When the American military arrived in Italy in 1943, the writer and aristocrat Curzio Malaparte was living in Naples. The city, wrecked from Allied bombs and artillery, was in ruins, its people sucking pieces of leather for nutrients, women selling themselves for a sip of wine. In *The Skin*, the American soldiers know nothing about Italy, nothing about the politics of the war; they laughed a lot, "like children, like schoolboys on holiday." Malaparte, at first, seems to find the Americans amusing. One soldier he befriends "would blush crimson" when he saw misery because Americans were embarrassed by it, like innocents. That concept, Baldwin's word, "innocent," I was finding, was all too common in foreign writings about the Americans.

But over time, Malaparte begins to discern something dangerous in the American soldiers' simplicity in the face of horror, their faith that "men can recover from misery, hunger and pain, that there is a remedy for all evil," much as Baldwin's Italian character in *Giovanni's Room* once accused an American expat of not believing in death, of believing "as though with enough time and all that fearful energy and virtue you people have, everything will be settled, solved, put in its place." *The Skin* is often grotesque satire, but in many ways, it is difficult to distinguish the American soldiers Malaparte is describing in the 1940s from those in Vietnam, or in the occupations of Iraq and Afghanistan sixty years later. The Americans succumb to the typical depredations of occupiers everywhere: they abuse local women publicly, go to obscene lengths for a good meal. For Malaparte, the Americans do not have good intentions at all; they come from a society, which he recognizes as a distinctly capitalist one, that was "founded on the conviction that in the absence of beings who suffer, a man cannot enjoy to the full his possessions." In other words, the Americans believe people must be subjugated so that they themselves can be free. They cannot recognize the irony inherent to the concept of an "army of liberation" because "they believe that a conquered nation is a nation of criminals, that defeat is a moral stigma, an expression of divine justice." As Christians, the Americans believe that the loser in the war deserved its lowly state, that the winners had been sanctified by heaven. Christianity, Malaparte writes, as Baldwin would, too, was often the Americans' "alibi" for their war making.

After a while in *The Skin*, a mysterious plague settles over Naples, the source of which Malaparte locates, darkly, in wide American grins. "The source of the plague was in their compassion," Malaparte writes, "in their frank, timid smiles, in their eyes so full of sympathy, in their affectionate caresses." The Americans' belief in their own mission on earth, in other words, kept them in Naples, obliviously occupying its people. In one of the last scenes of the book, Italians cheer on the sidewalks during an American victory parade, and amid the commotion, one of the U.S. tanks barrels into an Italian local, turning him into a "carpet of human skin," and then dumbly ambles on. "It is a shameful thing to win a war," Malaparte writes. But Americans rarely feel that way, certainly not about the war in Europe— not even about the fate of Japan.

In the period after Hiroshima and Nagasaki, the terrified world wrestled with the meaning of those events. Writers did not doubt the shadow it would cast over future generations. Mary McCarthy called the nuclear bomb "a hole in human history"; William Faulkner, in his 1950 Nobel Prize speech, wondered: "When will I be blown up?"; Doris Lessing's heroine in *The Golden Notebook* says to her psychoanalyst, "I don't want to be told when I wake up, terrified by a dream of total annihilation, because of the H-bomb exploding, that people felt that way about the cross-bow. It isn't true." In 1946, *The New Yorker* magazine devoted an entire issue to the writer John Hersey's reportage from Hiroshima. "The eyebrows of some were burned off and skin hung from their faces and hands," Hersey writes. "Others, because of pain, held their arms up as if carrying something in both hands. Some were vomiting as they walked. Many were naked or in shreds of clothing. On some undressed bodies, the burns had made patterns, of undershirt straps and suspenders."

Hersey's *Hiroshima* is an astonishingly effective catalogue of horror. But one critic at the time believed it left something out. In his review of the book, Gore Vidal pointed to a moral failing: that because it recorded the effects of the bomb in standard, objective American journalistic style—for which American journalists are usually lavished with praise—it had, crucially, avoided the larger political questions surrounding the bomb's discharge. *Hiroshima* did not, Vidal wrote, "even touch on the public debate as to whether or not there was any need to use such a weapon." Hersey likely believed that his spare representation of the terrible facts was itself the answer to the question of the bomb's "necessity," but Vidal's critique raises the question of whether the American style of journalism merely records history, rather than reckoning with it.

Vidal's point was that many people at the time, including members of the Truman administration, sensed that the Japanese, already devastated by the Americans' firebombing of Tokyo, which killed a hundred thousand people, were ready to surrender. Yet somehow, years after the publishing of *Hiroshima*, the conventional myth among Americans—including myself—became one in which, once again, the Americans had been driven by unfortunate events to do unfortunate things. Hiroshima, wrote Garry Wills, was "the moment when total war was turned into a way of waging peace." But I wonder how many Americans become what Wills called "Hiroshima liberals" by choice, by passive education, or by omission of facts—the particular kind of ignorance that Baldwin had once observed.

In 1994, the Smithsonian Institution sought to ask hard questions about Hiroshima in its fiftieth-anniversary exhibit of the bombings. Were the nuclear bombs unnecessary at that stage of the war? Did American justifications hold up to scrutiny? In the year of the Rwandan genocide, and the Bosnian war, and three years after the fall of communism, the Americans were finally facing their own most consequential violent act. But the plans for the exhibit were met with an uproar. Congress held hearings. Smithsonian employees resigned. John Dower, an American historian of Japan who would later win the Pulitzer Prize, had two of his lectures canceled. "In retrospect," he writes in an essay called "How a Genuine Democracy Should Celebrate Its Past," "it was naïve to imagine that serious treatment of the dropping of the first atomic bomb would be possible in a public space in the United States."

Censorship in America comes in quieter forms. It doesn't announce itself, as it seemed to in Turkey. In Istanbul, I had disparaged the mythmaking performed by museums and art spaces funded by a Turkish government more interested in preserving the nationalist ethos than in supporting the exploration of ideas. But in criticizing the Turks, I was comparing them to the United States, whose state institutions' independence and amply funded research is hardly ever called into question. I had never thought that American institutions, as Dower writes, had a mission "to praise, exalt, beautify, and glorify all that America has been and has done."

It is perhaps for this reason that Americans gradually became unemotional about mass death. Hillary Clinton once famously pledged on national television to "obliterate" Iran, Trump supporters speak casually of "annihilating" the Islamic State. *The Americans ended World War II. They did what they had to do to save the world.* Few Americans likely have any idea what happened after the bomb exploded, or the way straps of suspenders burned into the victims' skin.

One even lesser-known consequence of World War II was that the countries of Europe, and the nation of Japan, were broken, easily taken over by full-scale occupations in which the Americans rebuilt the cities they had destroyed, developed their capitalist economies, reminded them, at every turn, of why America was the greatest country on earth, and instructed them on the finer points of how to be free. The helpless pliancy of the Europeans and Japanese made Americans assume that the rest of the world, including Asians and Arabs emerging from their own colonial nightmares, would tolerate a new bunch of white Westerners dropping their bombs and telling them what to do.

AFTER THE WAR, the Truman administration passed the Truman Doctrine and Marshall Plan to much fanfare. They also pushed through a considerably less famous document called the Smith-Mundt Act, which enabled the State Department to engage in pro-American propaganda operations throughout the world. The act was a reaction not only to what were considered Soviet disinformation campaigns, but to the perceived anti-Americanism in Hollywood films. The American government declared that *their* propaganda would be the truthful kind of propaganda, the kind that was not actually propaganda. As the writer Frances Stonor Saunders has written, from 1950 to 1967 the State Department presided over a propaganda program in Europe, the central feature of which "was to advance the claim that it did not exist." Its partner in this endeavor was the

CIA. The agency's cultural activities abroad—its funding of *Encounter*, *The Kenyon Review*, and Radio Free Europe, its infiltration of labor unions such as the AFL-CIO, and of international student organizations such as the National Student Association—are by now well-known. But what is harder to understand is the era that the Smith-Mundt Act ushered in for Cold War entrepreneurs, so to speak, who saw themselves as crucial civilian foot soldiers in the fight against communism.

Years before the war ended, in 1940, Henry Luce published an essay called "The American Century," in which he exalted America as, in the historian Robert Herzstein's words, "a way station in humankind's attempt to build the City of God on earth," in order to strengthen American support against communism. "If we had to choose one word out of the whole vocabulary of human experience to associate with America—surely it would not be hard to choose the word," Luce once explained, sounding like George W. Bush, or Barack Obama. "For surely the word is Freedom . . . Without Freedom, America is untranslatable." Luce's family had been missionaries in China, and viewed themselves as not only converting a backward people but generously bestowing on them all the benefits of modern medicine and hygiene. Luce himself had lived on missionary compounds and barely interacted with the Chinese people. What he took away from China instead was the missionaries' idealized image of America and of its people as saviors.

It was this worldview that Luce disseminated to the American people in *Time*, an unabashedly patriotic weekly magazine. By 1945, before television and the ubiquity of the Internet, thirty million people read one of Henry Luce's publications, *Time*, *Life*, or *Fortune*, each week. According to Herzstein, what they found were stories that fueled the cruelty of the McCarthy era and harangued American politicians about "who lost China" to communism—for Luce almost a betrayal of his divine cause. Luce and his magazines had a similar kind of impact as Roger Ailes and Fox News. He often threatened anyone who didn't despise the enemy as much as he did, once even warning John F. Kennedy's father that if the president showed "any sign of weakness 'toward the anti-Communist cause,' then Time Inc. would 'clobber him.'" Herzstein recalls that Robert M. Hutchins, the president of the University of Chicago, once argued that Time Inc. did more to mold the American character than "the whole education system put together."

The Henry Luce phenomenon meant that a certain kind of magazine language—phrases such as "Who Lost China?" "Who Lost Vietnam?" "Who Lost Iran?"—would become embedded in American psyches, and were automatically deployed by editors and headline writers. We journalists always mourn the loss of a more independent, more vibrant, better-paying media, especially in the era of Twitter. But ostensibly independent magazines and television programs had not so long ago engaged in pro-American propaganda. It wouldn't be surprising if that legacy had lasted to this day, even if in watered-down forms. Was not the language of the war on terror—good versus evil, the identification of "enemies," a sense of Islam as an enormous, monolithic force—similar to these Luceian representations of a bloblike communism? In order for Americans to believe in their own superiority, they also had to avoid questioning their own lives and the system in which they lived. I wasn't sure I believed that American faculties, during this comparatively rebellious era of the 1950s and 1960s, could have been so easily disabled, until I came across a book called *Workshops of Empire.*

In 2014, the academic Eric Bennett uncovered the history of the University of Iowa Writers' Workshop, one of the most prestigious MFA programs in the country to this day. Iowa had been founded at a time when all over the country "American studies" departments were popping up to establish America as a distinct civilization, an endeavor that grew out of the era of Cold War attempts to counter the popularity of Marxism. Similarly, the University of Iowa writing program's patrons were Luce-like conservatives crusading for the United States in the Cold War. They wanted to design a literature program that "fortified democratic values at home and abroad."

To start, the University of Iowa founders sought out specific types of American writers. They disregarded people who were devoted to social justice and leftist causes that, in their view, were juvenile. They encouraged, instead, those writers whose work was "preoccupied by family and self." Once in the classroom, University of Iowa professors taught their students to avoid politics in favor of composing literature that would illuminate the human and smaller moments of life. As Bennett observes, a specific sensibility spread across America's landscape of fiction, one that celebrated beautiful sentences and quiet observations, suburban malaise and inward-looking anxieties, a literary form that would naturally tend toward the domestic. "Today's creative-writing department specializes in sensory and biographical memory," Bennett writes, "such as how icicles broken from church eaves on winter afternoons taste of asphalt."

One point of Bennett's book is that the University of Iowa's philosophy of fiction privileged the sanctity of personal experience—the preciousness of the individual—over the idea that our identities are shaped by the community or political systems or larger historical forces. Bennett believes that the University of Iowa not only drove writers away from exploring political ideas, but in the end undermined true artistic freedom. What if American creativity had been shaped in a way that was oblivious to the limits that had been set for it? Did that not mean American minds had those same limits? Was this why Kamila Shamsie found no American novelists inclined to write about the countries with which America was militarily involved? "The thing to lament is not only that we have a bunch of novels about harpoons and dinghies (or suburbs or bad marriages or road trips or offices in New York)," Bennett writes. "The thing to lament is also the dead end of isolation that comes from describing the dead end of isolation." It was possible that our highly valued American individualism might have been the ultimate force that detached citizens from the actions of their government, and from the fate of the country as a whole. Once I started looking, I found that the ethos of Cold War programming seeped into every public and private enterprise; under the guise of their own freedom, Americans were creating products that would inculcate in Americans a deep patriotism. Even things like international hotels didn't escape such ideological manipulation, which I discovered after a Turkish professor of architecture told me, "You need to research Conrad Hilton to understand America's influence in Turkey."

The hotel magnate Conrad Hilton was, like Henry Luce, a fervent Christian, capitalist, and anti-Communist. He believed that the Cold War should be fought not only with bombs but with room service. Hilton wanted to show off to the Communists "the fruits of the free world" with his hotels, which he explained, according to the writer Annabel Jane Wharton, were "not only to produce a profit, but also to make a political impact on host countries." So with funds from the Marshall Plan, Hilton opened his vertical "Little Americas" in Athens, Cairo, and Jerusalem. Hilton's most important hotel, however, was in Istanbul, whose proximity to the Soviet Union gave it symbolic and practical significance. The Istanbul Hilton would be America's last commercial outpost before enemy territory. Even the hotel's windows faced east across the Bosphorus.

As an advertisement for the modern ways of American life, the Hilton in Istanbul was a magnet to local aspirants. The hotel was where the wealthy Turkish secular classes held their weddings and social engagements and, as Hilton had hoped, learned to admire America. In the novel *The Museum of Innocence*, Orhan Pamuk's narrator says that "when I was ten, my parents attended the opening of the hotel, a very exciting occasion for them, along with all of Istanbul society, as well as the long-forgotten American film star Terry Moore," and that on Sunday evenings, they "would go as a family to eat that amazing thing called a hamburger, a delicacy as yet offered by no other restaurant in Turkey." Newspapers even dispatched reporters to the Hilton to break news of its latest technological innovations and design styles. For Turks who aspired to be "Western," there was no better place to be seen than the American Hilton.

But Hilton's hotels were intended not only to fill foreigners with dreams of America. They were also meant as a refuge for *Americans* when traveling abroad. Hilton wanted the hotels to remind all Americans of their paradise back home, their own polished, peaceful modernity: enormous, clean-lined, and spic-and-span foyers, ice water (rare in Istanbul then), the latest technological gadgetry, and unsurpassable hamburgers. The Hilton was there to discourage American customers from spending too much time in a foreign culture, from considering other ways of life. When I had visited the Hilton, I thought it was an emissary for corporate America, but had not considered that it might be a Cold War outpost for America itself.

Somehow this made the propaganda at the International Press Freedom conference I attended, where I had listened to the American journalist holding forth on the wonders of the military in Turkey, an even more profound occurrence. The ability to discern bias in political conversations or books was not enough. The totality of Americanism was something that often an individual *couldn't* see. It was too enormous, and too omnipresent. It might be embedded in the sentences of our novels. It might be embedded in the language we read in magazines, and in the language I myself as a journalist used. As Claus Offe writes, "The United States is no longer a spatially distant entity but a military, commercial and cultural *presence*, here and now, in a common space. American realities have in part become our reality." This global system, this common space, was no doubt in part due to American efforts during the Cold War, in which control, influence, and warfare needed to be unacknowledged in order to fully succeed in creating a global citizenry of American moderns who believed they came to their admiration for America on their own. If I had not known that magazines, plays, books, writing programs, newspapers—even hotels!—had all been produced to shape my sense of America's greatness, then what sort of individuality did I actually possess? Did I possess any at all?

AMERICANS REGARD THE 1950S as a golden era, a time when foreigners viewed them with admiration and longing; indeed, in Turkey and much of Europe, many defeated citizens would come to hunger for the advantages, the cars and fashions and prosperity, of the United States. But in this period of imperial expansion, many saw things differently. During and after the war, European exiles and expats, intellectuals and novelists, scientists and doctors, imbued with the wisdom of older civilizations, sensed deeper problems in American society. They were, after a while, alarmed.

Some of these European writers saw similarities, in fact, between American liberalism and the totalitarianism or German fascism they had escaped. The novelist Thomas Mann fled Germany in the 1930s for the United States, grateful for its sanctuary and dazzled by its promise. But by the 1950s, when the McCarthyites persecuted anyone Communist or insufficiently anti-Communist, he reversed his position on America, seeing it as a place with a diminished sense of justice. Theodor Adorno felt "an existential debt of gratitude" for America, but, like many fellow members of the Frankfurt School, hated its conformity, which reminded him of the fascism he had left behind in Germany. The Italian writer Italo Calvino thought American liberalism "a totalitarian structure of a medieval kind, based on the fact that no alternative exists." These foreigners saw something authoritarian in American rhetoric, American myths, and American confidence.

When he visited New York for the first time in 1946, Albert Camus wrote in his journal that America was a "country where everything is done to prove that life isn't tragic." In his view, "one must reject the tragic *after* having looked at it, not before." Here again was Baldwin's accusation that white Americans had no sense of tragedy, which I had begun to see operating in tandem with the country's terrible innocence about its own deeds. When they met in New York, an elderly Alfred Stieglitz, the photographer, told Camus, "Don't hope for anything from America. Are we an end or a beginning? I think we're an end. It's a country that doesn't know love."

Baldwin once explained that what he meant when he said Americans lacked a sense of tragedy was that they couldn't grasp that life itself was a risk, that there was no such thing as safety, that eventually we all suffer and die, and that the acceptance of this fact is precisely what empowers us to struggle and endure. Black spirituals, he said, conveyed this sense of tragedy. I can only guess that Camus and Stieglitz sensed that a country in denial of its own history of slavery—that had in fact, as I knew, defined its own best qualities against a prejudiced and hateful image of blacks—would become a country that at its root was hollow. Because the Americans had never looked their tragic history in the face, they could delude themselves into believing that their own comparable superiority might create a better world, a life so ideal that tragedy wouldn't even exist. It was an American dream that demanded the denial of all those who suffered from its hopeless pursuits, and could only be achieved if Americans stopped feeling. Octavio Paz, writing from Mexico, observed that the Americans' "self-assurance and confidence" didn't prevent self-criticism necessarily, but only as long as it was the kind of criticism "that respects the existing systems and never touches the roots." The sense of tragedy that Baldwin had been talking about would have been one Americans carried with them if they were aware that their miraculous country had been founded on a crime. The love that they couldn't feel, as Stieglitz had said, was the love they didn't manifest for all of their compatriots. Octavio Paz, as a Mexican well acquainted with the American way of empire, watched the coming half of the century with dismay. "It is impossible to hold back a giant," Paz writes. "It is possible, though far from easy, to make him listen to others; if he listens, that opens the possibility of coexistence."

From a distance, foreigners could see this American tidal wave enveloping their lives. Along with the CIA and the State Department propaganda schemes came the NGOs and the military, even to places as unfamiliar as Pakistan. There, observers recognized that something unprecedented was happening throughout the world; that their own lives would be affected by this new form of empire rising in the West. In 1954, a man from the American consulate in Islamabad asked Saadat Manto, a well-known short story writer, to contribute to the consulate's "magazine," which it published in order to sway Pakistani sympathies toward the United States. In his "Letters to Uncle Sam," Manto told a different story. As early as the 1950s, Manto saw that the demonization of communism in Asia would empower the only social and political force that might have the will to defeat it: Islamic fundamentalism. "I think the only purpose of military aid is to arm these mullahs," he writes. "I can visualize the mullahs, their hair trimmed with American scissors and their pajamas stitched by American machines in strict conformity with the Sharia."

But Manto knew the Americans only wanted to hear about their achievements, and so with the same sarcasm and faux flattery Malaparte employed about the good-natured, careless American soldiers of Naples, Manto praised the Americans like a schoolteacher.

"You have done many good deeds yourself and continue to do them," he writes. "You decimated Hiroshima, you turned Nagasaki into smoke and dust, and you caused several thousand American children to be born in Japan."

AFTER THE WAR, and the defeat of the European powers, the Americans suddenly found themselves able to take advantage of a ready-made empire of formerly colonized peoples that would come to be known as the "Third World." In response, the Truman administration conceived of what is known as his Point Four Program, a plan ostensibly meant to aid the benighted countries of the planet. "We must embark on a bold new program,"

Truman said, "for making the benefits of our scientific advances and industrial progress available for the improvement and growth of under-developed areas." Truman's words had the magical effect of turning a colonial endeavor into a humanitarian mission, in effect saying to the developing world, "We can help you be like us." "Modernization" would end up being the Americans' cleverest euphemism for empire building after 1950, and though the history of "modernization theory" has been deconstructed in countless academic books—Nils Gilman's *Mandarins of the Future*, Hemant Shah's *The Production of Modernization*, among many others—this most indestructible of American Cold War mentalities still seems to underpin Americans' fundamental sense of reality.

In the 1950s, a group of sociologists, economists, and political scientists that would over time include Daniel Lerner, Lucian Pye, Walt Rostow, and to a lesser extent "clash of civilizations" theorist Samuel Huntington, gathered under the auspices of the Center for International Studies (CIS) at MIT in Boston—at the behest of the CIA—in order to conceive of a new Cold War foreign policy. These white men knew better than to formulate foreign policy based on old racist notions of genetic superiority as the Europeans had done. Colonialism had gone out of fashion. Instead these white men conjured new racist notions in order to justify their involvement and expansion throughout the post-colonial world.

Among their decisions, in the words of the historian Michael Hunt, was to "diminish other people by exaggerating the seemingly negative aspects of their lives and by constricting the perceived range of their skills, accomplishments, and emotions." Once such backwardness was established in places such as Turkey, Iran, and Afghanistan, then the Americans could justify any kind of intervention, whether economic, cultural, or military. This "modernization theory" meant imposing the West's system of governance ("democracy"), its system of economy ("capitalism"), and its lifestyle practices ("freedom") on foreign countries in order to lead them down, according to Hemant Shah, the "irresistible and obviously superior path" to modernity. The Americans decided not to use the word "Westernization" to describe their theory, so as to appear neutral. As Gilman writes, the difference between the Europeans and the Americans was that the Europeans never even imagined that colonized peoples were capable of being as modern as Europeans. The Americans wholeheartedly believed they could make anyone into an American.

That is why, Shah explains, when Americans speak about foreign countries, they use a rhetoric of "development," words like "resistant to reform," "left behind," "spread of democracy and free markets," "a place of despair," and "strengthening civil society." Much of that language was language I myself used all the time. Even when I asked Turks the seemingly basic and obvious question "Will this country ever become a democracy?" I was not, as I thought, being a tough journalist. I was parroting the assumptions of modernization theory, the only paradigm I had for understanding the rest of the world.

The theorists of that time, however, had a problem: Americans did not want to think of themselves as imperialists, or occupiers. Someone else would have to force foreigners to embrace modernity. Who would it be? Modernization theorists feared that democratic leaders vulnerable to communism, Islamism, or any other enemyism of the United States would fail to carry through American industrialization programs and create a capitalist system. Instead, the types of leaders the Americans preferred to accomplish these tasks were military dictators. The popular argument that America had erred in the twentieth century by "tolerating" military dictatorships—Turkey, Pakistan, Iran, Egypt, half of Latin America—missed the point completely. The United States didn't tolerate military dictatorships; it fostered them.

In 1961, the CIS grandee Walt Rostow, whose book *The Stages of Economic Growth* was a bestseller in the 1960s, became President John F. Kennedy's national security advisor. To Rostow, modernization was "unidirectional," as if it were a path set by God. As Kennedy's advisor, Rostow's academic faith in America's missionary role in the modernization of other countries led to the invasion, occupation, and destruction of Vietnam. At the same time that Walt Rostow was "sincerely interested in improving the welfare of postcolonial peoples," Gilman writes, "he was directing the killing of Vietnamese peasants." Again, that word "sincere." William Appleman Williams and Nils Gilman seemed to be saying that Cold War Americans were sincere when they oppressed and killed people in order to transform their countries into one similar to America, which makes these American intellectuals seem sociopathic, or delusional, or both.

The Pakistani economist known as Inayatullah said at a conference in the late 1950s that the Americans were measuring the world "like the person who measures the competence of everybody on terms of his own special competence." Just as American settlers had defined their idealized selves against the prejudiced image they had of African Americans, our Cold War, empire-building intellectuals and politicians had very consciously pitted the modern American self against backward foreigners, this time with the same mistaken sense of its superiority. And like African Americans, the foreigners on the receiving end of these desperate demands would come to know the Americans far better than Americans would ever know them: as people with a myth about themselves they would do anything to prove.

In the twentieth century, the United States embraced autocrats willing to impose American ideas of modernization on Iran, Afghanistan, South Korea, South Vietnam, Taiwan, much of Latin America, and, indeed, my new home, Turkey. One of the most influential books on American foreign policy and modernization theory, one funded by the State Department, was Daniel Lerner's *The Passing of Traditional Society*, which was published in 1958. Most of Lerner's research was collected in a tiny village in Anatolia. In Turkey.

IN THE 1950S, Lerner had spent months in the Turkish Anatolian town of Balgat in order to study how new methods of media and propaganda could induce Turkish villagers—and uneducated peoples all over the Middle East—to embrace the United States as the quintessence of modernity. An epigraph from André Siegfried appears early in the book: "The United States is presiding at a general reorganization of the ways of living throughout the entire world."

My adopted home of Turkey, as it turned out, had been the Americans' original model modern country. They admired that Mustafa Kemal Atatürk was one of the first non-Western leaders to popularize the word "modernization." Turkey's and America's conception of themselves indeed evolved in tandem; in 1954, Senator J. William Fulbright would say that the Vietnam they were intent on transforming needed a leader "after the fashion of Kemal Atatürk, who made Turkey over" because it was "the best example of what should be done in an undeveloped country that I can think of in the last 30 years." No wonder so many Americans admired Atatürk; Atatürk was us.

The Americans recognized that they had to tread carefully in Turkey. "The Turk is a proud man. We must proceed with a reasonable caution to avoid surfeiting him with American omnipresence," one State Department briefing read. The first free elections in Turkey, which were held in 1950, had come as a pleasant surprise to the Americans: a largely peasant society had decided to vote for a party, the Democrat Party, that had been overtly praiseful of American capitalism. Soon the State Department, the Joint American Military Mission for Aid to Turkey (JAMMAT), and the CIA set up in Turkey and got to work on their modernization projects, around the same time that Engin Cezzar was studying theater in America, where he observed how little Americans knew about Turkey at all.

In reality, the Americans were busy in Turkey tackling all sorts of military, educational, and cultural deficiencies. In fact, the Americans almost completely remade the Turkish military, an institution I had imagined impervious to foreign interference: they founded an engineering school in Ankara, a commando training camp in Izmir, and schools that taught how to build artillery and ordnance. Turkish soldiers even took the same classes that American soldiers took. "American advisors wanted to replace Oriental obedience," writes the historian Nicholas Danforth, "with a more modern, liberal American ethos." Cultural programs cropped up in Turkey to promote a certain America-centric worldview. One radio show called *Hazırcevap* invited contestants to call in and try to win a trivia game, which revolved around questions like these: "Where are the longest bridges and tunnels in America?" "Among the weapons invented until now, are there any that are useful to human beings or nations?" "Where in America are the Redskins located?" "Do they make Turkish movies in Hollywood?" The Americans, it turned out, had also built the roads I loved so much in Turkey. The Turks had wanted to build roads that linked four major cities so they could easily transport their armies throughout the country in case of a Soviet attack, but the Americans overruled them and instead began building a different network of roads designed for economic efficiency. "It was more than a decade," Danforth writes, "before an unbroken paved road linked even such major cities as Istanbul and Ankara."

What, ultimately, were the Americans even trying to do? "U.S. officials believed that wanting to be modern was the first step toward being modern, and that being modern meant appreciating modernity," Danforth writes. "That is, showing off how modern America was would encourage Turks to be more modern themselves, and as they became more modern, they would develop an even greater appreciation for America, the most modern country of all." The Americans were creating a world in which no other future would be considered but the American one, which was both the source of change and the unattainable ideal.

When Rana had said much of her life had been defined by America, I had not understood what she meant. I had scoffed at the ways Turkish secularists used the word "modern," thinking they were snobs using some bastardized conception of the word, having no clue from where it came. I also unwittingly used that language of modernization when I moved to Turkey, and when I thought about Turkey, and sometimes when I wrote about Turkey. But I had not known, and did not suspect, the degree to which this way of thinking had been premeditated, developed, deployed, and enshrined in so many facets of American life by a handful of men. I had not even known it was a "way of thinking" that could be challenged, that could be flawed. I thought, indeed, that it was simply reality.

In retrospect, in my quest to break down the myths of America, to discern the outlines of its empire, I was also looking to defend my country. The idea of our good intentions must have had some basis in history. The British writer Anatol Lieven calls this imaginary period the "state of noble innocence." I kept looking for that moment, that moment when the state of innocence was real.

It may be an exaggeration to say that the magazines of Henry Luce still influence magazines of today, or that the recent currents of American literature still draw upon the University of Iowa's Cold War curriculums. By now, Daniel Lerner has been refuted by both foreign and American academics who recognized his book as a blueprint for imposing the American way of life on "traditional" people. And yet so much of what I read about Cold War programs has a deeply familiar ring of truth: so-called modernity trumped up as the antithesis of Islamic societies; globalization and neoliberalism accepted as natural, inevitable phenomena, just like modernization. I had a Cold War mind. The reason that I was not thinking about Erdoğan's economic policies—the reason I was not, as Rana said, thinking about *money*—was that deep down I had found Erdoğan's pro-business, American-sounding rhetoric deeply comforting, the obvious path forward for Turkey. The reason I thought myself uniquely capable of objectivity was that sixty years ago, American intellectuals and leaders declared America the greatest, most modern and evolved country on the planet—the end of the spectrum of evolution, as I had myself thought—all the while neglecting to inform Americans that that belief was itself an ideology, a form of nationalism, one no different from the Kemalism I scorned.

The American empire was harder to see because it had no beginning and no end. Ours was an empire that had not begun with conventional invasions. Our empire began with an invasion of itself. We were rebels against tyranny who made a nation out of tyrannizing others, we were the revolutionaries who exalted self-determination while robbing it from others. No romantic image was without its darker underbelly, as Caner had shown me was true of Turkey's myths, too—even during that romantic time of the nation's birth, whole civilizations were destroyed. Even during the "good war," the Americans had been a source of terror. There was no state of noble innocence. But that hadn't stopped American intellectuals during the Cold War from inventing one, thereby keeping the country's own citizens constantly in search of something they would never find.

4.

BENEVOLENT
INTERVENTIONS:
GREECE AND TURKEY

To defend your own reality and then impose it forcefully on the
outside world is paranoia.

—THOMAS MERTON

ONE OF THE GREATEST POSTWAR novels about Americans abroad,
Don DeLillo's *The Names*, takes place in Greece, in the late 1970s
and early '80s, when the Vietnam War and the Iran hostage affair brought
about an unprecedented crisis of faith in American power. The novel is set
in Athens, the expat characters' latest stop on their tour of an unacknowledged empire connected by mysterious corporate postings: in Egypt and
Nigeria; Panama and Turkey; East Africa, the Sudan, Lebanon, and finally
Greece. When it was published in 1982, the British critic Michael Wood

observed that for American writers, America "is not a place or a nation but a condition of the soul tied to a habit of the possession of power." DeLillo's novel might have come too early in the spread of the empire for individual Americans to grasp the ways in which their own identities were connected to this possession. I could only begin to understand the novel now that I lived in Turkey.

The Names, in fact, is a study in American ignorance; then as now, few Americans knew the difference between Sunni and Shiite, or how to pronounce Iran ("E-ron"). DeLillo's protagonist, Axton, is a risk analyst for an insurance company that counsels multinational corporations on pressing questions about the world. *Which country is risky? Where will the next bomb go off? Who creates the risk?* Axton is also, as my Turkish friends liked to imagine I was, an unwitting agent for the CIA, the spy who doesn't know he's a spy. "Are they killing Americans?" is his main question. Axton and the Americans abroad can't make sense of the world, can't grab onto anything. They are not so much arrogant as confused. They perceive their vulnerability, their noses wrinkling at smells in the air: "Wasn't there a sense, we Americans felt, in which we had it coming?"

A Greek man named Eliades, with the aspect of a grumpy sage, says to the Americans:

> I think it's only in a crisis that Americans see other people. It
> has to be an American crisis, of course. If two countries fight that
> do not supply the Americans with some precious commodity,
> then the education of the public does not take place. But when
> the dictator falls, when the oil is threatened, then you turn on the
> television and they tell you where the country is, what the
> language is, how to pronounce the names of the leaders, what
> the religion is all about, and maybe you can cut out recipes in the
> newspaper of Persian dishes. I will tell you. The whole world takes
> an interest in this curious way Americans educate themselves.

DeLillo's expatriates exaggerate their shame, apologize for not speaking languages, for not being able to figure out their own addresses or phone numbers in a foreign land. They survive on the "humor of personal humiliation," but there are worse humiliations. "'All countries where the United States has strong interests stand in line to undergo a terrible crisis so that at last the Americans will see them,' Eliades says. 'This is very touching.'"

I wonder now how deliberately DeLillo chose Greece as the setting for his novel about the American empire. In the late 1940s, Thomas Mann wrote in his diary that he considered what was happening in Greece under the Americans worse than what was happening in Czechoslovakia under the Soviets. To me, Greece would come to seem like the beginning and the end of everything.

WHEN MY FELLOWSHIP finished in 2009, the financial crisis whittled away any desire of mine to go home either in the short term—there were no jobs—or in the long term. The financial crisis made me stop looking at my future as I once had. My generation, somewhere between delayed adolescence and starting a family, felt the new economic limits in America acutely; it was no longer clear that our lives would get exponentially better, as our country had always promised us. It is a testament to how deeply capitalism had sunk into the Americans' consciousness that the financial crisis—the failure of capitalism—seemed to undo us more than September 11. If the economy was a sham, if the money was a sham, if the dream was a sham, then was anything they ever told us about ourselves true?

I stayed in Istanbul, where it was cheaper, and where, oddly enough, things were flourishing financially, because after the collapse of so many economies throughout the world, investors began directing their money to Turkey. The country, however, was still one that few magazines wanted to know about. I spent the last months of my fellowship studying the international activities of the Gülen movement. Just like the American missionaries of the nineteenth century, the Gülenists had built schools everywhere from Kabul to Nairobi, Japan to Indonesia, Mexico City and across the United States of America: Houston, Chicago, Washington, D.C. Many American policy makers embraced the Gülenists as a necessary moderating Islamic force in a world besieged by Islamic terrorism. I wanted to know whether the West's preoccupation with terrorism might have made them blind to the Gülenists' normal human flaws: destructive ambition, a desire for state power. But few editors were curious about Gülen, the imam who lived in America. One told me that he couldn't see why the Gülen movement, being peaceful and nonthreatening, had anything to do with American interests.

So I went to Greece. The financial crisis had gotten stuck there, drawing strength from the country's many dysfunctions. Everyone, at the time, looked down on Greece. Pundits scoffed that the Greeks had brought their stupendous crisis upon themselves, as if some deficit in their collective southern character, some deeply embedded depravity, had compelled them to destroy Europe. Just as with the investment bankers who couldn't muster any empathy for Americans who had lost their houses to bum mortgages, there was an international assumption that only an inferior (crazy, irrational, corrupt) people would have allowed such a calamity to befall them, not that the calamity might have been part of a larger calamity, and certainly not that the calamity might have begun, at least somewhat, in the United States. This was the strange way our sense of identity worked; we were omnipotent, and yet when a global financial crisis happened, we contemptuously shifted the blame onto other people, other countries. I didn't know much about Greeks, except for the remnants of the community in Istanbul, and I knew few growing up. It might have been their insignificance in my imagination that led me—perhaps unconsciously—to imbibe the spectacularly insidious prejudice of the time: the lazy, crazy Greeks. *This silly tiny country.* I arrived in Athens expecting a circus.

Though because I, too, was bewildered—horrified, ashamed—by the financial crisis in my own country, I felt myself more vulnerable to new ideas, and from the unlikeliest sources. On one of my first days in Athens, I interviewed a member of the Communist Party who sat near a painting of Lenin and peppered his speech with "comrade," all of which seemed absurd to my American sensibilities. But something in his sentiments, maybe just the outrage, felt wholly logical as well. "We deny this government propaganda that everyone is responsible for this situation," he said. "We don't agree with the EU idea that the banks are too big to fail, because they are still making millions in profits. It's an illusion that it'll be in the favor of people if we return to growth and development."

Greece, I discovered, was a place where hammers and sickles and "Fuck the Police" graffiti decorated the city walls; where references to civil wars and world wars and an American intervention came up in daily conversation; where immigrants fleeing war and economic plunder scrambled atop the life raft of European shores and festered in Athens. To Americans, the Greek crisis seemed separate from the Arab Spring, which seemed separate from, say, East Africa, but later I would meet a Kenyan activist who had been incorporating such diverse movements as Occupy Wall Street, Syriza, gay marriage, and political stirrings from Cairo to Jakarta into her own development of Kenyan activism. We don't count the early Greek protests as part of Occupy or the Arab Spring, but that wave of dissent might have kicked off in Athens, as early as 2008. Ideas and images were ricocheting around the world at new speeds, but they also settled in people's psyches forever. In Greece, their rage was broad, bigger than Greece. Their rage, like that of so many others during that time, was against history.

THE STREETS OF CENTRAL ATHENS are lined with tables and in spring, when the sun is still pale yellow and soft, they are full of people. Greece is a café civilization, and yet visitors seeing this for the first time react defensively: What financial crisis? Look, every table is filled with Greeks. Shops were still open, crowds ballooned out of the Metro exits, cars clogged the streets. People were laughing. They gave street dancers their coins. The Acropolis hadn't fallen down. How could we measure this new suffering in beautiful, quaint Europe when everything looked so nice? Only the Greeks themselves, as my friend Olga explained to me, would look at that souvlaki joint with the tables outside and tell you that a souvlaki and Coke cost only four euros, that that young man sitting there for hours was unemployed and didn't want to sit in his apartment or he would kill himself, and that that elderly pensioner sitting with him had lost his pension and probably had been nursing that same draft of beer all day. The foreigner, the German bureaucrat, and the IMF representative couldn't see that, and so for the young man and the old pensionless pensioner, there would be no limit to their suffering.

For much of the last century, Greece had been run, on and off, by the Papandreou family. They were Socialists. The first Papandreou, Georgios, became prime minister in 1944; his son Andreas took over in 1981. When

I arrived in Athens, Andreas's son, another George, had assumed the prime minister's office, and thus had the unfortunate task of pushing through austerity measures to ward off economic ruin. I couldn't get to George for an interview—he was busy—so I settled for Nick Papandreou, George's very tall brother. When I met him, Nick was sitting at a long table at the Andreas Papandreou Foundation, a beautiful old house in a run-down part of Athens. A terrace off the back overlooked the city's ancient graveyard. Black-and-white family photos hung on one wall; Nick's novels and books, and pamphlets about his father, Andreas, lined another. Nick, who had an American mother and grew up in Canada and the United States, among other places, sounded American. The Papandreous, I would soon discover, had a long and tangled relationship with the U.S.

Nick told me a story about riding the Metro in Athens:

"Nick! Why did your brother bring in the IMF?" one passenger called out.

"No choice. It was either that or no one gets paid come July first," Papandreou replied.

"Well, I am glad to see you taking public transport," he said.

"What do you do for a living?" Papandreou asked the man.

"I'm a doctor."

"Did you ever take side money from your patients?"

Everybody was listening. "Yes."

"Are you still taking money on the side?"

"Not anymore."

"Why?"

"Because now, the way things are, I'd be lynched."

The fact that cracking down on *doctors* counted as a positive development in Greece was a sign of just how troubled Greek society had become. The Papandreous' country was more than 300 billion euros in debt, which represented 115 percent of the country's GDP. The European Union and the IMF agreed to bail the country out only if the government passed austerity measures like raising taxes and cutting social services. But reforming Greece required nothing less than a societal revolution that would upend the way people usually operated: from doctors and tax collectors and lawyers who took bribes to cabdrivers who didn't give receipts. Greece also had a bloated, mismanaged public sector and a stunted private one, both legacies of a political system prone to clientelism and corruption, which had caused the demon-word "socialism" to creep into the censorious Western rhetoric about the country. I wondered how the West had ever allowed Greece, a member of NATO, to become so *Socialist* in the first place.

The conventional story about Greece went like this: When Greece joined the European Union, it was poor and fractious. Andreas Papandreou, who came to power on a platform of fiery anti-American populism, reunited the country by offering generous social services, all of which were buoyed by European Union money flowing into the country. Bad habits continued: employment for life in the public sector, politicians with stuffed pockets, an aversion to foreign investment, snail-like growth, a communal lifestyle that kept people happy at the taverna table but stifled individual creativity, a national belief that beating the "system" was something the smart people did. Then, the world economy collapsed. In Greece, the old habits became harder to conceal, but like the wife of an alcoholic who refuses to notice the vodka bottle stashed in the closet, the European Union looked the other way.

The Greek people, however, were watching. In 2008, riots tore Athens apart. The Greek police shot a fifteen-year-old kid named Alexis Grigoropoulos, and for weeks afterward, high school students and anarchists charged through the streets. "Fuck sixty-eight, fight now!" declared the protestors. The Greek youth lacked jobs, adequate education, and, in a country riven by cronyism and nepotism, a future. They had also noticed that the new flood of money from the West had not filtered down to their own lives, or to the services and universities they needed. "The flames may die down but the coals will simmer," one young protestor told *The Guardian* at the time. "One little thing, and you'll see it will ignite again. Ours is a future without work, without hope. Our grievances are so big, so many. Only a very strong government can stop the rot." The kids cited 1967 and 1974—neither dates about which I knew much—as inspirations for 2008. "They have no hope in the current system," a Greek shipping magnate told me about the young people in the streets, "and their only hope is in breaking everything and starting anew." When I visited, the protests had continued, the riot police—outfitted with shields, billy clubs, tear gas guns, and nine-millimeters—following clusters of anarchists wearing black hoodies, boots, and backpacks, the international uniform of the twenty-first-century's warrior class.

The rest of the protestors looked rather upscale. They walked slowly and patiently to the head of Syntagma Square, where the lovely yellow Parliament building overlooked the area from a hill. At sunset, in that truly celestial Athens light, the rest of the square would be in shadow, but the Parliament building glowed. This was where the protestors of Athens spent their days shaking their fists and trying to break down the doors. Greeks ignored, if not tolerated and condoned, a certain level of dissident violence. The Greeks believe in protest, this is how they live, I thought, at that point still having no idea in what such a belief had been rooted.

ONE EVENING I WENT TO SEE where the refugees lived, in a neighborhood called Sofokleous, which was close to the center of the town but tucked away from the tourists. The whole world seemed to be there: the Congolese and the Pakistanis, the Bangladeshis and the Afghans, the Kurds, the Iraqis, the Somalis, the Moroccans and the Nigerians. They dreamed of being smuggled deeper into Europe, but if they got caught by the police, they were thrown back to Greece, the first European country they entered. The Greeks were suffering from a financial crisis wrought by the West and a refugee crisis brought on, to a large extent, by the wars of the West. Long before the war in Syria sent thousands more refugees to its shores, the world crises were converging in Greece.

It was a Sunday, and the Sofokleous streets were empty. My friend Iason, a journalist who had reported from Iran and Afghanistan, told me to leave my handbag at home and to dress down, in the hopes that we'd appear like heroin addicts looking for a fix. Only three years ago, this had been a stylish part of town. Then the police decided to push the refugees out of the main city squares where they often lingered, essentially corralling them into these back streets. In a country with little industry and few jobs, there wasn't much for these foreigners to do but sell handbags, toys, drugs, or their bodies.

I expected to see a neighborhood similar to the bad parts of West

Philadelphia, but I was wrong. As we began our walk down the main thoroughfare, beautiful Athens seemed to fall away, and off a dystopian cliff: Sofokleous was where the dispossessed had been sent to rot. Some refugees looked healthy, selling socks off the sidewalk, screaming at one another. But others were bloodied and beaten, their clothes half ripped off, shoes missing. To our left, we saw three men sticking needles into their ankles; to our right, a woman sidled up to a man for some drugs. One woman's flesh seemed to be melting off her. Iason told me to walk quickly.

Turning up a side street, we spotted a man sitting inside a taverna called Klimataria, which first opened in 1927, when Athens was a cow town. Big barrels of wine stood against one wall; enormous pots hung from the ceilings. It looked like a happy place. It was empty. Business had declined by 70 percent, we were told, and soon the restaurant would be moving. The owner, Pericles Spiridou, had thick, wavy white hair, like the gods, and sat alone at a table with a pen and notepad.

"The immigrants sometimes attack each other in the street with swords," he said.

Tourists who came to Klimataria fled with fear. Spiridou was a liberal-minded person. He didn't disparage the immigrants themselves. Instead, he spoke of politics.

"Where is the regulation?" he said. "Where is the police? The state does nothing. No one has any control."

The state was at fault, but his words conjured notions of forces too big, of changes too massive, coming from places too mysterious. Spiridou was still waiting for some sense to be made of it all. Who were these people? Would anybody do anything about it? Where would they go? Spiridou was forty-nine years old. He had existential concerns. He was sitting at his taverna, seeing a financial crisis coming from the west, refugees coming from the east and south, and his restaurant becoming too dangerous to operate.

"We've lived through many things," Spiridou said. He looked heart-broken for a moment, and then angry. "Civil war, a dictatorship, the fall of communism. Now what I hope is that I live to see the fall of capitalism. That's my dream. And I will see it."

His leftist language surprised me then, but soon everyone would be discussing capitalism in this way, like any other phase of history, one that would pass.

I USUALLY BEGAN my interviews in Athens with the same question: "How did Greece get to this place?" The narrative for why the Greeks were so angry was first explained to me by a political scientist named Stathis Kalyvas. I was relieved to find Kalyvas, and of all the nuances and details he explained to me that day, I clung to the one statement of his that fit into the worn lock of my consciousness like a key.

"The best way to think of it is to think of Greece as a teenager," he told me. "Many Greeks view the state with a combination of a sense of entitlement, mistrust, and dislike similar to that of teenagers vis-à-vis their parents. They expect to be funded without contributing. They often act irresponsibly without care about consequences and expect to be bailed out by the state—but that only increases their sense of dependency, which only increases their feeling of dislike for the state. And of course, they refuse to grow up. But like every teenager, they will."

The reason Kalyvas's explanation appealed to me, I later realized, was because it recalled the language of modernization theory, whose intellectual proponents thought of postcolonial nations as rebellious adolescents. According to Nils Gilman, the image of foreign nations as " 'young' or 'immature' appears throughout the literature on modernization." At the time of my interview with Kalyvas I hadn't known anything about modernization theory. But I hadn't needed to. Mainstream newspapers such as *The New York Times*, a million television news broadcasts, likely even most of my college history courses all used the same language of the maturity and immaturity of nations. That rhetoric was not only condescending, but a kind of Trojan horse: it implied progress and hope—*You, young Greece, may be a miserable mess now, but you, too, will grow up one day to be just like us*—and so seemed somewhat harmless. But in the process weren't all foreign countries condemned to failure so that the United States could remain the ideal? These countries would be selected as candidates in need of endless salvation by the United States—and, by extension, me, one of its foreign journalists asking that patronizing question, "*Whatever in the devil went wrong here, guys?*"

But Greeks don't let journalists and their superficial questions off so easily. Almost every Greek person of whom I asked that question did not begin in 2008; they did not even begin in the twenty-first century. They started with one of two dates: 1946 or 1949.

"So what happened here?" I would say.

"Look, in 1946 . . ." they would begin.

"Papandreou handed out pension plans by giving one to everybody who fought in the 1946 to 1949 civil war," one said.

"What civil war?" I asked.

Even if they started with Greece's early years in the European Union, their statements inevitably led back to this much earlier history. This shared history was one of the few things that united them: the conservative academic and the Communist apparatchik, the shoe salesman and the novelist, my friend Iason and the random guy I spoke to on the street. My interviewees kept referring to "the junta" and "the intervention," and something called "Polytechnic," all of which I gathered, with a slowly building dread, had something to do with the United States. Greece's economic system might have been poorly managed by the Greeks, but this system had emerged in response to political events that had been equally devastating.

"The intervention, as you know . . ."

"You know, because of the U.S. intervention in Greece . . ."

"Didn't you know the first U.S. intervention of the post–Cold War period was in Greece?"

In *Greece*?

As I sat with them, not knowing about these things—about my own country—I felt as if a physical separation lay between us, as if I inhabited an entirely other universe. I had been charged with writing about them, for a magazine thousands of people would read, and yet whatever I wrote would to Greeks inevitably be read as if the magazine had dispatched an alien from another planet. Spiridou has seen a connection between the financial crisis and the refugee crisis, as if it was the dominant political structure of the world that was responsible for Greece's catastrophes. If a crisis of this magnitude could happen, could it possibly be only a few years old? Didn't it in fact mean that the entire economic architecture of the world was somehow faulty? And wasn't it to some degree *our* architecture? Wasn't this the American Century?

THE AMERICANS' AFFECTION for fascism in the 1930s fell disproportionately on the small country of Greece. (The Americans at that time also supported Mussolini.) The threat of Bolshevism overshadowed any American concerns about the authoritarian tendencies of the right-wing military dictator General Ioannis Metaxas, but at the heart of American policy was a belief that the Greeks could not govern themselves. The American ambassador in Greece at the time, Lincoln MacVeagh, said he supported Metaxas because the Greeks possessed immature political institutions. A *Foreign Affairs* magazine article in 1936 argued that the Greek problem was a problem of "national character"; yet another writer at the time called this problem a "disinclination to obey a leader and the concomitant tendency to split up into cliques and groups." *Those crazy Greeks*, indeed.

American concern for Greece's "democracy" was minimal. When MacVeagh returned to America, he called the unpopular and often sinister dictator Metaxas the "savior of the country." And yet, "Greece is still Greece," he wrote, "slowly modernizing out of its backward depths . . . and inveterately disobedient and individualistic whenever immediate and constant pressure is not applied." The supposed Bolshevik threat may have served as the United States' practical, strategic reason for backing a right-wing dictatorship, but it would be the Americans' deep belief in the Greeks' backwardness that excused that dictatorship's violence—and eventually the Americans' violence, as well.

One of the less famous examples of Nazi horror during World War II was its occupation of Athens. During their three-year occupation of the country, the Nazis wreaked havoc on Greek society, subjecting the population to starvation, torture, imprisonment, and death, and forever rending the bonds among the Greek people. Inevitably, the terror gave way to an insurgency by Greek rebels who were, to varying degrees, leftists and Communists. When the war ended, those who organized the leftist resistance continued fighting with the royalist Greek army that had tolerated, and at times collaborated with, the Nazis. It was, as the Greek novelist Nikos Kazantzakis, put it, a fratricide. The Greek Civil War was also one of the first battles of the Cold War.

The Greece that the United States inherited from the British after World War II was not only poor and war-torn, much of the population homeless, but also corrupt, oligarchic, and violent, ruled by a despised king, a tiny right-wing elite, and a vast network of thugs, port dwellers, and longshoremen, who served as the king's underground army. Up in the mountains, Communist guerrillas, many of them former resistance fighters who had battled the Nazis on behalf of the Allies, as much as for themselves, continued their ugly war. If they were beholden to anyone, it was to Tito's Yugoslavia, not to the Kremlin; Stalin had little respect or concern for the Greek guerrillas. That fact didn't matter to the Americans. As they saw it, all of the countries around Greece had fallen: Czechoslovakia, Poland, Bulgaria, Romania. Greece would be the place where the West would take its stand. The Americans' "domino theory," introduced to American students in lesson plans about Vietnam, originated with Greece, which was seen as the first piece to fall before knocking down Iran in one direction and Italy in the other. Greece would stay anti-Communist at any price. In 1947, Truman went to Congress and pleaded with them to pass the Truman Doctrine.

The president's language seventy years ago sounds surprisingly familiar. "The very existence of the Greek state is today threatened by the terrorist activities of several thousand armed men, led by Communists, who defy the government's authority," the president told Congress:

> The United States must supply this assistance. We have already extended to Greece certain types of relief and economic aid but these are inadequate. There is no other country to which democratic Greece can turn. No other nation is willing and able to provide the necessary support for a democratic Greek government.
>
> I believe that it must be the policy of the United States to support free peoples who are resisting attempted subjugation by armed minorities or by outside pressures.

Totalitarian regimes like the Soviet Union would "undermine the foundations of international peace and hence the security of the United States,"

Truman said. "I believe that we must assist free peoples to work out their own destinies in their own way . . . The free peoples of the world look to us for support in maintaining their freedoms. If we falter in our leadership, we may endanger the peace of the world—and we shall surely endanger the welfare of our own nation."

I believe that we must assist free peoples to work out their own destinies in their own way. Thus began a key component of American exceptionalism: the idea that America's duty to the world was to liberate foreign peoples. What Truman had meant was that this liberation would come only to those who imitated the American way of life. The catalyst for most of the foreign policy of the postwar era, the foundation of the new world order, the place that enshrined a moral rhetoric and self-belief in all Americans, was Greece, a country whose history few of us cared to learn. This was part of the "American intervention" I kept hearing about: the Truman Doctrine.

ONE OF THE FIRST VICTIMS of the Cold War era was the American journalist George Polk, who was murdered one evening in Thessaloniki. Polk was handsome, flirtatious, outspoken, ambitious, and skeptical of the American project in Greece. "We have to stand for decency and for freedom," he said. "We're no better than the Russians otherwise." He stood among several prominent reporters of the time—William Shirer, Edward Murrow—who saw dark clouds in Truman's vision. In Greece, they observed the beginnings of America's imperial reflex; a satellite country only had to cry "communism," and more funds and weapons would follow. Polk repeatedly questioned the wisdom of Truman's policy and exposed Greek political corruption. His reporting undermined American aid to Greece and threatened America's collaboration with the Greek government against the Communists. When his body washed up in a Thessaloniki bay, the authorities pinned the murder on the reds.

Some fifty years later it emerged that the American journalist was most likely killed by Greek thugs hired by the Greek regime, which was covered up with the assistance of American embassy staff, high-ranking CIA officials, and even American journalists. Every year, awards in George Polk's name are given to American journalists—I had friends who had been recipients—but never had I heard anyone mention that one of the most prestigious American journalism awards was in the name of an American journalist who had been silenced with the collusion of his own country.

In the late forties, the United States was giving hundreds of millions of dollars a year to Greece in economic and military aid. The USS *Missouri* paid a visit to Athens, as it had to Turkey. Greece soon experienced the circus-troupe invasion of Pax Americana: advisors, soldiers, teachers, spies, businessmen, diplomats, and agronomists. "Americans are now so numerous here that practically every large café in Athens prints its bill of fare in both Greek and English," said Polk, according to his biographer Kati Marton. Americans worked in Greek government ministries. They set up shop at the embassy near the royal residence; many of the Americans lived in the same building off Constitution Square. According to the bilateral agreements signed around the administration of economic aid, the historian John O. Iatrides writes, "American officials were given authority to supervise virtually every function of the Greek state."

The rest of the American money went to the military, with which the Greek government began a series of emergency measures to purge Communists and disloyal citizens from society. On some of the thousands of islands strewn across the Aegean Sea, the Greeks constructed internment camps, where citizens were "reeducated" and forced to renounce communism. The government tortured them with truncheon beatings, and gave them electric shocks, and bound their skin with wire. So-called and supposed Communists—or anyone who criticized the regime—were regularly executed, cities locked down under curfews. The streets of Athens were festooned with American military regalia.

But unlike the stream of images we see today from war-torn places, in Greece, as Marton writes, there were "no cameras to expose the ravaged faces of hunger, the broken bodies of those held captive on barren islands merely on suspicion of Communist activity." Many newspapers and magazines, including *The New York Times* and Henry Luce's *Time*, instead reinforced the Americans' and Greek royalists' propaganda. It was *these* policies, the American policies, that drove more Greeks to join the dreaded Communist resistance.

In the countryside, the Greek military launched offensives against the villages of these rebels, with the help of U.S. intelligence agents and napalm bombs. What the Americans did not know, the Greeks never forgot; a Communist Party member told me in 2010 that the Americans "first tested" napalm on the Greeks (it was after they used it on the Japanese during World War II). Those years also saw the first counterinsurgency operation in America's history led by the fledgling Central Intelligence Agency, which in turn trained Greek intelligence agents in counterinsurgency and interrogation "techniques." James Becket, a lawyer who later lived and worked in Greece as a representative of Amnesty International, wrote that all of this energy, money, and lives were expended for a myth, because in Greece "an omnipotent Communist Party taking orders from the communist monolith in Moscow does not exist."

But at the time, it was dissenters within the American apparatus, like George Polk, who were labeled "not objective." "In the Cold War lexicon," Marton writes, "the word 'objective' had thus assumed a new meaning." I wasn't sure that legacy wasn't still with us. Long ago, I had accepted that the foreign Communists of that period had been our true enemies—that Communists existed, in fact, wherever the Americans said they did. I never questioned their guilt; I certainly never thought that perhaps "enemy" might simply mean someone who believes in a different political system. The outlandishly brutal actions of America abroad in the 1950s required compensatory rationalizing language, a language equally violent in its distortion. It was a discourse that defined "objectivity"—indeed, "reality"—according to the requirements of American power, and that, as much as in Greece, was created in Latin America.

THE AMERICAN AMBASSADOR in Athens during that era was a man named John Peurifoy, and he became one of the primary executors of postwar American policy. Peurifoy was known to participate in Greek security meetings, even intervene in discussions at Parliament. When the Greeks were debating which electoral system they preferred—proportional representation, which most politicians favored, or a majority system, which the prime minister wanted—Peurifoy warned in so many words that if the

Greeks chose the proportional system, he would cut off American aid. Today, a Greek friend told me, Greeks still use the word "Peurifoy" to refer to the bullying manner in which a foreigner condescends to Greeks.

After Greece, the State Department sent Peurifoy to Guatemala. "I have come to Guatemala to use the big stick," he announced upon arrival. Guatemala's popular new president, Jacobo Arbenz, had been implementing agrarian reforms, which to Americans seemed similar to those in Communist China. Guatemala, the Americans reasoned, threatened to go Communist as well. "Public opinion in the U.S. might force us to take some measures to prevent Guatemala from falling into the lap of international Communism," Peurifoy told *Time* magazine. Overthrowing Arbenz was the CIA's top priority, and in preparation they distributed violent how-to manuals to their Guatemalan conscripts, and began training them for war. On the day of the Guatemalan "revolution," Guatemalans, organized by Peurifoy and the CIA, invaded Guatemala to overthrow Arbenz and liberate Guatemala from "communism." If Greece was one of the Americans' first occupied satellite states after World War II, Guatemala would count as one of its first military coups.

The coup in Guatemala, according to the British historian Alex von Tunzelmann, spurred "a shock wave of anti-American feeling" across Latin America. Pedro Mir, a Dominican poet, said at the time of Americans: "You do not want Walt Whitman, the Democrat, but another Whitman, atomic and savage." If there is one region about which Americans know their imperial history, it's likely Latin America: the United Fruit Company; Coca-Cola and Del Monte working with Latin American death squads; David Rockefeller's Business Group for Latin America conspiring with the CIA to bring about coups; the School of the Americas, an American military college in Fort Benning, Georgia, which trained seemingly every Latin American dictator in, among other things, torture techniques. There is no place of such thoroughgoing capitalist-imperialist horror as Latin America. But there is a tendency among Americans, even those marginally well-read, to rely on a number of assumptions about their history—for example, that the Soviets did pose a genuine threat to the United States—which serves to diminish the emotional impact of such imperial actions. How else could we still think of the 1950s as a period of innocence? In fact, it was during this decade, and largely in Latin America, that the American government began to find rhetorical ways to deliberately obscure its intentions. When President Eisenhower observed that the word "capitalism" had become associated with imperialism, he was disturbed. From then on, according to von Tunzelmann, he decreed that capitalism would be replaced with words such as "free enterprise," "the free world," or, most simple, "freedom."

As in Greece, there wasn't as great a Communist threat throughout most of Latin America as the Americans believed. Most Latin Americans were religious, unlikely to be swayed by godless communism; and Stalin himself had little interest in a region he saw as "the obedient army of the United States." But the right-wing dictators throughout Latin America seized on the United States' irrational fear of communism, and conjured a Communist menace whenever necessary for their own power and survival. The Americans supported monsters like Trujillo in the Dominican Republic and Papa Doc Duvalier in Haiti, as well as military regimes throughout South America, political eras from which those countries still have not recovered. "Do nothing to offend the dictators," said the American secretary of state John Foster Dulles. "They are the only people we can depend on." Years later, Arthur Schlesinger Jr. would admit that the Kennedy administration simply did not understand the many shades of leftist and progressive politics in Latin America, or anywhere.

In Latin America, the Americans would eventually stage or support six more military coups: Argentina in 1962, Guatemala again in 1963, Brazil in 1964, Bolivia in 1964, Uruguay and Chile in 1973. What might have been a last resort had become an easy habit—yet one that did not quench American desire for global power. Despite destructive influence in the Western hemisphere, the Americans' failure to fully wrest control over the region would inspire them to look elsewhere for self-renewal. President Kennedy, so embarrassed by the Bay of Pigs invasion, needed to show that U.S. power was credible. And so from Greece to Latin America and across Asia, the Americans searched for the vulnerable country where they could forever prove their authority. Kennedy's adviser, the modernization theorist Walt Rostow, told the president: "Vietnam is the place."

Those decades of interventions, coups, and invasions had been justi-fied by Truman's benign words and intentions. My perception of the

Truman Doctrine had been mostly all benevolence and protection. It is one of our origin stories. Even after the invasion of Iraq, there are few things that happen militarily, politically, or economically—the IMF hammering Greece, the many American-sponsored dictatorships whose brutality inspired the revolts of the Arab Spring—that do not recall this very illusion of largesse, this language of virtue and progress, and this iron core of cold, imperial self-interest. In an essay called "The CIA in Latin America," Gabriel García Márquez quoted from a book called *Inside the Company*, written by a whistleblower and former CIA officer stationed in Latin America. The officer, Philip Agee, wrote: "The key question is to pass beyond the facts of CIA's operations to the reasons they were established—which inexorably will lead to economic questions: *preservation of property relations and other institutions on which rest the interests of our own wealthy and privileged minority* [italics mine]. This, not the CIA, is the critical issue."

I WASN'T SURE what interests Agee was talking about, but I would learn about them from a young economist who was among the many Greeks protesting in the streets in 2010, whom I interviewed years after. His father had come to Greece from Cairo in the 1940s, at the beginning of the Greek Civil War. Upon his arrival, a policeman asked him to sign a paper denouncing communism, which he refused to do. He was not a Communist, but he reasoned: "Look, I am not a Buddhist, either, but I would never sign a denunciation of Buddhism or Islam or the Jewish faith." The police "beat the shit out of him" and sent him to a concentration camp, where he became a member of the Communist Party. The economist himself had been a student activist and had belonged to the party PASOK, led then by the anti-American Andreas Papandreou. During the 1970s "junta" era, the economist explained, it was very hard to avoid being political.

The economist's name was Yanis Varoufakis. Over the years, he developed a theory about the worldwide financial crisis that showed how the Truman Doctrine and Marshall Plan years of the 1940s and '50s had long ago set the calamity in motion.

"The story is one in which the postwar period is characterized by two different phases, both of them featuring the United States as the protagonist," he said. "The first phase is Bretton Woods—I call it the Global Plan, because it's not just Bretton Woods, it's bigger. Bretton Woods was the monetary system the Americans established—a system of fixed exchange rates and the IMF and all that.

"But they did something else, too: the United States tried to augment the fixed exchange rate with something quite remarkable, which I call a surplus recycling mechanism. This was not the first time we had an exchange rate. We had the gold standard in the interwar period. Why did that collapse? Because you didn't have a mechanism for recycling surpluses from the surplus countries to the deficit countries. When you don't have that, the moment there is a recession, the deficit countries fall into a black hole and drag everyone down with them. The New Dealers who went through the Depression understood this very well, and it was the same New Dealers who designed the postwar world."

"They set out to design the postwar economic system?" I asked.

"Yes. If you look at the Senate papers of the period between 1946 and 1947, you will find lots of statements by James Forrestal and Dean Acheson to this effect."

At the time of the Bretton Woods conference, a *New York World-Telegram* editorial put it this way: "The kid who owns the ball is usually captain and decides when and where the game will be played and who will be in the team."

"Look, it made perfect sense to them," Varoufakis went on. "They understood why American capital collapsed in the Great Depression. They also understood that by 1945 the world economy was finished, and Europe was finished, and America had a historic duty to reset the scene and rebuild global capitalism. They felt that duty and they did have that duty.

"What was the Marshall Plan? It wasn't just a plan stemming the advances of the Soviet Union. The economic minds behind the Marshall Plan needed the Marshall Plan to create this surplus recycling mechanism. American factories were overproducing at that time. They needed the Europeans to buy their goods, but the Europeans had no money. So they put two and two together and said, *Okay, we'll give them money.* That's surplus recycling. And this worked brilliantly, until a very important linchpin fell off this global plan."

The Marshall Plan, in other words, had not been the act of charity so many Americans and foreigners celebrated. It was a global economic scheme. But then the exuberant postwar economy of the 1940s, '50s, and early '60s began slowing, while others abroad improved.

"America suddenly stopped having surpluses. That started an economic disintegration—in the period between 1965 and 1971, from LBJ to Nixon. It was their idea to do the second phase of the global plan. It was also Paul Volcker's idea. He was central."

"Paul Volcker? The financial crisis guy? Seriously?" I said. Paul Volcker assisted President Obama in regulating Wall Street after the 2008 financial crisis.

Varoufakis laughed. "Americans tend to have a memory that spans a maximum of ten years. Volcker said: What are we going to do now? How will we retain our hegemony if we don't have surpluses to recycle? Then he said: If we can't recycle our surpluses, we'll recycle everyone else's surpluses. And this is the second phase of the global plan."

I wanted him to say whether these economic decisions were good or bad; it was still difficult for me to interpret American history any other way.

"I try not to make moralistic judgments," he replied, looking at me worriedly. "At the time, America was losing control of the Europeans. The Europeans were incensed—especially French president Charles de Gaulle—that America was not doing austerity. The argument from the European side was, *Look, if you don't have surpluses, then you must do austerity.* And LBJ and then Nixon said, *We'll be damned if we are going to shrink our economy for your benefit, damn you!* They were not going to destroy the system they created for someone else's benefit."

And these must have been at least some of the interests that Philip Agee, the CIA officer, had said the Americans would never let go. Varoufakis wrote in his book *The Global Minotaur* that Volcker would later give a speech in which he admitted that the Americans had unleashed "a controlled disintegration of the world economy."

"So the Americans unpegged the dollar from gold," Varoufakis continued. "Then Volcker comes in in the late 1970s, and pushes interest rates up. Suddenly, there is a complete reversal of the old plan. Before the 1970s, you had America being the surplus country: exporting products to Europe and Japan, importing a surplus of capital, and then taking this money and loaning it back to them. When these surpluses ended, they engineered something else. American consumers were now *buying* products from Europe and Japan and later China. What was financing America's deficits? German and Chinese profits. They were flying into Wall Street."

And then the whole thing collapsed.

Varoufakis was speaking from an economic or scientific point of view, but all I could think of was an ordinary Greek's emotional or psychological reaction to this history, the sense of helplessness when the European Union suggested that raising taxes or cutting pensions would somehow assuage a crisis sixty years old. The Greeks, like many other peoples around the world, had once been victims of a military coup, and thus would not necessarily assume such calamities could be entirely their own responsibility.

ON THE DAY of the Greek junta, the writer Neni Panourgia was a child. She remembers walking outside and seeing only military trucks instead of cars. Military music played on the radio, but the world otherwise felt hushed. In the next weeks, thousands of people were arrested. Books and rock albums were banned, press freedoms curtailed, prisoners tortured. The Greek military establishment, which was close to the Pentagon, had been worried about the rebellious rule of Prime Minister Georgios Papandreou, whom they accused of installing left-wing generals in the military in order to foment revolution. His son, Andreas, was also an outspoken critic of the United States. On April 21, 1967, Greek colonels launched an anti-Communist military coup. Some of the colonels had been educated at the War College in the United States, and some had been torturers in the Greek internment camps.

Many Greeks at the time wondered about the so-called American Factor. In her book *Dangerous Citizens*, Panourgia recounts the experience of two Greek prisoners in a cell on the very first night of the dictatorship. One man, Tzavalas Karousos, hears someone saying, "This smells like Indonesia. American stuff." He was referring to the coup of 1965 against Indonesia's President Sukarno, a nationalist who sympathized with his country's Communist Party. What followed was a campaign of lawless violence, in which the military incited militias of ordinary men to behead, shoot, and stab anyone Communist or accused of being Communist. Between five hundred thousand and one million people were killed. Today, thanks to the 2001 U.S. State Department publication *Foreign Relations of the United States, 1964–1968*, it is known that CIA officers and embassy officials supplied the army with a target list.

Tzavalas Karousos didn't know the details of the U.S. role in Indonesia, but there was a kind of shared consciousness among the citizens of the non-American world, acquired mostly through news reports, images, and intuition. Did Karousos also think of Arbenz in Guatemala? Did he think of Mossadegh in Iran? Did he think of Lumumba in the Congo? Was there an archipelago of shared memory—experiences strung together with news from across the world? Those men in the Greek jail already had a sense of forces larger than them; a feeling of helplessness. "The unknown weighed heavily on us," Karousos says. "This is the result of the modern disease, anticommunism." After the junta, a statue of Truman in Athens would be repeatedly knocked down and defaced.

The years that followed in Greece were not as bloody as Indonesia, but no less damaging to the unity of the nation. That year of the coup, James Becket, an American lawyer for Amnesty International, arrived in Greece to investigate allegations of torture by the new regime. He had been hoping that the Greek victims might appeal for assistance from the American government, but State Department officials were defensive. As he investigated further, interviewing torture victims and their relatives, he discovered that the United States' "involvement in torture went beyond simply moral support." In his book *Barbarism in Greece*, he writes, "If American support is obvious to the Greeks, it is vital to the torturers":

> The torturers themselves not only use American equipment in
> their military and police work, but they rely on the fact that the
> U.S. supports them. Hundreds of prisoners have listened to the
> little speech given by Inspector Basil Lambrou, who sits behind his
> desk which displays the red, white, and blue clasped-hand symbol
> of American aid. He tries to show the prisoner the absolute futility
> of resistance: "*You make yourself ridiculous by thinking you can do
> anything. The world is divided in two. There are the communists on*

that side and on this side the free world. The Russians and the
Americans, no one else. What are we? Americans. Behind me there is
the government, behind the government is NATO, behind NATO
is the U.S. You can't fight us, we are Americans." [italics mine]

Contrary to Truman's hopes to rescue a people from the pressures or occupation of an armed Communist minority, Becket writes, "The Greeks, a
free people, would be subjugated by a minority armed by the United States,
and the outside pressures would be American."

Panourgia draws a line from the Greek case to the usage of illegal deten-
tions and torture in the Americans' twenty-first-century war on terror, which
she argues "has a history that reaches back to a space and place used as a
laboratory for neo-colonialism at the outset of the imperial expansion of
US power after the Second World War: namely, Greece after the Truman
Doctrine and under the Marshall Plan." Like the Greek man in his jail cell
thinking of Indonesia, Panourgia also draws on a constellation of shared
experiences to make sense of her world.

"Polytechnic," it turned out, was the night that Greek college students
rose up and eventually brought down the Greek dictatorship, in 1974. In the
years that followed, Socialist parties redressed the wrongs of the civil war and
the dictatorship by offering financial restitution to civil war fighters, as well
as generous social and economic policies to their constituents, which over time
grew into bloated and unnecessary patronage for votes. This restitution of the
left and others, went the story, was the foundation of Greece's dysfunctional
policies that helped lead to the financial crisis of 2009. The reason all the
Greeks I met still talked about the civil war, and the American intervention,
was that there was no way otherwise to explain what had happened next.

George Papandreou, the prime minister in Greece I was writing about
in 2010, the one charged with saving the economy by implementing austerity measures imposed on him by the West, was the grandson of Prime
Minister Georgios Papandreou, who had been deposed by a U.S.-supported
military coup. The current Prime Minister Papandreou was also the son of
the outspoken American critic Andreas Papandreou. I had interviewed his
son, Nick, the one who rode the Metro, with none of this knowledge. To
write about Greece in 2010 as a basket case of its own making was an abne-
gation of responsibility and even accuracy; to pronounce the ways in which

it was "behind" was to parrot the language of modernization theory, and to belittle it as such without awareness of the political intervention and military coup my own country instigated, and which arguably, if anything, set the country "back," was to be disrespectfully disconnected from the historical experience of my own subjects and indeed from my own country. Greece always seemed a pleasant European country to my American sensibility. Now I knew, well into a twenty-first century in which the word "counterinsurgency" rolls off all American tongues, that Greece was where my country's concept of "counterterror" found its first violent home. I left beautiful Athens haunted by the palliative effects of my own ignorance.

Anatol Lieven writes that Americans have viewed their own "unpleasantness" during the Cold War as necessary evils foisted upon innocent souls desperate to defeat a truly evil foe. The state of innocence Americans constantly return to—this little sand berm on an ocean of misdeeds—exists because Americans say it does, but when you actually read the history of foreign interventions, you do begin to wonder where it *ever* came from. In Guatemala, a country whose democratically elected president we overthrew in one of the foundational American military coups of the post-1945 era, the vicious military would become known for smashing babies' heads against walls, punching pregnant women until they miscarried, and burying people alive.

Was I not actively endorsing the American way—of committing acts and forgetting them, of living in this denial—if I wrote about a foreign country without first understanding the American relationship with it, a relationship that transformed that country's development and produced my way of looking at the world? This was where objectivity as an ideal was undemanding; objectivity for Americans would require first a full reckoning with history, the sort of truth and reconciliation commission of the soul that William Appleman Williams advocated for as early as the 1950s. This utter distortion of reality, in which an American journalist could be killed by people who considered themselves "Americans" and his death blamed on Greek Communists, makes even terrorist acts seem rather like an insistence of reality, as when the Athens Hilton hotel—whose enormous building spanned countless city blocks and ruined the view from the Acropolis—was bombed by Greek leftist rebels in 1969, a terrorist act that was also the beginning of a slow clawing toward anything that resembles truth.

· · ·

ONCE, A SHOPKEEPER whom I saw almost every day in my Istanbul neighborhood—I bought my milk and soda water from him—asked me whether I was ever returning to the United States. I replied that I was, in fact, traveling to New York that month, but would come back to Turkey in a few weeks. "You know"—I grimaced theatrically—"New York is a difficult place." I always said such things, more as a tribute to Istanbul, because I knew some Turks—usually upper-class Turks, or anyone who still dreamed of the West as a salvation—also found it surprising to hear that I loved Istanbul more than New York City.

My shopkeeper was not an upper-class White Turk; he was Kurdish. He looked at me sympathetically: "Ya, your country really has exploited the world, hasn't it?"

The verb he used, *sömürmek*, has many meanings, which out of curiosity I looked up when I got home. The online dictionary most young Turks used for English usually proffered an array of colorful English translations. For *sömürmek*, it said:

exploit

to suck all the nourishment from

to eat up (everything in sight)

to exploit, use (someone, something) wrongfully for one's own ends

to exploit, to presume on; to gobble

trade on

to suck (a liquid) (into one's mouth)

sweat

milk

put upon

use

presume on

presume upon

make capital out of

It was because of the Communist crisis in Greece that the Americans included its neighbor Turkey in the Marshall Plan and Truman Doctrine. After helping the Americans fight the Koreans in 1950, the Turks had welcomed admission to NATO; some of them, like I had, even viewed the Truman Doctrine as a rescue operation. By the mid-1950s, the United States had erected its own army, navy, air force, and intelligence stations all over Turkey; Incirlik Air Base, near the southern Turkish city of Adana, was to be America's Middle Eastern outpost, and the place where America kept many of its nuclear weapons.

Within a decade, some thirty thousand Americans, mostly military personnel, came to live on Turkish soil. NATO flooded the country with pro-American propaganda—it was in fact a condition of the Marshall Plan that it be allowed to do so—and strengthened ties "between Turkish labor and anti-communist international labor federations." The intent, the academic Amy Austin Holmes writes, was to make Turkish labor unions "economic rather than political," or, in other words, pro-American rather than Communist. The union most directly influenced by the Americans in those years was Türk-İş, the union that had failed to protect the miners of Soma.

In response, Turkish leftists began to believe that NATO membership did not guarantee security as much as ensure that Turkey would remain a capitalist country. The Turkish people became uneasy about the strange social mores of their new American neighbors. Although the Americans were stationed in Turkey ostensibly to protect the Turks from the Soviets, Turks feared that they were being saved from one threat only to be savaged by another. The novelist Yaşar Kemal, whom a CIA officer once tried to convince to leave the Workers' Party because he would sell more books in America that way, wrote a letter to American newspapers in an attempt to spare them "from the disgust of other nations," and accused Americans of "entering our hearts like a traitor's dagger":

"You have created slaves and compradors in Turkey . . . Your soldiers can bring into the streets tens of thousands of Turks by being disrespectful to Turkish women. Your soldiers constantly tear down and trample Turkish flags. They run over people in the streets and are not even tried in Turkish courts."

The first democratically elected prime minister of Turkey, Adnan Menderes, a champion of the United States, had by then been in power for almost ten years. The long period of power corrupted him; he also had begun to wreck the Turkish economy, displeasing his American patrons as well as the Kemalist generals. In 1960, Turkish military officers staged Turkey's first of many military coups, and Menderes was hanged on the island of Imralı. In response to Menderes's authoritarianism, the generals drafted a new constitution intended to strengthen civil society. When Baldwin arrived in Turkey in the early sixties, he landed in a country in which newspapers, writers, playwrights—and, in effect, leftist movements—had been newly set free.

The turning point in American and Turkish relations was a crisis that broke out between the Greek and Turkish peoples on the island of Cyprus in 1964. President Lyndon B. Johnson intervened by threatening both the Greeks and Turks with a loss of U.S. weapons and aid, which effectively paralyzed the Turkish military and prevented a war. To the Greeks, Johnson said: "Fuck your parliament and your constitution . . . We pay a lot of good American dollars to the Greeks, Mr. Ambassador. If your prime minister gives me talk about democracy, parliament and constitution, he, his parliament and his constitution may not last long . . ." To the Turks, Johnson wrote a letter saying pretty much the same thing. For Turks, men and women, children of Atatürk who believed themselves the liberators and guarantors of their nation and resented the direct intervention of any foreign country, the Johnson letter was the ultimate shame.

In 1968, demonstrations across the country broke out against the U.S. naval brigade that patrolled the Mediterranean. A leftist student declared: "Istanbul is not the brothel of the Sixth Fleet. We will continue our fight against imperialism." The following January, the U.S. ambassador Robert Komer came to Turkey from South Vietnam, where he had been serving in Johnson's war as its "chief of pacification," the overseer of the "hearts and minds" department of Operation Phoenix, which targeted Vietcong agents and caused the deaths of twenty thousand Vietnamese. When Komer arrived to give a talk at Middle East Technical University in Ankara, in January 1969, a group of students who belonged to the Marxist-Leninist movement Dev-Genç set his car on fire. The violence in Turkey against American targets escalated: unlike the warm welcome given to the USS *Missouri* in 1946, thirty thousand people protested the arrival of the Sixth Fleet to Istanbul. Riot police killed two people and injured hundreds (it was called Bloody Sunday). Bombs went off at a military installation in Ankara, assailants shot security guards outside the American embassy, and a radical group kidnapped four U.S. Air Force personnel and demanded four hundred thousand dollars in ransom, inciting a nationwide manhunt.

A young American woman named Maureen Freely—her father, John Freely, a professor at Boğaziçi University, was a friend of James Baldwin—was living with her family in Istanbul at the time. She spent her childhood gazing dreamily out the window at military ships passing through the Bosphorus, and attended Robert College with children whose parents were spies. Gritty, unfashionable Istanbul in the 1960s exuded an atmosphere of skulduggery and suspicion. Freely, who would write a series of novels about the Cold War, never seemed to shake the terror of the time, or her own complicity in Turkey's fate. "It was widely believed that the military, the prime minister, and everyone beneath him were US puppets," Freely wrote later in her novel *Enlightenment*. "In the popular imagination, it was CIA pulling their strings."

For three decades after the USS *Missouri* docked in Istanbul, Turks fought their version of the Cold War on city streets. Labor unions and leftist parties faced off against neo-Fascists and Islamists, all sides seemingly backed by foreign powers no one could see. These were not petty street fights. An average of twenty people died every day, often from leftist violence, but more so by mysterious right-wing-perpetrated murders and assassinations that would never be solved, forever making Turks "paranoid," or "conspiracy theorists," or skeptics, like Emre, like the Greeks, like the Guatemalans, the Indonesians. Right-wing paramilitary violence, as had been used in Greece and Latin America, however, wouldn't quell the Cold War crisis in Turkey. There, the Americans would become so terrified of the rise of communism that they would soon encourage the Turkish government to use an unlikely force against it: Islam.

5

MONEY AND MILITARY COUPS: THE ARAB WORLD AND TURKEY

What the hell do the Americans want, ignorant people?

—SAID ABURISH

S OME YEARS BEFORE THE REVOLUTION, I visited Cairo as a tourist, taking the requisite camel ride to the pyramids, trying on Bedouin dresses in the souk, getting lost among the mummies in the antiquities museum. It was a short, superficial, and sensual trip, about which most of my memories are visual, including the shock of seeing blond American girl tourists in tight short shorts outside a mosque, which filled me with shame. The week before, I had flooded my downstairs neighbors by absentmindedly pulling at one of the haphazard pipes that lived on the outside of the apartment's nineteenth-century walls, drenching the Turkish rugs that lined the stone floors, eliciting screams from below. I had no idea how to stop the water, so clueless was I to the phenomenon of central water controls in apartment buildings. I had no friends in the building to call on, and all my efforts to learn the language yielded few intelligible words as I screamed from my front door. I was dressed in my pajamas, a tank top and shorts, and terrified of running out and exposing myself that way, so I stood for a while before the pipe, trying to hold it together with my hands as the water belted me like a hose. I was lonely and clumsy, wreaking havoc on things I knew nothing about. There was no worse feeling in a foreign country; it was easy for such small, manifestly human events to take on heavy symbolic significance. Random things said to me on a touristic visit seemed weighted with significance, too, as when, one evening in Cairo, a young activist told me he admired the Turks because "they built their Metro themselves."

We were walking through the center of the city at night, the streets empty, craning to admire the marble colonial facades that had survived the fires of the late colonial era and the poverty of Mubarak's. The Egyptian activist had been in jail before for criticizing the regime. The Turks didn't have foreigners build their Metro for them, he said. I was not sure that was true, but I got the point; Turkey was seen as a more independent country, a country that built itself. Yet, at the time, I didn't know what this statement meant in the Egyptian context, or what it meant more broadly. My understanding of global economic systems was still so limited that instead I was surprised the Egyptians did *not* build their Metro themselves—who else would have done it? (The French, and others.) We Westerners talked of Istanbul's sea views. Egyptians spoke of its metros.

Turkey was in fact building more metros, more bridges, more airports, more office parks. By the time of the Egyptian revolution in 2011, Istanbul's city limits were exploding with development, office towers shooting up as if in some real-time video sequence. Turkish friends saw the European side of Istanbul from a boat on the Bosphorus and noted how striking this new stock-market-graph skyline was, how there used to be hills carpeted green here and poofs of trees there. Everywhere there was the knocking of hammers and hum-screeching of saws; festivals and biennials;

decrepit buildings sandblasted into hotels overnight. Western cities, cowering shamefully from the financial crisis, suddenly, according to countless travel articles, seemed places of the past—the new world was east.

That time in Turkey was exuberant, people and places came alive as if they had been mummified in the amber of Kemalism and now were free again. The old Ottoman bank building in my former neighborhood, the bank receipts and handwritten notes of Armenians and Greeks collecting dust in its basement, was turned into a multimillion-dollar art space called Salt, where Arabic script had been carved into the marble: "He who earns money is God's beloved servant." Its founder, Vasıf Kortun, told me the Turks didn't know their own history, and now they had the means and freedom to discover it; Kortun put on exhibits about Armenian photographers, the 1980 military coup, defunct leftist literary magazines. "In New York it feels like the best years are behind us," a woman from New York said. "In Istanbul it feels like the best years are yet to come." Turkish friends counseled caution. "Many of the reasons the West thinks a place like Istanbul is optimistic is linked to the idea of private money achieving things," one artist told me. "Yes, private money is doing things right now, but it's too early to know whether it will benefit artists. It hasn't been tested. If Western history is a guide, it will find that in capitalist societies, consumer culture is not a way to find new ways of living. For this Istanbul could be interesting. We're a very young country. And when you're young you tend to believe in ideals."

There was a disconcerting paradox at the heart of Turkey's prosperity, which was achieved to a large degree because the government was selling off all the country's public works companies. In the shadows, in vastly complicated and inscrutable judicial maneuverings and police actions, the optimism of democratic beginnings was being steadily undermined by a leader both insecure and arrogant. The Gülenist allies of the government that had come to dominate the judiciary had been mounting aggressive cases against secularists, and countless journalists and military officers once associated with the old secularist regime languished in jail. The Gülen movement had seeped into the police force and intelligence departments and was wiretapping everyone's phones. The AK Party seemed to be taking control of every institution in the country, just as Rana had warned.

Yet to the outside world, Erdoğan equaled stability. Turkey looked good. In fact, in the eyes of policy makers and journalists, Erdoğan's Turkey had gone from being the secular model for Iraq before the invasion to an Islamic-democratic model for the entire Arab world: some religion, some democracy, some investment-fueled economic growth. Pundits called it the Turkish model, an example of an Islamic country that managed to become democratic. But the analysis hinged on multiple false assumptions. Turkey had always been, and still was, an authoritarian country with democratic electoral processes. Unlike the Arab world, Turkey was never colonized by foreign powers, or humiliated by Israel, and it rarely appeared to be overly subservient to the United States. It always maintained an illusion and a narrow reality of democratic and economic participation. Even with four military coups and decades of violence, a certain confidence and pride in Turkishness prevailed. Turks had not suffered in the way the Arabs had, and it did not have the same grievances.

Before the invasion of Iraq, protests had erupted around the Arab world. The journalist Anthony Shadid said that in conversation with Arabs at that time, he rarely heard the word "freedom"; instead, Arabs talked about "justice." I don't think that by 2011, when Egyptians filled Tahrir Square, the Americans cheering them on knew the difference between those two words. By the time Mubarak resigned, many Americans watching from afar believed this to be a righteous conclusion to a thrilling revolution. They thought themselves the kind of people who supported democratic protest, and as I watched the Egyptians dancing in the streets I did not feel the shame I had when I saw bare, fleshy American legs outside a mosque, or that I felt while flooding my neighbor's apartment with dirty pipe water, because in the case of the Egyptians I had not at all been conscious of the history that we shared.

IN THE FALL OF 2011, six months after the revolution, I went to Egypt to write about the legacy of Suzanne Mubarak, Hosni's wife and fellow dictator of thirty years. I was consumed with the narrow details of the story: Did she oppose his policies, was she an advocate for women's rights, where was she now? I saw her as an evil woman, an easy villain. Suzanne, sequestered somewhere with Hosni and her sons, wouldn't give me an interview, so I spent my days among her associates and antagonists. One of them I visited on a sun-dappled street in the upscale neighborhood of Mohandeseen, its weeping willow trees with limbs like ballet dancer arms sweeping the streets.

Suzanne's right-hand woman, Farkhonda Hassan, was sitting inside the new office of the National Council for Women, which had been Suzanne's most important initiative; the old offices on the Nile had been set on fire during the protests. Hassan was bemoaning the new space, as if a revolution hadn't just happened.

"You should have seen our old building!" she cried. "We had three floors! They were so beautiful. And everyone had their own office."

"Was Suzanne surprised by the revolution?" I asked.

"She didn't realize how bad things were," Hassan said in a plaintive voice. She spoke about the revolution and its effects on her as if she were part of a company that had been downsized.

"They loved her!" she said. "Why people turn so quickly from support to extreme criticism overnight is very strange."

The West had also celebrated Suzanne from afar. As the Mubaraks often justified their thirty years of rule by invoking the threat of the Muslim Brotherhood, Suzanne presented herself as a secular-minded woman who protected women's rights, and would counter the pernicious effects of Islamic fundamentalism. "Egyptian at Center on Rights of Women," went one *New York Times* headline in 2000. But feminists I sat with in Cairo said that Suzanne had not been a champion of women. In a country where women lacked basic rights, Suzanne always stuck to a conservative platform of "family values." (The phrase was championed by Erdoğan as well, though a Turkish feminist once told me *he* swiped the language from the playbook of the Republican Party of the United States.) One evening in Cairo, Nawal El Saadawi, one of Egypt's foremost feminist activists, sat with her long, white braid in the middle of a modest apartment, surrounded by fellow activists, and told me that the Mubarak regime in fact sidelined, banned, and harassed feminist NGOs. "They really fragmented the feminist movement," she said. The mandate of the National Council for Women—Suzanne's organization—was to be the *only* representative of Egyptian women.

Dr. Amal Abdel Hadi from the New Woman Foundation spoke of Suzanne in the same way. "All the very vibrant movements were crushed, very harshly," she said. A pattern of co-optation was established. "We worked hard on establishing the woman's right to pass the Egyptian nationality onto their children even if their husband is not Egyptian. From the Mubaraks, there was a strong resistance. Suzanne claimed that the President said it was a national security issue, and *we'll never do that.* Until the last moment they were against it.

"And then suddenly they were for it! So the law was changed. It became *their* victory—all the women's organizations worked for years to bring something she had opposed, and then they took it over! If you were calling for a radical change, they opposed you. If you were going to succeed, then they appropriated it."

Amal Abdel Hadi was describing only one aspect of the Mubaraks' relationship to civil society. From afar, outsiders heard about the violence, about imprisonments, repression, and torture in Egypt—all of which should have been a searing enough indictment of the U.S.-backed regime. But what Abdel Hadi was elucidating were the more subtle—and to foreigners almost invisible—ways in which a dictatorship worked. Once again, as in Turkey under the Kemalists, the illusion of Westernization that the Mubaraks projected for their American patrons was the opposite of liberation.

"Suzanne wasn't a feminist, that's for sure," Abdel Hadi said. "She was pro women's rights, but she acted in a way that's not really for women's rights. If you dismantle the feminist movement, then women's rights will not come to communities like ours. Feminism is not a popular issue. It needs a lot of work and it needs a real movement. She wasn't an anti–women's rights person. But she's not a human rights defender. And she's not a feminist. She was doing this as part of her personal glory."

THE REVOLUTION TOOK the Mubaraks by surprise, people told me, because they saw Egypt through a gilded peephole. For them, cars were towed, walls scrubbed, flowers planted, grass grown, Egyptians bribed to smile. When Suzanne arrived at unfamiliar buildings for meetings, her

staff replaced the soaps in the bathrooms. Roads in a city of clamorous traffic would be shut down for their convoys. Egyptians offered various expla-
nations for the Mubarak psychosis—absolute power begets corruption, the
oligarchs insisted they stay, the Mubaraks believed Egypt would crumble
without them. On some basic level, however, all such ideas made sense and
strained credulity at the same time: What kind of people, even out of self-
preservation, wouldn't notice how much they were despised?

I went to meet one of Suzanne's family friends at his office in Zama-
lek. It is an upscale neighborhood with an air of colonial romance, though
outside the window traffic blared as if a fleet of garbage trucks dumped
their wares all at once. The man's elegant demeanor—he was handsome,
and smoked as if the cigarette were but another of his elegant appendages—
was accompanied by a steadily building sense of menace in his words.
Since his family had been close to the Mubaraks, I had expected that he
would defend them, but he, like many others, had lived a double life: the
one in which you survived under a regime, and the one in which you despised it.

"I want to emphasize that my opinion of her from what I know personally and from my dealings with her is completely different from my political opinion," he said. "I knew her very well. She and my mother went to
the same school, they remained very good friends all along. She was a very
shrewd woman, serious, cultured and interested in culture, and somewhat
charismatic."

"What was important to her?" I asked.

"Housing for the poor, poverty alleviation, education for children, literacy," he said. "I must tell you I genuinely believe she meant well, she wanted
to have a better educational system and combat poverty, and she wanted to
meet and talk to people, but the security measures were simply insane, which
caused them to be isolated."

"People have said that they barely knew Egyptians."

"I must tell you, it is not the person as much as the institution," he
said. "I have seen the gradual change through the years—I have seen what
they were and what they have become. It is not only them; it is this whole
system that caters to godlike people—that caters to people who are
worshipped.

"There's only so much you can do to resist that, and in thirty years you cannot, so you become so isolated, you become literally insane. Privilege comes with a wide range of people who feed it. I have never seen so much corruption and audacity, or such a widening of the gap between rich and poor, or such a horrific police state, one that only cares about the privileged, like I have seen during this regime. When was the last time they touched a car handle? When was the last time she actually saw money? Do they have a wallet? It is a life that is so corrupting. I am really blaming a culture and a system for putting unprepared people in such high positions. I don't blame the people because they are very ordinary people.

"But when you allow your close entourage to be what it was—villains—then that says something about you. We didn't know the magnitude of the corruption. It is horrific. Egypt became like a little farm or something, it wasn't a state anymore. Talk to me about gas, talk to me about all these state security companies, talk to me about wheat, about petroleum—this is where money is, this is where the corruption is."

"Do you think she approved of the violence against the protestors during the revolution?"

"I wouldn't be surprised if they thought this kind of violence against protestors could be a solution for them to stay," he said. "I wouldn't be surprised at all. We know the Muslim Brotherhood was subjected to the most brutal torture. It was taken for granted that the Mubaraks would run Egypt forever. They thought they were the only people holding the country together, and if they left, the Muslim Brotherhood would take over. They actually believed that, one hundred percent. I think she was a woman of duty."

I wondered if before the revolution, he would have felt comfortable talking about them this way to a journalist.

"No, I would not feel comfortable criticizing them to a journalist. When they were upset with you, it was their bodyguards who would take care of it. It's not them, it's the institution. They have very innovative ways of destroying people."

He kept saying that same thing: "It's not them, it's the institution." The "institution" he conjured was one that had been built of forces enormous and historical, something beyond the Egyptian people's control.

. . .

THE YEAR AFTER the regime fell in 2011, it appeared the Muslim Brotherhood was poised to take power after the country's first democratic elections in decades, which filled many Egyptians with fear. Since its founding in 1928, the Muslim Brotherhood's Islamic network had functioned like a parallel society—richer members provided its poorer members with food, medicine, and clothing through annual financial donations, and millions of Egyptians sought refuge in the Brotherhood's supportive social networks. The organization's goal was to create, through proselytizing, a nation that fulfilled the dictates of God's law.

When Hassan al-Banna and later Sayyid Qutb led the Muslim Brotherhood in the early to midcentury, one of their primary motivations had been to resist Western imperialism, first British, then American. These men, like many of the peoples from the countries of the former Ottoman Empire, had been dismayed by the Americans' betrayal of the Arabs after World War I. The texts Qutb wrote in jail were radical enough that they would eventually inspire al-Qaida. For thirty years, Hosni Mubarak was able to use the Brotherhood's existence as justification for his undemocratic policies: it was either Mubarak, a corrupt dictator who tortures and loots but accepts America's military aid, or the Brotherhood, religious fanatics who hate Israel.

One evening, I visited one of the Brotherhood's financiers, Hassan Malek, in Heliopolis, a neighborhood of high-end shopping malls and Italian restaurant chains, modern apartment buildings and ornate nineteenth-century villas. Under Mubarak, Malek had spent four years in "prisons not fit for animals, let alone for humans." Inside the Malek family's apartment, a large, brown stretch of leather on the wall had been engraved with the ninety-nine names of Allah. Malek's twenty-six-year-old son passed out chocolates and talked about how "everyone should help their country." His sixteen-year-old daughter shyly displayed her artwork, a portrait of a woman with long hair. Another son played peekaboo with the toddler, who ran around screaming. The Maleks gave off an earnest "ask not what your country can do for you" vibe, as if dispatched to the twenty-first century from a less cynical era.

That evening, Malek was concerned about the demands of the IMF to reform the economy, which for the Egyptians sounded in many ways like the West's crippling economic demands in the past.

"We don't have a preconceived position against the IMF," he said. "But they have to listen to us. They can't impose on us conditions that are not good for Egypt. We will deal with the Egyptian society in a transparent way. Our society should become self-reliant from now on. I believe that the West and particularly the United States furthered the injustice that befell us because they supported the regime," he said.

"And even despite that, we are willing to turn the page completely, even with America, but under one condition: that they too change the way they deal with our country and our people."

Those weeks, I met more leftist dissidents and Muslim Brothers imprisoned by the Mubaraks, the heads of anti-poverty NGOs and feminist NGOs, the former dean of Al-Azhar, people suing Suzanne Mubarak for illegally purchasing villas, young activists who broke from the Muslim Brotherhood, Salafis who had lived in the United States, labor organizers who had been protesting long before the revolution, young women attacked in Tahrir Square. Corruption and torture and repression were common themes of our conversations, but even more prevalent were references to international economic policies. I began to know what people were about to say before they said it. Implicit in all of these statements was a recognition of American power.

We are sick of aid conditional on turning a blind eye to Israel.

They give us money and tell us what to do.

The Sinai is underdeveloped because the Camp David agreement says we can't populate it or develop it, because that makes Israel feel safer.

The "international economic network" that forced structural reforms caused the disaster that resulted in the revolution.

Part of the revolution was because of corruption but also because of poverty.

Before structural reforms, we had a productive economy.

Foreigners are working in Egypt and sending their money abroad; we have a skilled population and nowhere to work.

We want a relationship based on fairness with Israel.

They're taking 25 to 40 percent of our oil reserves in exchange for developing them. We don't do it ourselves.

The Americans knew if they could sideline a country with the history and power of Egypt, that would take care of much of the Arab world.

Central Cairo, the neighborhoods surrounding Tahrir Square, had wide boulevards and stunning architecture, the atmospheric cosmopolitanism of the Mediterranean. Even with the grime and smog and trash—and even without the minorities that contributed to such cosmopolitanism— you could feel the pulse of a divine city. And yet something had happened to Cairo, the worst kind of neglect and contempt for its people—an entire country of promise left to decay. Forty percent of the population lived on two dollars a day; fifteen million lived in shantytowns, many of which had no water or electricity. In the last twenty years, manufacturing has eroded, the economy has become service-oriented and stratified, and unemployment has risen among the middle class. Much of Egypt's exports were energy products that did very little for job growth at home. And this was the country that received more American aid than any other country besides Israel.

How could this couple, the Mubaraks, any couple, any leader, have allowed their country to suffer this way? How had they stayed in power? The Mubaraks had not been clever people. "The truth is, they were just mediocre," one Egyptian man said to me. They could not have stayed in power for thirty years unless they had been held there by an outside force. The evening that I saw Nawal El Saadawi, only six months after the revolution, she was already warning of the future that was to come, and said to the room of young activists: "We are facing a very dangerous counterrevolution. Who is the counterrevolution and who is against women? It is the United States of America, Saudi Arabia, Israel, the Mubarak regime, and some of the military class inside the country. All these powers internal and external are working to abort the revolution."

There was a long history to explain why the United States ended up in such terrible company. The Mubaraks had been our people, I thought. I believe that this was the first time, standing on the other side of a revolution that had inspired such transcendent hope for the future, that I felt wholeheartedly that America was me, and I was it. This recognition did not feel like a form of guilt at all, something that can be indulged, regretted, and forgotten. It felt like learning, say, that I had a whole second brood of relatives whom I never knew about, and that to some degree my denial of their existence had allowed for the prosperity and happiness of my own.

Nawal El Saadawi once wrote that she was often invited to conferences in the United States and asked to talk about her Egyptian identity. "It makes me turn your question round and round," she said. "Why does no one ask you, what is your 'identity'? Is it that American 'identity,' American culture, does not require any questioning, does not need to be examined, or studied or discussed in conferences like this?"

THE AMERICANS MAY not have had a European-style colonial past, but they did arrive in the Arab world at the beginning of the nineteenth century, long before Charles Crane's expedition. The first missionaries, Pliny Fisk and Levi Parsons, left Boston in 1819 for the Ottoman Empire, or Palestine, "to attempt to evangelize the lands of the Bible" and reclaim them from "a withering infidel grasp," writes the historian Ussama Makdisi (who is himself a descendant of Arab Protestants). But the Americans would not have an easy time converting the infidels of Palestine. They had a faulty belief that the entire religion of Islam would soon collapse. Other successful military conquests in the East—the British conquest of India, for example—had convinced them that Christians could convert the entire world.

At that time, the Ottomans sometimes called the Americans "aliens," or *müsteminler*, and some Arabs referred to Americans as "the English." That they were American meant very little; no one knew anything about the United States. The Americans didn't know anything about the Ottoman Empire either. The missionaries' first five years at Mount Lebanon passed without a single Arab Christian convert. They had not realized that the Ottoman Empire was multireligious, where coexistence was possible because Ottomans tried not to "openly blaspheme or insult other people's religions," as Makdisi writes. The Maronites, Muslims, Jews, Druze, and Armenians shared a way of life. The Ottoman authorities viewed the American intruders as a "threat to diversity." Protestantism was unquestionably alien.

The American missionaries did not believe they needed to understand a culture before attempting to wrest someone from it. The imperial nature of American Christianity and the Christian nature of American imperialism had become entwined during the wars against Native Americans, and now this particular fanaticism had come to Palestine. The missionaries sent long, tortured letters home about the supremacy of their own Promised Land. "I cannot tell you how much like a paradise America appears, as I view it from this land of darkness," said one missionary, referring to the city of Beirut. They saw all non-Westerners, all people of the East, as backward and savage.

Recognizing that their efforts to convert Arabs to Christianity were failing, the Protestants instead began to sell them on the idea of America. The Protestants' schools did not require conversion to Christianity, and offered Arabs a kind of scientific education common in the West. In turn, many Arabs did come to believe in America as a symbol of modernity. After graduating from the Syrian Protestant College, two Christian Arabs named Faris Nimr and Yaqub Sarruf started a journal called *al-Muqtataf*, which was meant to provide Arabs with the knowledge to become a "literate, scientific, and secular modern citizen."

But Nimr and Sarruf quickly realized that the Americans were not entirely open to every aspect of the Arabs' modernization. The missionaries excluded Arabs from professorships and high positions. "Sarruf and Nimr extolled scientific modernity as a vehicle for Arab emancipation," Makdisi writes, "without realizing that it was the same historic force that had given rise to powerful Western, including American, ideas about the fundamental superiority of the white Anglo-Saxons over all other races." Some years later, in 1910, Theodore Roosevelt visited a restive Cairo to tell the Egyptians to abandon their fight for independence from the British.

The Arab intellectuals of the time were outraged that the American president would betray his own American ideals. They felt "Roosevelt should act as an American, not as an imperialist European."

The Arabs, however, still had faith in the American missionaries. It was one of these imperialist missionaries with good intentions, Howard Bliss, who stood before the world leaders in Paris after World War I and proposed that a commission be sent to Syria and Lebanon to ask the Arab people whether or not they wanted to be ruled by a foreign power. President Woodrow Wilson agreed. A Western leader had decided to listen to the natives. Thus began the journey of Charles Crane and Henry King.

If the Sykes-Picot Agreement was an act of imperialism, Makdisi writes, the Arab writer George Antonius saw the King-Crane Commission as the manifestation of American goodness. Crane wrote home that "even the Bedouin of the desert knew and appreciated what America had done for Cuba and the Philippines," and that Arabs said that should they not be granted independence, they would accept the guardianship of the United States. "They declared that their choice was due to knowledge of America's record," King and Crane wrote, "their belief that America had no territorial or colonial ambitions, and would willingly withdraw when the Syrian state was well established as her treatment both of Cuba and the Philippines seemed to them to illustrate . . . From the point of view of the desires of the 'people concerned,' the Mandate should clearly go to America."

The Arabs were misinformed about Cuba and the Philippines, and Crane and King were clearly biased, but in any case, the remarkable contents of the King-Crane Commission were cast aside for European ambitions. Syria and Iraq were handed over to the French and British, mainly for their oil fields, and Western-backed rulers installed in their capitals, as well as in Cairo, where independence riots were repressed. Writing decades after the event, the journalist Muhammad Haykal recalled that the decision fell on the Egyptians "like a bolt of lightning," especially because of the betrayal by Woodrow Wilson. "Here was the man of the Fourteen Points, among them the right to self-determination, denying the Egyptian people its right to self-determination," Haykal writes. "Is this not the ugliest of treacheries?!"

Despite King and Crane's grave warnings against it, the Americans would also support the establishment of a Jewish state. It was to be the first in a series of turning points over Israel. The Arabs who admired America so much saw American support for the Jews as "bigotry." Antonius had believed that the American missionaries had been crucial to the Arab national movement. He had even dedicated his book to Charles Crane. But the ultimate test of the Western-Arab relationship was whether the West would force Palestinians from their land so that the Jewish people who suffered during the Holocaust might have a refuge: "To place the brunt of the burden upon Arab Palestine is a miserable evasion of the duty that lies upon the whole of the civilized world," Antonius said. "It is also morally outrageous. No code of morals can justify the persecution of one people in an attempt to relieve the persecution of another."

The Arabs who found their lands once again conquered were vulnerable and helpless. They had no modern armies, few sympathetic representatives abroad. Arab intellectuals debated the correct response to such a catastrophic betrayal: nationalism or Islamism, democracy or authoritarianism, pro-Western or anti. The Arab thinker from this general era that Americans may know today is, again, Sayyid Qutb; after September 11, his texts were pored over to understand Muslim fundamentalism, the hidden strain of Arab life that explained everything. But Arab intellectuals were grappling with the crisis of Israel and the Arab world with varying analyses and prescriptions that didn't involve an Islamic revival. Many, such as the intellectual Constantine Zurayk, who used the term *nakba* to describe how the establishment of Israel wounded Arab souls, continued to embrace Western progress as a guide for the "wholesale revolution" within Arab society.

On the question of Israel in Palestine, however, there was no debate. The pro-American Arabs of this era, those who had been raised in American schools and who had thrilled to American ideas, would become heartbroken and disillusioned. The Americans, who had by then embraced the spirit of their missionary forebears, found themselves the patriarchs of a region, one of uncommon riches and uncommon despair.

After the missionaries came the oil speculators. Abdelrahman Munif's novel *Cities of Salt*, about the arrival of the first American oil explorers in the 1930s in the eastern Saudi province near Dhahran, is one of the few

Arab testimonies translated into English about the United States as an explicitly colonizing force. To see "the American" portrayed this way is contradictory to our sense of ourselves as liberators rather than colonialists, especially because we also rarely see American characters portrayed as mysterious and menacing foreigners, the way Arabs and Asians are so often depicted in our own newspapers, films, and books. "The Americans were something completely new and strange," Munif writes, "in their actions, their manners and the kind of questions they asked, not to mention their generosity, which surpassed that of all previous visitors." Like Malaparte, Munif writes of this new people's immature qualities, "who looked and behaved like small children, showed endless, unimaginable surprise and admiration." The Arabs sent to work on American oil fields watch their huge American ships arrive, gape as the bare-armed women disembark, laughing, and despair as the foreigners waste water carelessly. "Why did they have to live like this, while the Americans lived so differently?" Munif writes of the Arabs' wonder. "Why were they barred from going near an American house, even from looking at the swimming pool or standing for a moment in the shade of one of their trees? Why did the Americans shout at them, telling them to move, to leave the place immediately, expelling them like dogs?"

Cities of Salt is a novel few Americans read, and its initial reception in 1988 might have something to do with why. That year, John Updike wrote in *The New Yorker* that Munif was "insufficiently Westernized to produce a narrative that feels much like what we call a novel." He called the writer "a campfire explainer": "There is almost none of that sense of individual moral adventure—of the evolving individual in varied and roughly equal battle with a world of circumstance." This was an odd expectation of a novel about an event in which the collective experience is paramount, and in which the larger moral point is that there was nothing "equal" about the Americans and the Arabs. "Arabs are discomfited, distressed, and deranged by the presence of Americans in their midst," a concept that, for Updike, "wears thin." Munif's novel was banned by the Saudi family beholden to American oil interests. In the United States, the country's leading man of letters, John Updike, in its leading magazine, *The New Yorker*, concluded that "the thought of novels being banned in Saudi Arabia has a charming strangeness, like the thought of hookahs being banned in Minneapolis."

The great Arab novel, for an American critic, hadn't been modern enough; for Updike, the experience of Americans in a foreign land simply wasn't important to American ideas of literature, while for Munif, the discovery of oil and the American occupation of Arabia "was a breaking off, like death, that nothing and no one could ever heal."

THE HISTORY OF the Arab world had so often been reduced in America to a battle over Islamic extremism, but rarely did Americans question from what Islamism had emerged—why it had become such a potent political force in the first place. In the postwar era, there had been other hopes for liberation in the region, especially in Egypt, with the rise of Gamal Abdel Nasser. At the time, neither nascent Islamic fundamentalism nor Constantine Zurayk's notions of Western progress had compared to the appeal of Nasser's secular nationalism. The Americans even supported Nasser's coup against the Egyptian monarchy and the British, because they wanted an Atatürk, someone "ruthless and efficient" to rule the country, as the academic Hazem Kandil writes. In the beginning of Egypt's independence, the Americans preferred a strongman in power.

Nasser, enjoying the adoration of the region, quickly proved himself an independent-minded pest. Though he welcomed American aid, he would not go as far as joining the anti-Communist Baghdad Pact, which brought together Iraq, Iran, Turkey, Pakistan, the United Kingdom and, informally, the United States, against the Soviets. Nasser favored something called "positive neutrality" in the Cold War. This was the decade of the Non-Aligned Movement and the Bandung Conference, when leaders such as India's Nehru and Indonesia's Sukarno promoted the possibility of independence from both Cold War behemoths. When Nasser nationalized the Suez Canal in the name of Egyptian sovereignty, President Eisenhower defended the Egyptians, hoping his support would eventually convince Nasser to become a bulwark against communism, rather than a full-blown nationalist. Time and again, the Americans saw nationalism as support for Moscow, not an assertion of independence.

Eisenhower would eventually turn his back on Nasser, and Woodrow Wilson's principles of self-determination, completely. By 1967, the Americans supported the war of Israel against the Arabs in hopes that it would bring about Nasser's downfall; Charles de Gaulle even called Israel's war an American proxy war. Israel's defeat of the Arabs was the beginning of several humiliations that would undo the promises of Arab nationalism. "Nasser may have fallen, and with him the dreams of a generation, but Pax Americana helped usher in an age of defiant religiosity, resistance, and cynicism," Ussama Makdisi writes. When Nasser died, citizens around the world wept. The antagonism of Arab nationalism by the Americans helped to open a social vacuum for Islamism, and, in Egypt, for the Muslim Brotherhood.

The total capitulation of the new Egyptian president, Anwar Sadat, to the demands of the United States during a series of negotiations after the 1973 war with Israel sent Egypt hurtling down a path of subservience and economic devastation. Kissinger, amused by the Egyptians' prostrations, encouraged Sadat to sell out his entire country; according to the agreement, the Suez Canal would never be closed to Israel, Egypt would supply Israel with energy products, President Nixon would be received in Cairo by cheering crowds. Even that wasn't enough. During the Camp David Accords five years later, the Americans wanted the Egyptians to accept a degradation of their own military prowess in order to elevate Israel as the dominant force in the region. The foreign minister of Egypt said afterward: "I almost died of disgrace, disgust, and grief as I witnessed this tragedy unfold."

The American-Egyptian relationship soon approached a level of the grotesque. The United States paid for Sadat's security detail and trained his guards, provided him with street cameras and electronic devices for spying on Cairo streets, and began loaning Egypt millions of dollars on the condition that they buy American weapons. Sadat opened Egypt up to American corporations. *Al-Infitah*, as this period was called, ushered in a different kind of desolation in Egypt, "a perpetually dependent market on foreign products." In his novel *The Committee*, the Egyptian writer Sonallah Ibrahim catalogued the parade of Western companies invading Egypt: "Phillips, Toshiba, Gillette, Michelin, Shell, Kodak, Westinghouse, Ford, Nestlé, Marlboro." The era of the 1950s when Europeans and others embraced American goods slid into an era of unease about the new corporate imperial onslaught.

I had not made the connection between such products and imperialism when I visited a small museum in Istanbul near my house called the Museum of Innocence. The novelist Orhan Pamuk had famously built the museum—in one of the remaining wooden houses in old Beyoğlu, down the street from where I now live—as a memorial to his novel of the same name. In essence, it was a fictional museum; on each floor, meticulously constructed dioramas portrayed the many scenes in the novel, which was as much about obsessive love as it was about the 1970s, the years before Turkey, too, opened itself up to Western markets. Pamuk's museum, a museum of old Turkey, is a paean to the old Turkish products—the Turkish wine, the Turkish fruit soda, the Turkish cologne—before the market was subsumed by Western ones. An American oblivious to this notion of national sovereignty could not have known how the arrival of Colgate would eventually disturb the Turkish or Egyptian people. Ibrahim's *The Committee* includes a long, satirical tirade against the tyranny of Coca-Cola: "While the words used for God and love and happiness vary from one country to another and from one language to another, Coca-Cola means the same thing in all places and all tongues."

In Ibrahim's novels, corporations like Coca-Cola are regarded with almost the same anguish as an insolent army, and I could see a deep nostalgia in Pamuk's museum, with its little bottles of Turkish shaving cream and, of course, the locally produced Samsun cigarette packs that preceded the Parliaments I smoked while speaking in Soma to a group of former tobacco farmers. The Egyptian activist who told me wistfully in 2007 that the Turks built their Metro themselves had been referring, in part, to the Egyptians' even more devastating period of *Al-Infitah*, as had been so many Egyptians I met in 2011 and 2012. But in those years, Egypt's Mediterranean neighbor to the north was also trying to hold on to its dignity. In Turkey, the 1970s were the last years of political alternatives, before the country settled on a direction from which it never turned back.

IN 2014, VASIF KORTUN, the founder of the art space Salt, told me that he was saddened and fascinated to rediscover speeches by one of Turkey's leaders during the 1970s, Bülent Ecevit. "We have completely lost this history," Kortun said. "We have no memory of it."

Kortun looked melancholy, largely because of the disappointment that had set in over the authoritarian and religious conservative tendencies of Tayyip Erdoğan. I looked up Ecevit's speeches and discovered one from 1974, after he announced his decision to continue poppy production in Turkey against the wishes of the United States. "Our nationalism is not just inscribed on street walls," Ecevit cried into the crowd. "Our nationalism is inscribed on the soil of Cyprus, the seabeds of the Aegean, and the poppy farms of western Anatolia." His last clause was a response to American pressure to halt poppy production, which sustained the lives of thousands of Turkish farmers, because too much heroin was flowing into New York City.

The anti-American fury of the 1960s had temporarily ended in 1971 with another military coup, for which many Turkish leftists suspect the involvement of American spies. The coup did little to quell the fractiousness of the nation. Instead, Turkish nationalism, my old obsession, mutated even more into a nationalism of self-protection, which split between two general political spheres. One was Ecevit's leftist nationalism. The other resembled the anti-imperialist Islamist nationalism of the Muslim Brotherhood. In 1969, Necmettin Erbakan, who would someday be mentor to a young man named Recep Tayyip Erdoğan, had founded the Islamist movement called Milli Görüş, or national view, which counseled Turks against accommodating the West, urged a closer relationship with the Muslim world, and advocated for a more Islamic society. Turkey would split between these left and right spheres even more violently in the 1970s.

On the leftist side were Maoists, Communists, Leninists, Socialists, trade unionists, students, and social democrats, many of whom shared the sympathies of Ecevit. The pro-American trade union Türk-İş split in two, and a radical new union emerged, DİSK, which was anti-American and Marxist. The influence of these godless trade unionists prompted a harsher response from the right—including from Islamists, right-wingers, nationalists, the Gray Wolves and, often, members of the Turkish army. They were known in leftist parlance as the "Fascists." It was unclear who exactly was behind this civil war. Both sides believed that the other was being used by one of the two Cold War powers: the left by the Soviets and the right by the United States.

The spiral of violence continued throughout the decade. On May 1,

1977, unknown snipers fired into a crowd celebrating Labor Day in Istanbul's Taksim Square, killing some forty people and injuring hundreds. In the Anatolian city of Kahramanmaraş, in a single week in December 1978, a movie theater was bombed, left-wing assassins hit a coffee shop frequented by right-wingers, two teachers were murdered, and another's home was bombed. More than one hundred Alevi citizens, many of them leftists, were eventually killed in a right-wing pogrom. The journalist Mehmet Ali Birand compared the atmosphere to 1920s Chicago's, gang-style violence, a daily cycle of attacks and retribution. Prime Minister Ecevit began questioning whether the United States' "stay-behind organizations" were responsible for some of the carnage. He discovered that these extrajudicial groups had been established in the covert operations section of a 1959 bilateral treaty with the United States, as a way of mobilizing secret fighters in the event of a Soviet invasion. These groups were suspected of being part of what would become known as the "Deep State."

While Turkey's towns and cities were being wrecked by fighting, Ecevit contended with global pressures, mainly an arms embargo by the Americans for invading Cyprus, and an IMF credit squeeze during an economic period in which breadlines were common. But during that miserable year of 1979, Turkey became even more important to the Americans. The Soviet Union had invaded Afghanistan. The rise of the Ayatollah Khomeini in Iran had further imperiled America's interests in the region. Inside NATO meetings, American generals began to complain to their Turkish counterparts about the chaos in their country: *When will it end? When will you do something?* The Turkish army had pulled off two military coups before, they knew what NATO was saying. When the Turkish expert at the National Security Council Paul Henze said to a Turkish general, "I hope that you will not allow things to get out of hand in Turkey," the Turkish general replied, *"Merak etmeyin"* (Don't worry).

The military coup in Turkey on September 12, 1980, was a trauma from which the country never recovered. Fifty people were hanged, three hundred died in custody, and five hundred thousand were imprisoned, many of them artists and intellectuals. "Should we not hang them?" General Evren asked crowds at public rallies. "Should we go on feeding them?" Turkey became known for its torture techniques, the most notorious of which were *falaka*, or the beating of the bottoms of feet, and the act of forcing prisoners to eat their own excrement. "The policy was not necessarily to kill you in jail," said one former prisoner, the painter Orhan Taylan. "They would abuse you to the point of death, then release you so you would die soon on the outside." Thousands more lost their jobs, often university professors and journalists, and countless leftists and rightists, accused of militancy, fled the country. DİSK, the radical labor union that would descend on Soma in the wake of the mine accident, was shut down, while Türk-İş, the one to which the miners would belong, remained open, albeit with severely limited bargaining power. The day of the military coup, in the White House Situation Room, an officer had made a call to Paul Henze: "Your boys have finally done it!"

Caspar Weinberger, President Reagan's secretary of defense, said later, "We admire the way in which order and law have been restored in Turkey," and the United States quadrupled its aid to the military government. Some Americans and Europeans pushed for the inclusion in the new government of a man named Turgut Özal, who would go on to become Turkey's prime minister in the 1980s. The West, and especially the IMF, admired Özal for one reason: he pledged to bring capitalism to Turkey, just as Sadat had done in Egypt. Turkey soon passed sweeping IMF-mandated reforms to open the country up to foreign markets.

Military coups and economic intervention abroad had profound effects on the generations that experienced them, including their growing suspicion that they were not in control of their own lives. In 1972, a year before he was killed in an American-backed military coup, the Chilean president Salvador Allende spoke at the UN about "serious aggression" from the World Bank, the Inter-American Development Bank, and USAID, against the state companies of Chile—an array of forces "more subtle, more cunning and terrifyingly effective in preventing us from exercising our rights as a sovereign state," he said. "The entire political structure of the world is being undermined." The news video of the coup attack on Allende's palace is worth watching, as I suspect that many Americans sometimes think that such military coups are pulled off in some gentlemanly fashion, if only to later maintain plausible deniability. During the attack, the Chilean military bombed the presidential palace on a city street almost as dense as in New York. It would be as if someone fired on the New York Public Library.

A military coup, as much as a war, is a horror. Imagine a military coup in the United States staged by China or Russia or Iran. Imagine the imposition of political and cultural ideas completely antithetical to your own. Imagine the outrage, and the paranoia one might have, forever suspecting that some incalculably arrogant force might come and upend your life forever. Imagine this as an *American*, for whom the definition of one's identity is to be forever impervious to such an unimaginable fate. I met many people over my time in Turkey for whom the 1980 coup was the most formative experience in their lives. A taxi driver once held up his hands to show me where the military regime had tortured him so badly that he lost half a finger. For the young people of my generation, there were less visible scars. In 2016, the Turkish writer Kaya Genç, who is my age, recalled the years after the coup:

> We lived in a country totally isolated from the world. We lived
> in a continuous present—talking about history was dangerous,
> historians were despised. A repressive nationalism demanded from
> people to repress their individuality, religious and ethnic identity.
> The modernist coup was a big project to cleanse public life from
> "dirty" things like identity, individualism, religious beliefs,
> expressions of sexuality. With my family I used to travel to London
> and feel surprised about how, despite being a constitutional
> monarchy, Britain was a much freer society: they were okay with
> having a history, veiled women on the street, punks protesting the
> state, conservatives and leftists in the parliament, etc. Back in
> Istanbul, it was all clean and military-like and soulless and dead.
> The coup made us all self-repressors.

THOSE WHO DID NOT self-repress barricaded themselves against the Turkish state in other ways. The true-blue leftists I had met over the years in Turkey—the young Communists throwing rocks at May Day parades, the Kurdish intellectuals who merely wanted to preserve their independence, the members of the labor union DİSK who still sounded like they lived in the 1960s—were frozen in time at the point where they had been cut off by the 1980 coup. Entire neighborhoods of Istanbul existed in this parallel universe, still holding on to not only their leftist values but a part of their history. This rebellious leftism eventually, for some, became focused on ethnic identity. The long-oppressed Kurds, the ones who rebelled against Atatürk's daughter Sabiha Gökçen, who could not legally speak their language or watch Kurdish television shows, and who suffered from discrimination in the workplace, on the street, and in school, began agitating for independence. Many Kurds joined a militant group called the Kurdistan Workers' Party, or PKK. When I moved to Istanbul, in 2007, most of the Kurds I met had a family member who had, as they said, "gone to the mountains," to join the PKK and fight the Turkish state.

One of the Kurdish neighborhoods in Istanbul was called Okmeydanı, which I began visiting in 2013. Okmeydanı had once been a *gecekondu* area, made up of homes illegally "built overnight," some of which still had little yards, as if in the countryside. Other buildings sagged from neglect, and most had been decorated with leftist graffiti, the names of martyrs painted and stenciled across storefront facades. One evening, boys giggled on street corners in the poor street lighting, like on some film noir set, and a lingering fog hung in the air. It was actually tear gas: every week—seemingly every day—the people of Okmeydanı clashed with the police. Originally many of the migrants who came to Okmeydanı were left-wing Alevis from the east, who traditionally had opposed right-wing Sunni Turks like Erdoğan. In the 1990s the Kurds fleeing the military's war against them arrived, and Okmeydanı took on the character of resistance. "Thugs" or "Fascists" didn't dare come to Okmeydanı, just as they didn't go to Gazi Mahallesi, or Sultangazi, because they knew that the Kurds who lived there would fight them. In Okmeydanı, residents who suspected an imminent attack by Fascists—or the police—sometimes openly policed the neighborhood with guns. As the war against the Kurds began again in 2015, the police intensified its daily harassment of Okmeydanı.

"The armored police vans have been circling, peering inside shop windows, which is a provocation," one storekeeper told me. No one in Okmeydanı wanted me to use his name. "There is a lot of rage waiting to explode."

The Kurds had even begun to look elsewhere for true independence from their Turkish overlords. Kurds from Syria, allied with those in Turkey, began to form an independent state in a Syrian region called Rojava, which was even attracting leftist intellectuals from my friend Caner's university and beyond. I met one man in Okmeydanı who had lost his son in Syria. He had been fighting against ISIS for the PKK. "The Kurdish youth knowingly go to death—they stand in front of the tanks," the father said. "It's a very brave fight and I'm proud of it." He looked at me with tenderness and some pity, knowing that Americans couldn't understand why the Kurdish people are willing to die for such beliefs.

I left his house that evening with Caner, and a group of Turkish and Syrian Kurds who lived nearby.

"I can't speak Kurdish—you know why?" said one, laughing. "*This animal country*. They would lock me up in a room if I spoke Kurdish."

"Why doesn't America help the Kurds build a state?" one asked me, the American. "There are thirty million Kurds."

"They don't. No one does!" said another.

"They only help the Kurds when the Kurds help them," I said.

Silence.

"Kurds always help them!" Caner said.

"I know, they always claim to love the Kurds, but they don't ever really help them," I said. "Now because of Erdoğan . . . they love him. I mean, they don't love him, they hate him, but they need him."

"It has always been like that," he replied. "The United States prefers the large states more than the people without power."

IN SOME WAYS, military coups were no more violent during the 1970s and 1980s than economic intervention—especially in Egypt, where, by the time of the invasion of Iraq, the period of forced political and economic submission had become unbearable. Under Hosni Mubarak, American-style neoliberalism meant that "the collective well-being of the nation is depicted only in terms of how it is adjusted to the discipline of monetary and fiscal balance sheets," as the academic Timothy Mitchell writes. Through its myriad aid agencies and NGOs, America administered an insidious form of empire. But why hadn't the Turks or the Egyptians ever said no to the United States? "Simply because we are forced to say yes," writes the Egyptian economist Galal Amin. "Coercion is not exercised directly by the hand of the colonizer but at the hand of his local agents." Thus the schemes of modernization theory through right-wing dictatorships that had been drawn up at the most esteemed educational institutions in America had succeeded in vanquishing human will. When Egyptians protested the invasion of Iraq of 2003, the Mubaraks threw them in jail and tortured them on America's behalf.

Americans tend to believe the Muslim hatred for the West is irrational. "Since the rejection of the West is existential, the argument goes, Western nations can do little to appease Arab and Muslim wrath," the historian Salim Yaqub writes. But the problem with the theory of the clash of civilizations is that it dismisses grievances against the West that are completely genuine: its blind support for Israel, its propping up of dictators, its brutal economic policies, and its stunning carelessness with Arab lives. "Bin Laden rejected the secular, liberal language of universal human rights and international law," Makdisi writes, because "they had done nothing to protect Muslims around the world." The Americans have over the course of sixty years made the Arabs feel as if they could be broken. By 2013, a military dictator was back in power in Egypt. The Egyptian-American journalist Mohamed Soltan, who was sent to jail under this new regime, later spoke of his experience in the notorious Egyptian jails. "The one thing that everybody in the prison had in common—the ISIS guys, the Muslim Brotherhood guys, the liberals, the guards, the officers," he said, "is that they all hated America."

The Iraqi man I met in Istanbul in 2012 said to me, "Your country had so much to do with what Iraq was like in the eighties and nineties. We know so much about you. And you don't know anything about my country at all." There had not been even a hint of accusation in his voice, though I couldn't know his true feelings. He sounded as if this particular difference between Iraqis and Americans was but one in a constellation of millions. To me, it was like a burst of wind, that old revolutionary shock, and then the customary slamming of mental doors; the force of what he said brought to life, once again, my resilient and cowardly American reflexes:

Why would Americans know anything about life in Iraq? I thought. I still had no control over those reflexes. What I meant was: why would it be necessary, why would they bother, *you are just one country of many.* This was it, this was the gulf, this was the distance between us. This imbalance of power between people and nations was violent even in the absence of violence.

What did he mean, my country had everything to do with what Iraq was like then? There I had the usual problems. One, I did not know the history. Two, I did not know to imagine how that history affected people on an individual level. Our foreign policy, our wars, almost never affected Americans. What did he mean? He meant the bombs of 1991, which nearly destroyed Baghdad and killed thousands of people, and he meant the support for Saddam in the 1980s, which prolonged the Iran-Iraq War. And he meant the sanctions, which destroyed the livelihoods of men and families, plunged people into poverty, and caused as many as five hundred thousand children to die. (About which Madeleine Albright—today a feminist icon—once said, "We think the price is worth it.") The sanctions were still in effect when we invaded Iraq in 2003, but I remember hearing little about them. The Iraqi man said he despised America for the sanctions above all else.

If as an American I merely ignored, was not incensed or heartbroken by American actions like sanctions, then it must have been because I somehow believed that those Iraqis were deserving of sanctions. What this does in the end is create a distance between myself and those foreigners I thought deserving of sanctions. It is one that cannot be bridged. The difference between us and them is that our country has created this universe in which sanctions are acceptable punishment for everyone except our country. It means that no other country can force my father to lose his job, or force my family to go hungry, or to break up my family, or to forever distort my future, but my country can do that to almost any other foreigner, including the man sitting across from you at a café.

One of the assumptions that allowed for sanctions was that life under the madman Saddam Hussein was terrible anyway, which was true, it was terrible. But what Americans likely didn't know was that the Iraqi government had for a long time provided its people with adequate health care, schools, and social programs. "Baghdad University in the 1980s had more female professors than Princeton did in 2009," according to the British-Pakistani writer Tariq Ali. Literacy was almost ninety percent, people had gone to university for free. Sanctions only hastened Iraq's decline. Before the invasion, some optimistic Iraqis might have hoped that the United States, in promising them freedom and prosperity, would herald a return to the golden age of the 1970s, when Baghdad was, according to the journalist Anthony Shadid, a libertine paradise of vibrant cultural production and dazzling street life. While the Americans were promising a fantasy version of American life—all freedom and democracy—Iraqis likely envisioned a better version of *Iraqi life*, one rooted in history and reality. Americans never grasped that Iraqis might have their own idea of what a good life would entail. In the first days of the American occupation—and what would turn out to be the next decade—Iraqis were bewildered that the United States could not even provide them with electricity, Shadid writes. In 1991, after the first Gulf War, Saddam got the lights back up within months.

But such was our sense, rooted in modernization theory, that all other nations were decades behind us and thus needed our interference, all of these fantasies we held on to even as America's own infrastructure—its airports, its roads, its hospitals, its schools—deteriorated. In his introduction to Daniel Lerner's *The Passing of Traditional Society*, David Riesman writes, "The Arabs were once a great civilization. The illiterate in his depression, and the modernizer in his impatience, live amid the ruins of greatness. How open and how empathic will Americans be, how magnanimous, if our turn comes to live amid the ruins of our modernity?" Instead, like the featherweight symbols Americans had turned themselves into, they believed their mere presence in Iraq would incarnate some illusory democracy. It was because we did not see Iraqis as humans that we did not know that "democracy," a word by then sucked of most of its meaning by the American century, might have mattered less to most parents than the ability to feed, house, educate, and protect their children.

"Either you're with us or you're with the terrorists," President George W. Bush said before the invasion, echoing Truman. For sixty years, all over the world, people struggled with the binary universe Americans created—wouldn't someone want to resist it merely because of the hypoc-risy? *You can be free as long as you want our freedom.* Such dichotomies, such totalitarian views, created many little monsters in its image. It is shocking to read Shadid's *Night Draws Near* now and notice that Abu Musab al-Zarqawi, the ideological founder of ISIS, emerges during the first years of the occupation. The book was published in 2005, eight years before ISIS became known to the world.

In 2017, the articles still appear with anguished regularity in the pa-pers: "Who is ISIS and what do they want?" When ISIS first declared it-self, so many American policy makers said its existence wouldn't have been possible without the collapse of Syria into civil war. But ISIS was born from the Iraqi occupation; it came from the Americans. It may have grown from the darkness, because the Americans couldn't make the elec-tricity work. It may have grown from the world we created in Iraq: the night raids by scary hulks draped in weaponry, kicking open doors and humiliating men and dishonoring women, the bombs from the air, the tanks in the street. Our mercenary thugs, the Blackwater men sitting off the backs of trucks with machine guns and wraparound glasses and leath-ery skin, grimacing at everything that moved, lawless individuals attached to no army, were no less terrifying to an Iraqi child than is ISIS to us, with its black flags and hoods and macabre videos. It was hardly noticed, as ISIS ran across the map of the Middle East, gobbling up pieces of land like an amazingly fast zombie free-for-all, that this militant army now occupying lands was born during an occupation, that they were thousands of occu-pied men who likely knew of no better way to gain power than to imitate the occupier, to defeat him at his own game.

6.

LITTLE AMERICAS: AFGHANISTAN, PAKISTAN, AND TURKEY

When we revert to the final solution of kill or be killed, all
warring parties in the name of clan tribe nation religion violate
the first law of civilization—that human life is precious. In this
general collapse, one of the first victims is language. Words are
deployed as weapons to identify, stigmatize, eliminate, the enemy.

—JOHN EDGAR WIDEMAN

A FEW YEARS AFTER the financial crisis, America's jobs, it seemed,
were in Kabul. I knew a lot of journalists and photographers in
Istanbul who worked there regularly, and they would return with terrifying stories of night raids and Taliban ambushes and rides in Black Hawk
helicopters, at the end of the day collapsing into bed, caked in dirt. But it
seemed journalism was not the only reason to go to Kabul. At the time, an
unemployed American friend in Istanbul could not get any government
jobs in D.C., but in any case, he said, "all the good jobs," those for a

hundred thousand dollars a year or more, were in Kabul. For a lot of those jobs, you had to have a master's degree, at least; even in their desperation for applicants the American government maintains high standards for positions with inexplicable purposes: "program officer," "regional governance specialist," "communication and reporting officer." A recent Harvard graduate I met in Istanbul was furious that she wasn't qualified to work in Kabul—so many of her friends were there, and she had even studied Dari, and "wouldn't it just be interesting to go?"

My boyfriend at the time, a journalist, first brought up the possibility of my visiting Kabul at my parents' dinner table: "Suzy's really gotta come to Kabul," he said in a way that sounded like, "You really gotta get out to Des Moines some time." The table had fallen silent, that being the first time my parents reconsidered how much they thought they liked my new boyfriend. "Are you insane?" I said to him with my eyes, my hands frozen on either side of my plate, but he was chewing his steak and rhapsodizing about how beautiful we'd all find Afghanistan. Foreigners fall in love with Afghanistan like they would a young girl.

My family, by then, had come to accept my life in Istanbul. They even visited several times, shocked by how beautiful and modern and gentle the country was. Not only was I safe there but, post–financial crisis, there were fewer opportunities for me at home. My parents were pragmatists, little different from the Americans Googling for high salaries in Kandahar. Americans were trying to figure out how to either take advantage of or survive in this new world.

At that time, suicide bombers struck Kabul once a month, but my journalist friends said it was safe, compared to Helmand. Foreign correspondents had well-honed ways of deflecting fear. At night they still filled up Kabul's one Italian restaurant or Thai place, marveled over how they got that kind of fish in Afghanistan. I wanted to see this parallel world that had been created in the semipeaceful headquarters of our nine-year war. "But remember, it's not really like an occupation," I was told. The military had recently announced, in the eerily professional and nonsensical jargon with which it announces important battles, that they would invade Kandahar soon, and "reverse the momentum and gain time and space for the Afghan capacity." To protest this incursion in their "political and spiritual center," the Taliban began firing rockets; journalists in Istanbul put in their requests for a seat on the bus.

Many reporters and photographers chose to live in Istanbul, but rarely covered Turkey, mainly because American newspapers couldn't make much sense out of its Islamic-democracy-secularist-autocracy mishmash, and also because, at the time anyway, there were no wars in Turkey. Some reporters would come to Istanbul from places like Basra or Karachi and gush anew at the wonders of Atatürk, still the main reason in their minds that this "Muslim country" was so stable, that it didn't have suicide bombers, that women in spaghetti straps danced on tables by the Bosphorus. Istanbul was the relief, but also the exception, which might have had the unintended consequence of reminding them the Muslim world was hopeless, and that only the West could save it.

Machismo almost necessarily amplified the latent savior complex, if not a secret thrill for violence, in so many of us. Yet despite war correspondents' reputation for superficiality and adrenaline addiction, the ones I knew were idealists, so much more so than the self-centered New York writers I had known. I was surprised at first to hear the sincerity in the correspondents' voices, the concern for the fate of other countries. They had a necessary belief in the importance of journalism, not only because it was among the ways they could justify why they imperiled their bodies. These Americans had a purpose for living I had not yet glimpsed in my generation, and I suspected that the snide remarks often made about war journalists—that they were self-important—likely came from a place of profound envy and longing to do something for the greater good of the world. But what power did journalists have? How often did we hurt the very people we claimed to represent with our own muddled vision of the world, of America, of ourselves?

In retrospect, the dissolution of the Arab world also meant the dissolution of a certain kind of foreign journalism. Before it, the West had set up their wars in Iraq and Afghanistan with elaborate infrastructures. In Afghanistan they had an easy blueprint to follow; the Americans had a muscle memory of the occupations in Germany and Japan, and a convenient amnesia of the German and Japanese people's total devastation and easy capitulation to them. America was not the same country in 2001 as it was in 1945, but Americans thought it was, so frozen was their conception of reality in those myth-production years. The contemporary occupations would instead become temporary containment strategies for chaos, market economies for occupation, a dream factory of empire. Later, a foreign friend observed harshly that perhaps ISIS went after journalists because during the war on terror, journalists had become associated with that vast infrastructure of the American military. The country's imperial soul had hardened into a vulnerable exoskeleton, all of us visible to anyone who wanted to attack it. In those years, I, too, participated in my first and only American occupation, in Kabul.

IN MAY 2013, over ten years into the war in Afghanistan, an Afghan writer named Qais Akbar Omar penned an op-ed for *The New York Times* titled "Where's My Ghost Money?" Omar had heard that the CIA was secretly paying Hamid Karzai in cash in suitcases and plastic shopping bags, and wanted to tell Americans that if they would secretly give him money, he would "do the things we thought the Americans were going to help us do when they came to Afghanistan nearly 12 years ago." These things included digging wells in villages and building modern water systems in the cities; constructing sewers to replace the "open drains in the streets," because "Afghans, like Americans, use toilets every day"; and repairing broken hydroelectric dams to bring electricity to the two-thirds of the country that still didn't have it. Instead, he observed, the Americans had spent billions of dollars building cobblestone streets "our donkeys cannot walk on," and teaching farmers to "grow hot red peppers that Afghans do not like to eat." I could see Americans snapping, "But you should be grateful. Eat the peppers." The Coalition Provisional Authority in Iraq, which was established in Saddam's old palace, served meals laden with pork products in a Muslim country. I can imagine that Americans—who cannot live without their hot peppers or pork products—did not consider that perhaps there were foods that Iraqis and Afghans also cannot live without.

I finally went to Kabul because I had heard from a friend, in passing, that the roads in Kabul were not paved. This didn't make any sense to me. The image contradicted my romantic image of a country that prized its own fine roads, and even once built roads for the nation of Turkey. When you rebuild a country, don't the roads go down first? Were we rebuilding the country? Of Afghanistan, I had imagined military compounds and broken buildings and Westerners huddled in armored vehicles, but I assumed, if only for our own ease of transport, or to signal progress to the world, that we had repaired the Afghans' roads. These were the twilight years of our time in Afghanistan. If we hadn't done that, what had we done?

In the check-in line at Dubai International Airport, where I transferred planes for Kabul, everyone going to Afghanistan was white. I met one stocky American guy with a jockish voice (that sounds as if a cave lies at the back of the throat) and a muscular body. I asked him whether he was in the military. "Nope. I'm a contractor. Just like everyone else in this line." I watched nearby as a large white man with electric-white teeth, his plain white T-shirt tucked tight into khaki pants, laughed with wild panic as he crashed into another middle-aged guy, his skin bronze as a penny. "Hey, man, how ya doin'! Ha- ha!" The Dubai waiting area for the flight to Kabul was as exotic as Columbus, Ohio. The whole room was littered with people who made money off the war, which, I couldn't help but acknowledge— as I smiled widely back at them in some automatic species-response signal— included me as well. We were all contractors now.

Like the unpaved roads, contractors hadn't played a big role in my imagination of the occupation; they were too new. My imagined American occupier—who of course, to me, was never called an occupier—was still a fit and dignified soldier in uniform, even after all the satirical war movies I had seen: *Three Kings, Jarhead*. The men in this room reminded me of Wall Street guys at a strip club, hedge funders launching into a round of steaks. Some of the American men looked positively deranged: tanned and wiry, wound up like teenagers on steroids, their horse-saddle skin betraying abuse of tobacco, alcohol, sun, and near-death experiences. This was who we were attracting to Afghanistan; it felt like a massive illegal operation as shot by a Hollywood director.

We boarded the plane, and finally cut loose from strange Dubai, where the sky and the water melt into an aluminum-hued oblivion. Dubai had recently become the world's most disreputable construction site. Now it served as the Kabul elite's vacation spot. Western war profiteers cooled off in Dubai hotel pools and the Afghan criminal elite bought houses on a man-made island shaped like a palm. They were buying up the waterfront property, one resident told me, in anticipation of the day Kabul collapsed.

KABUL, FOR THE TIME BEING, was the boomtown. President Obama had in recent years launched a "surge" of troops to finally win the decade-long war. In Kabul, that meant a surge in wartime entrepreneurship. A strange ecosystem of soldiers, aid workers, businessmen, journalists, and other civilians flourished in the base of the bowl-like city. Kabul, land-locked, ringed with improbably steep mountains, felt like a defiant fortress with its inhabitants peering out into the wild. A fragile, jagged peace saturated the everyday life, as if the manic effort to house, feed, and protect the executors of the war mostly amounted to staving off the chaos outside. Someday, America in Kabul would vanish. It was impossible to imagine what the city would look like when it did.

When I visited, modern midlevel high-rises and wedding halls as gaudy as anything in Vegas rose above the traditional mud houses. SUVs in white, a rich man's clean-city color, had ascended to prominence as the power-status symbol of choice. Shiny grocery stores were stocked with vitamin supplements and condoms and *The Economist*. But the presence of Westerners didn't mean any part of the city met Western standards, not by a long shot. People delighted in reminding me of the percentage of fecal matter in the air—10 percent, 16 percent, 30 percent—which bothered me far less than the prospect of tripping into one of the drains that lined the roads. Some of the roads were indeed so rocky and cratered that driving on them recalled off-roading in Colorado. To my driver, Arif, and many other Afghans, I expressed surprise that "we" hadn't even bothered to fix the roads of our imperial city in nine years, but they blamed Karzai instead.

Afghans were also terribly poor, and far away from the dynamism of the city center, some lived a bleached existence, relying entirely on the one family member who managed to land a job with the "dog washers," the Afghans who returned from abroad, or with the "Michaels," as foreigners were sometimes called. One young man who worked for Global, the security company that ran the Kabul airport, supported eight families on seventy dollars a day, and that was a fortune. The Afghan elite lived in enormous "poppy palaces," the Central Asian disco version of a McMansion, homes so unbearably ugly and ostentatious, they seemed to be engaged in satire. In some sections, the city felt warm and pleasant. Huge acacia trees canopied the Kabul streets, fat roses grew tall as fences, women wore outfits other than the cinematic blue burka. Kabul's buildings were low-slung like in New Orleans, many of the streets hummed with urban normalcy: Small-time entrepreneurs taught their sons the family trade—ice cream churning, kebab spinning, deli owning. Small girls in black pant-suits and white head scarves carried parasols and walked to school in cheerful groups. Indian music consumed the traffic. Shakira's World Cup theme song was popular. The rest of the country, I was told to remember, was nothing like Kabul.

The main Western neighborhood was called Wazir Akbar Khan, once Kabul's wealthiest enclave. As in many Muslim cities, walls ringed the yards of the homes, so everywhere there were gates. Where there were a lot of foreigners, there were also blast walls: big, flat upright slabs of concrete, Hesco crates filled with sandbags and topped with barbed wire. A local could tell you what's beyond all those walls: "To the right is Special Forces, ahead of you is the American embassy, to the left is the International Security Assistance Force [ISAF], then the Spanish embassy and the Italian embassy, and beyond that the CIA and Camp Eggers, and then the British embassy, the Pakistani embassy, a Karzai relative's house, the Canadians." Walls obscured everything, so the streets felt like hallways—like a massive, mazelike skateboarding ramp, or a mental institution. You saw only the walls and the checkpoints and the sky. I had wondered whether Kabul would feel like an occupation, but it felt as though, rather than occupying the city of Kabul, the international community was occupying itself.

An Afghan woman would eventually warn me of the differences between Afghans and Americans. Often, she explained, Afghans politely lied to their Western patrons about their true opinions, refraining from leveling criticism out of courtesy. Americans took everything at face value. Communication broke down for cultural reasons. I was told this, yet for my first days in Kabul, part of me still believed one thing the Afghans said—that despite our many failings, they hoped the West wouldn't leave. I couldn't help it; they all said the same thing.

I WENT TO the Gandamack Lodge to meet its owner, Hassina Syed, one Thursday night in June. Since the Muslim day of rest falls on Friday, Westerners let off steam on Thursday nights, and that evening they filled up nearly every seat in the Gandamack's resplendent garden. The lodge, a two-story house with a wraparound porch, was hidden behind two gates and several guards with machine guns. Syed, only thirty years old and full of energy, wore a beautiful peach pantsuit and patterned scarf around her neck, which fluttered behind her as she made her rounds. Lanterns on tables lit up the smiling faces of the customers, their pale skin hanging in the night like many moons.

The daughter of a mujahideen father and an illiterate mother, Syed had founded a women's organization and was experimenting with new farming technologies. She had a lot to say about what was happening in Kabul. To her, Afghanistan—its apples rotting on the ground, its factories rusting, and its lapis lazuli mines inactive—was a kingdom of untapped wealth that hadn't become much improved with the influx of aid projects. If Afghans in the countryside complained about bombs, Afghans in Kabul complained about USAID.

General Stanley McChrystal's surge (and Obama's) had meant billions of more dollars for USAID, which built schools, "implemented farming initiatives," and set up weaving looms for poor women, generally serving as the kinder face of America in the world. But USAID, too, was in a state of decline. In the past, USAID had undertaken ambitious and expensive modernization projects in Afghanistan. In the 1960s, "Little America" in Lashkar Gah in Helmand Province was a manufactured utopia with irrigation projects and schools; Afghans and Americans lived together and never, goes the story, locked their doors. Little America grew out of America's faith in modernization theory. But many of Little America's programs failed, and the community was finally destroyed by Afghanistan's many wars.

In the post-9/11 years, the United States spent $67 billion on civilian-aid programs in Iraq and Afghanistan, but Afghans like Syed knew that much of this money went to America's own companies. After September 11, USAID was flooded with funds, but not with employees; the staff couldn't manage such large sums. Aid organizations that have too much money rushed to spend it, and the easiest way to do that was to quickly give the projects to someone else. So if USAID officials decided to build a medical clinic, instead of erecting it themselves, they hired Louis Berger Group to do so. Louis Berger Group was then free to hire a whole slew of private subcontractors, and ultimate accountability vanished into the recursive transactions. When the windows in the clinic didn't close in winter, was it the responsibility of USAID or of some corporation they outsourced to?

The Afghans had trouble winning these bids entirely. "The contracts always say you have to have 'past performance'—who in Afghanistan has that?" Syed said. "Afghan women don't have 'past performance.' How can we compete with retirees from the U.S. Army? Please don't invite foreigners to compete with ordinary Afghans. The money should stay like concrete, in Afghanistan." She ground her spoon into her bowl. "The soldiers and USAID people don't bring their families here. They will leave. We need sustainable projects."

Syed told me that she had been invited to ISAF to listen to a talk about a much-vaunted USAID program that encouraged the foreign occupying forces to buy local Afghan products. After the presentation, Syed stood up and inquired why the three types of bottled water being consumed at the conference were from Spain, Pakistan, and Dubai.

"We have water!" she said to me. "We have bottled water. Why weren't they buying our Afghan water?"

Syed got up and socialized with her guests. I recognized a stocky British woman curled up in the corner, smoking, who earlier that week I had seen at the popular lunch spot the Flower Street Café. While discussing some internal politics, I assumed, at the British embassy, she had said, "Oh, no, but you can't say *that*! Whatever you say—we're *not leaving*. This is not Basra!" So many foreigners in Kabul had worked in Iraq, too. They always hastened to declare Baghdad far worse than Kabul. This woman laughed loudly, but I detected a gentle panic trailing in the wake of these Western conversations. There was a sense that we were there to get things done very quickly, what James Baldwin had called America's "funny sense of time," as if "with enough time and all that fearful energy and virtue you people have, everything will be settled, solved, put in its place." You could see that alarm in the USAID workers' frantic smiles as they showed off the latest farm project.

When I went to the bathroom, I saw a Brit gripping the end of an artificial leg as if playing with it. "See, I told you!" he said, laughing to his friend and pointing. I followed his finger's direction until I saw an elderly man selling Afghan souvenirs in the foyer: lapis lazuli bowls, jangly chain belts, silver jewelry. He rested his stump on a chair. The drunk was outside waving the old man's prosthetic leg around like a lightsaber.

I returned to Syed. She reminded me that Americans' taxpayer dollars were turning to dust. I wasn't sure how to explain to her that most Americans didn't know whether or not their taxes had been raised to fund this war; that in America there was no draft; that in America we had an army staffed by farm kids and ghetto boys; that in America wars were waged because in America wars were easy to wage.

"Go to this event with Ambassador Eikenberry tomorrow," Syed said, handing me an invitation. "You'll see."

THE DAY OF the Afghan Chamber of Commerce meeting with Ambassador Karl Eikenberry at the five-star Serena Hotel—the only five-star hotel in Kabul—three or four Afghan guards stood dressed in full body armor and holding AK-47s, in front of two gates so high they resembled a drawbridge. Gunmen had attacked the Serena a few years earlier; at a party, I met an Afghan-American who had hidden in the basement while the militants shot up the gym. At both ends of the street, more guards stood upon little round stages, checking cars before they could pass in front of the hotel. A long row of Land Cruisers, Pajeros, and 4Runners, mostly in white, lined up to wait for their masters. Guards and drivers, representatives of Kabul's security economy, draped their thin bodies over the hoods, smoking and staring.

When I stepped into the conference room of the beautiful hotel, Eikenberry stood at a lectern, speaking to a large audience. USAID women, their heads uncovered, sat in front. One hundred Afghan men, some in Western suits, some in traditional *shalwar kameez*, sat motionlessly, listening. No cell phones rang, though one man taped the speech with his camera phone. The event had the formal air of a midwestern business conference, but with much more luxurious surroundings.

Eikenberry had brought up the same aid problem that Syed had: foreigners were not buying Afghan products. To rectify this, the American embassy had recently launched a new program called Afghan First.

"We are purchasing as much local procurement as possible," Eikenberry said. "Especially from local woodworkers . . . I'm very proud that if you go into our video teleconferencing room, our emblem of the United States was made here in Kabul. So every time the president sees me, he's looking at an emblem made here in Kabul . . . The USAID economic growth program will increase and improve capacity building . . ."

Everybody in Kabul loved the phrase "capacity building." Everyone talked about capacity building, building capacity, getting capacity up, improving, growing, and discovering capacity in the Afghans. I heard it so much that I wondered how it translated, whether bureaucratic jargon was actually translatable. Eikenberry said he was very proud to announce that "the new Afghan First website will be available in Dari and Pashto," the native languages of Afghanistan.

He didn't seem embarrassed to make this announcement nine years after the invasion, as if it were an important accomplishment rather than the most basic act of international friendship. Eikenberry was by all accounts a sincere man who cared deeply about Afghanistan, someone who tried his best. But I felt a crushing kind of pain in that room, to see an American leader behave in his faux jovial press-conference American way, seeming to believe his kindness was all that truly mattered. As he spoke, I was again reminded of the way Baldwin and Camus and so many others had described Americans, as people with no sense of tragedy.

Eikenberry offered the Afghans a chance to ask questions.

"An American contractor took money from me and fled," said one.

"Why are cars being bought from Russian companies? I sell cars."

"We have seen millions of dollars spent every year to help the private sector," said a software developer, dressed in a Western suit. "But the same service we want to provide is also being provided by an NGO that gets funding from the EU. How can we compete with them?"

Eikenberry, an amiable, big man, fumbled a bit and deferred to the USAID staff. A woman stood up. She talked about China.

"That's not just an Afghan problem but a global one . . ." She was grasping. "But, you know, it hasn't been a problem for Bill Gates."

I leaned over to the Afghan man sitting next to me. "Did she just say Bill Gates?"

He waved me away. Americans rarely took the blend-in-with-society approach to nation-building. I remembered the USAID woman I'd met on the plane, who had been transfixed by Sudoku pads and had gorgeous long, golden hair. When I'd asked her whether I should put on my head scarf before disembarking, she had just shrugged and said she never wore one. I was all ready to get angry at a fellow American for her cultural insensitivity, but I realized that the reason she never had to wear a head scarf was that she probably never left her compound at all.

Eikenberry stood up again and joked that he wished he could distract everybody with the promise of the great food waiting for them in the reception area so he didn't "have to answer such hard questions."

"I have to get back to the office for a teleconference with my president," he said. "He will not be happy if I am late." I wondered why Americans always spoke to grown men in foreign countries as if they were children; why in fact the Americans behaved like children.

We filed outside for food and drinks and business card trading, but many Afghans hung back, quietly standing in line to speak to the USAID folks one-on-one. The foreigners in that room controlled the Afghans' livelihood. This was their chance. On my way out, an elderly American man exclaimed upon recognizing a friend, "Hey! Yeah, you know. Just another event at the Serena!"

I found Arif wolfing down some snacks in the foyer.

"What did you think?" I asked.

"They are just wasting our money." He flicked his hand at the hotel and the food. "All this waste."

. . .

AMERICA HAD a much longer history in Afghanistan than most Americans knew. Saadat Manto's prediction in the 1950s that the Americans would resort to using the mullahs and the mujahideen to defeat the Soviet empire in Afghanistan came true. As early as the 1970s, even before the Soviet invasion of Afghanistan, the CIA, the Pakistanis, and the Iranians began funding religious fighters to subvert the Socialist regime in Kabul. Islam, they believed—as they would in Turkey—was the only force strong enough to defeat communism.

The effect of this American policy was felt strongly in Pakistan, where it helped bring to power that country's Islamic military dictator, Zia-ul-Haq. When the Pakistani writer Kamila Shamsie expressed outrage that American novelists never wrote about America's actions abroad, she was in part thinking of America's support for Zia. Then, the first time Americans were championing the "Afghan people's right to freedom and self-determination," they cared little that Pakistan's dictator Zia was staging "public floggings and hangings, or when he passed a law which made it possible for a woman who had been raped to be stoned to death for adultery." Karachi, the city where Shamsie grew up, was overcome by what she calls Kalashnikov culture. The Karachi port was the main conduit through which the United States sent arms to the Afghan mujahideen, and many of those weapons ended up in the hands of criminal groups and others throughout Karachi. "By the mid-eighties," she says, "Karachi, my city, a once-peaceful seaside metropolis, had turned into a battleground for criminal gangs, drug dealers, ethnic groups, religious sects, and political parties—all armed. Street kids sold paper masks of Sylvester Stallone as Rambo; East met West in its adulation of the gun and its hatred of the godless Soviets." There was so much trouble in her city that schools were regularly closed, and kids had to go through drills meant to protect them in case of bombs or riots. Security concerns even stopped cricket matches for almost two years.

For Shamsie, the face of "Islamicization" was Zia, the ally of Saudi Arabia and America. The weapons came with the building of more "Wahhabi mosques and madrasas." Zia placed Shamsie's uncle, a pro-democracy politician, under house arrest. The future of Pakistan was changed forever by this American intervention, not only the political landscape and the possibilities of violence, but the way individuals related to God. As she notes: What was once devotion became fundamentalism. When American pundits and politicians lashed out after September 11 about the dangers of Islam, Shamsie thought such emotions terrifying in their reckless hypocrisy. During the Soviet-Afghan war, the United States and Pakistan together, in a supremely cynical alliance, had created a generation of Islamic fundamentalists—designing jihadi textbooks and sending MANPADS into Afghanistan. Many of these fundamentalists also stayed behind in Pakistan, destabilizing the country, and eventually attracting hundreds of American drones to Pakistani skies.

"Please explain," Shamsie asks, "why you are in our stories but we are not in yours." She generously assumes that Americans want to fuse their own national stories with those of others, that they aspire to a greater complexity and understanding of their own motivations and actions. But as would become clear in Afghanistan, that was not at all what the Americans were trying to do.

IN 2009, GENERAL McCHRYSTAL had promised a new counterinsurgency doctrine, which purportedly focused more on protecting Afghans and less on air strikes. At that time, many policy makers suggested that America was failing in Afghanistan in part because it was distracted by the war in Iraq, which was as comforting an argument as the one that explained away the loss in Iraq by invoking the Bush administration's unpreparedness. Both arguments implied that Americans can and should win wars.

They served to distract from the more awful truth: America's killing, in the stale military language of the time, "eliminated" no "enemies"—it killed people and created more enemies. According to the journalist Anand Gopal, military language obscured the realities of death and injury in Afghanistan, not just "errant bomb strikes" or the "mishandling" of "detainees," but the intentional killing and torture of suspects and civilians. The Americans' mandate was to track down any member of the Taliban, but since they did not know the country, they relied on the only people with the status, knowledge, and firepower to help them: violent Afghan warlords who fingered their own rivals so they would be persecuted by the United States. Across the country, the Americans, not unlike what they had done throughout Latin American countries during the Cold War, "carried out raids against a phantom enemy, happily fulfilling their mandate from Washington," and in the process became a sort of warlord corporation in their own right. One American leaflet dropped by a plane in Kandahar read, "Get Wealth and Power Beyond Your Dreams. Help Anti-Taliban Forces Rid Afghanistan of Murderers and Terrorists." Many of these Afghans—bread bakers, politicians, teenagers—were sent to the Americans' jails at Bagram and Kandahar airfields, and at Guantánamo Bay. They were innocent. Many had even supported the American invasion.

Gopal reports that some Afghans believed the Americans were colonizing them like the British, but even that characterization is kind. Here is one typical example of how these Americans conducted their night raids on innocent Afghan villages:

> As the soldiers approached a home, a dog growled and they shot it. A villager ran out, thinking a thief was on the premises, and they shot him too. His younger brother emerged with a gun and fired into the darkness, yelling for his neighbors. The soldiers shot him as well, and the barrage of bullets also hit his mother as she peered out a window. The soldiers then tied the three bodies together, dragged them into a room, and set off explosives. A pair of children stood watching, and they would later report the scene. An old man stepped out of the neighboring house holding an oil lamp. He was shot. His son ran out to help, and he, too, was shot.

McChrystal wanted to rectify some of this unpleasantness. "All ISAF personnel must show respect for local cultures and customs and demonstrate intellectual curiosity about the people of Afghanistan," he said. The Americans developed a program called the Human Terrain System (HTS), the brainchild of idealistic anthropologists and disillusioned military veterans who believed that sending social scientists out with soldiers would help America win wars and kill fewer people. HTS drew on an argument of Marine General Anthony Zinni: "What we need is cultural intelligence.

What makes them tick? Who makes the decisions? What is it about their society that's so remarkably different in their values, in the way they think, compared to my values and the way I think in my western, white man mentality?" Out in the field, the HTS research scientists discovered that U.S. soldiers did not know not to smile when Afghans read from the Koran, did not know not to crowd disrespectfully into an Afghan house, did not know that rural Afghans didn't have mailboxes. They could not connect with the people.

But even after the American anthropologists went through the multimillion-dollar HTS training program in a military basement in Kansas, the same problems of cultural ignorance and indifference and purposelessness persisted, as did the most obvious truth—the most elusive one for Americans in denial—which was that Afghans would never accept Americans as their overlords.

The HTS began to suffer from the typical flaws of the corporate occupation: cost cutting, rushing to *get the job done*, the overweening priority of profit. More than one HTS expedition ended in death, both Afghan and American. "If you could have found a way to project on a big screen the nation's mixed feelings about its role as the sole superpower in a post–Cold War world, this was what it would have looked like," the journalist Vanessa Gezari writes in *The Tender Soldier*. "American exceptionalism tempered by the political correctness of a postcolonial, globalized age and driven by a ravenous hunger for profit. The Human Terrain System was a cosmic expression of the national zeitgeist, neatly encapsulating both a justification for the war and the intoxicating belief that war could be less lethal, more anthropological. We claimed we want to understand the Afghans. What we wanted was to understand ourselves."

What Gezari was characterizing was the particular trajectory of American liberalism, which for people from minority races and cultures had become only superficially inclusive, and which was further undermined by an economic system so corrupt that it could not sustain all livelihoods. Acceptance to this system was always dependent on imitating the modern ways of the rulers. As usual, the Americans—after September 11, after Iraq, after the financial crisis—had sought in the delusions of empire proof of their own exceptional traits and strength. *Why couldn't we manage this*

occupation? If we can't do this, does it mean everything we believed about our-
selves is false? Why don't they want to be like us?

THE LARGEST EXISTENTIAL threat to Americans might have been admitting the Afghans would be better off without them. In western Kabul,
not far from the city center and across from a narrow riverbed filled with
trash, a historic park called Bagh-e Babur, or Babur Gardens, extended from
the road up to the top of a steep hill. From the crest you could see the entire
city of Kabul. Babur, the first Mughal emperor, had ordered the gardens
built in the mid-sixteenth century. The ongoing late-twentieth-century
violence in Kabul destroyed the gardens as well as its palace. In 2003, the
Aga Khan Foundation, one of the largest private employers in Afghanistan,
began reconstruction of the park. It was one of the most beautiful places I
had seen in Kabul.

I visited the gardens with its development director, a South African
architect named Jolyon Leslie, one late Friday afternoon, when thousands
of Kabul Afghans had gone there to enjoy their day off. The lines to get
into the garden were long. Afghan guards gave Afghans a once-over before
letting them pass. No body patting, no bag X-rays, no closet where women
were dispatched to be felt up by other women. I realized what had made
the difference in security: as many as seventy thousand foreigners lived in
Kabul, but that Friday at Babur Gardens, I was the only foreigner in sight.

The entryway spit us out into the lovely courtyard of a caravan-
sary. Women, in varying degrees of concealing dress, held tight to their
daughters' hands, little girls in miniskirts. Inside, the steppes of the park
rose before us, and beautiful paths lined with trees shaded us from the
brutal sun. The Aga Khan Foundation had set aside areas for women and
areas for men. The marble palace and a tiny, ornate mosque hung above the
city like magic orbs.

The garden was not without its problems; people did drugs and got
into fights. Leslie, who had lived in Afghanistan for twenty years, ticked
off these issues as if Kabul were just any other city. It didn't make sense;
this was a war zone! Wasn't this a great place to smuggle in a bomb? Yet
here a segment of the population of Kabul lived a normal day: kids ran

around a jungle gym, men danced, women picnicked under trees. Up near Babur's tomb, an elderly tour guide spoke to a rapt group of boys. He was teaching them their history.

"This was built by an all-Afghan team," Leslie said.

"Really?"

"I'm sick of people saying Afghans can't manage anything," he said. "I'm from South Africa, and we call that racism."

Everyone looked so happy. Inside the palace, Afghans were setting up for a film festival. In one of the palace rooms, the U.S. embassy had installed a new exhibition called *Picturing America*: reproductions of Joseph Stella's Brooklyn Bridge and N. C. Wyeth's *The Last of the Mohicans*; images of Selma, Alabama, in 1965; Abraham Lincoln; Yosemite Valley. To me, too, they looked like postcards from a foreign country. None of the park goers frolicking on the grass were inside at the exhibit puzzling out images from America's history. It was only me, the American.

On the way home, passengers who were stuck in traffic, their cars squeezed together in the narrow streets, smiled at one another and waved. I watched a man and a woman chat as they waited to cross the street. I could not stop staring at them, and since I was in typical Kabul traffic, I could have stared at them for the next half hour. Just a man and a woman chatting on the street in Kabul before they crossed to the other side, where men twinkled their bicycle bells, and a girl in a sequin tutu chased after her mother. Whenever we got stuck in traffic in the days prior, I'd grow anxious that this would be the moment a bomb would go off. That day I was mesmerized by the casual banter of the Afghan man and the Western-looking Afghan woman, their hand gestures and smiles, and also by the fact that while I was watching them live their normal, unfettered lives, nothing terrible happened at all.

WHILE I WAS IN KABUL, I heard from everyone—from the Afghans who worked at the house I was staying in to upper-class politicians—that the best school for children in the city was, hands down, the "Turkish school." From the road, it looked no different from the other pastel-hued bureaucratic buildings in Kabul, the kind that could have been a hospital as easily as it could have been the Department of Public Works. But inside I found myself in Turkey, not only because the school was sparklingly clean and well ordered, but because there hung on the walls a giant photograph of Atatürk. The school, however, was not some last-ditch attempt at Kemalist evangelism; the school was run by the Gülenists.

The Gülenists by then had established thousands of schools in hundreds of countries; Central Asia was one of their most important regions of influence. The other was the United States. With the schools came fleets of Turkish teachers and their families, nonprofit organizations and cultural festivals, and eventually, Turkey's foreign policy apparatus. Erdoğan recognized the international diplomatic and financial potential in countries where the Gülenists had made such inroads, such as Somalia, Indonesia, and Japan. Through their schools, the Gülenists had created diplomatic outposts all over the world, which made doing business in those countries a lot easier, and in turn made the spread of the Gülen movement a financial reality. As one man formerly affiliated with the movement told me, "Those schools are not only there because they care so much about education. Those schools are there to further the movement." I was too blind at the time to realize that the Erdoğan government was building an empire.

In fact, the period of the Gülenists and the AK Party's power expansion had begun around the same time Zia-ul-Haq was using Islam to quell communism in Pakistan and funding the mujahideen in Afghanistan. Zia had shared his ideas with Kenan Evren, the military general who staged the 1980 coup in Turkey. It is one of the ironies of Turkish history that it was the Kemalist-secularist military's coup that would usher in Turkey's era of political Islam.

At the time, NATO approved of using Islam as a green belt, or a "wall," to stop the advance of communism. Following this lead, Evren, and later Turgut Özal, the prime minister who eventually succeeded the general, took a series of radical measures that changed Turkish society forever. Engin Cezzar had tried to explain this history to me when I visited his apartment. "I'm very sorry, but this awful American policy is killing us," he said. "They want Turkey to be a mild Islamic republic." I hadn't listened.

Months before the coup, Turkey accepted an IMF package that would open up the country to global markets. Evren, who needed more capital to rebuild the country after the economic paralysis of the 1970s, turned to a country flush with oil revenue: Saudi Arabia. In 1976, an Islamic conference had been held in Pakistan called the *Siret-i Nebi* Congress. It was organized by Rabitat, which had been founded by the Saudis in 1962 in reaction to the rise of Egypt's Nasser, and later Iran's Ayatollah Khomeini. Rabitat, according to the scholar Banu Eligür, "aimed at propagating a strict religious fundamentalism in the Muslim world," by supplying countries with books, money for mosques, and salaries for imams. In 1981, the Saudis even began paying the salaries of imams in Turkish communities in Germany and Belgium.

Evren's sudden alliance with Saudi Arabia set off a furor in Turkey, but he defensively praised the "improvement of our relations with the Middle East and Islamic countries." Turkey is "an inextricable part of the Islamic community," he said, words that for some were blasphemy. After the instability of the 1970s, Evren had come to believe that if the state did not offer a strict and moral religious upbringing for its citizens, then an inevitable void would be filled by Marxism or fascism. To counter such threats, Evren adopted something called the Turkish-Islamic Synthesis, which had been developed in the 1960s by a group of right-wing nationalist intellectuals. These "idealists," as they called themselves, saw the rise of Marxist militancy, as well as the Kemalists' desperation to imitate the West, as an attack on "Turkishness" as well as on Islamic culture. "Both 'red imperialism' and 'capitalist imperialism' aim to destroy the Turkish nation by turning people against each other and provoking internal disorder," a primary text on the Turkish-Islamic Synthesis suggested. "In order to achieve these purposes they alienated people from their religious and national values and conquered their souls and hearts with the fake ideals of equality and freedom." Imperialism in all forms was to blame.

Once, Atatürk had sought to adopt Western lifestyles, while denouncing the West's foreign policy. Under Kenan Evren, the Turks reversed course. Though Evren was pro-American, he wanted to wrest control of the Turks' identity. Evren's new Turkish ideology emphasized loyalty to the state, to the mosque, and to the family (i.e., the father). He saw Sunni Islam as a "useful tool for creating citizens who would be respectful and loyal." Turkish students were required to take a course on Islam called

"Religion and Ethics." Evren began building hundreds of *imam-hatip* schools, which offered students a religious education, as well as many more mosques. "In this way," writes Banu Eligür, the professedly secular military "tactically opened up a social and political space for Islamist mobilization in Turkey."

The civilian who eventually took over from Evren, Turgut Özal, would propel Turkey further in this nationalist-Islamist direction. Özal was himself pious, and a member of the Nakşibendi brotherhood, the country's largest Islamic sect, which had been banned during the Kemalist revolution. With Evren's blessing, and Özal's enthusiasm, a measure of freedom and independence was returned to all of Turkey's brotherhoods in the 1980s. Among these brotherhoods was the Nur, which spawned the Fethullah Gülen movement. The Gülenists, who had been proselytizing underground since the 1960s, were allowed to flourish—even more so with the help of a liberalizing market economy. Gülenist businessmen founded holding firms, publishing companies, newspapers, radio stations, and, crucially, schools. Turgut Özal championed them.

Özal loved America. He had studied engineering in the United States and came to believe that the country owed its success to liberalism and capitalism. "His dream was to make Turkey another America—his role model," writes the academic Sedat Laçiner. "It can be said that one of the main pillars of Özalism, with its Turkism and Islamism, was liberalism and American-type democracy. For Özal, all these principles were compatible, not contradictory . . . Özal's ideology consisted of American secularism, American democracy, American capitalism and American liberalism." Once again Turkey was imitating America, but *this time*, Turkey turned itself into a model of Reaganite and Thatcherite neoliberalism (Özal loved them, too). Many Islamist politicians would mimic Özal's way of combining Islamism and capitalism. Özal empowered the Islamic youth of Turkey. Most prominent among them was a young man who once sold *simit* on the streets of a decrepit Istanbul neighborhood: Recep Tayyip Erdoğan.

THE 2010 FOURTH OF JULY party at the American embassy in Kabul started at nine in the morning on July 3. My driver dropped me off far outside the gate of the embassy. The whole road was blocked off; many roads in Kabul were like this. Sandbags lined the sidewalks. You'd walk for a while, and you'd pass a checkpoint, and then another. To the left were the white USAID trailers, and to the right, the old and new embassy buildings. A large sign read: THE U.S. EMBASSY WOULD BE GRATEFUL IF ANY OF OUR FRIENDS WHO HAVE INFORMATION ON TERRORIST ACTIVITY OR THREATS TO PLEASE COME TO THIS GATE.

A receiving line waited for foreigners and Afghans to meet Ambassador Eikenberry, his wife, and the newly arrived General David Petraeus. They stood before a giant wooden American flag. Red, white, and blue bunting hung from the drab modern embassy buildings. Off to one side Afghan men stood around a kebab stand and some tents. USAID had set up tables about their various programs, like at a county fair. The popular local band Kabul Dreams, made up of four young Afghan boys, played "Knockin' on Heaven's Door." Hassina Syed stood in line, waiting patiently to shake the general's hand. She wore a gray pantsuit and head scarf—"the other me," she said. General Petraeus, now in for his second war, looked older than his years.

After the American and Afghan national anthems, we gathered around the lectern for some speeches. First, Eikenberry read a message from Secretary of State Hillary Clinton. Throughout the day, red, white, and blue balloons had been spontaneously popping, due to the heat— even the snipers up on the tops of buildings sat under a big striped sun umbrella—and the sound of the loud pops did much to set an already jittery crowd on edge, a sea of slightly jumping shoulders.

"Welcome to America's birthday party," Eikenberry read. "I'm delighted we can mark it together . . . All of us have to take responsibility to work together."

Those bland, company-man words. In Kabul these words sounded criminal. These were loveless, soulless words. How could we speak to Afghans like this? I saw a country and a people completely divorced, alienated, severed from itself and its reality, as if superimposed on someone else's photo. Our administration of all these little empires had rendered all of us into half-hearted automatons; no one believed in the words they were saying, and yet this language was about real things: flesh and death and war, people's homelands, and their children.

"Let us use this to make new connections."

Pop!

"... Find solutions ..."

"... challenges ..."

Pop!

Petraeus was up next. I hoped for better.

"We cherish the relationship."

"Your success is our success."

Pop!

"What an all-star team has been assembled here in Kabul."

I glanced around at the pink American faces, the blue and white polka-dot scarves, the dreary midcalf navy skirts and hopeful red ties. Somber Afghan men in Western suits bore name tags that revealed they were professors. We smiled at one another like bored students at a class assembly. *Progress. Mutual objectives. Thank you for raising your hand and answering the call.*

The language reminded me of a tiny book a friend gave me before I left for Istanbul; she had found it in a used bookshop. It was called *A Pocket Guide to Turkey*, and had been produced by the U.S. Department of Defense for all the soldiers heading to one of their first Cold War satellites, in the early days of the postwar empire. People liked to say of Afghanistan that the occupation failed because we weren't good at occupations anymore, but I suspect we were always the same way:

> Of course Uncle Sam isn't sending you to Turkey to observe social trends. You have a couple of jobs to do. Your bread-and-butter job is to teach the Turks all you can about American military know-how. That's plenty important. The Turks wouldn't have invited you over if they didn't think it was worth while—if they didn't feel that you knew your stuff.

The Americans in Kabul brought out a five-by-seven-foot flag made out of cupcakes. I saw a platter of potato skins and, feeling an unexpected rush of nostalgia, grabbed one. Karl Eikenberry thanked "sponsors" for the event. Apparently, local Afghan and foreign businesses had paid for the American embassy's Fourth of July party.

The embassy band was singing "I Heard It Through the Grapevine." Hassina Syed seemed upbeat. She said this Fourth of July party was better than last year's.

We shuffled out to wait for our drivers. The cars whipped and halted around a monument to Ahmed Shah Massoud, the Northern Alliance leader who was assassinated two days before September 11. The dust and the noise and the heat—it all felt different out there. Big cement trucks paused in front of the gates. Life felt uncertain. A few of us backed away from the traffic to wait behind a pile of sandbags. I wondered whether the Afghans driving by knew it was our Independence Day.

"Ha," Arif said, when he picked me up. "We've had like four independence days. Independence from the British, independence from the Soviets, independence from the Taliban, and . . . *inshallah*, someday, independence from you."

A few weeks after I left, a truck full of American contractors killed four Afghan civilians on the road, and Afghans torched the cars and screamed "Death to America!" So often walking through Kabul, I wished I'd never come to Afghanistan. It was my mere existence, I felt, that did damage enough. I wanted nothing else but to withdraw myself.

In "Shooting an Elephant," George Orwell writes: "All I knew was that I was stuck between my hatred of the empire I served and my rage against the evil spirited little beasts who tried to make my job impossible." Such were the ugly confessions of the Englishman sent to work for the empire abroad; I suppose there are American soldiers, spies, diplomats, even embassy chefs who might sometimes share the same crisis of conscience and thrill of anger, even if we don't hear about it much. Mostly, though, we don't think of ourselves like the British at all. That month, as an American journalist in Kabul, attending embassy parties, and living in homes behind blast walls, and enjoying the privileges of being a white person in Asia, I had a feeling similar to Orwell's, except for a few key aspects. The dominant reflex was not hatred—the desire to "drive the bayonet," as Orwell had written—but indifference. In Greece and Turkey, in the 1940s and 1950s, Americans had descended on Athens and Istanbul for their specific nation-building tasks, while their CIA and military counterparts deployed direct imperial muscle, as they would throughout the world and up until this day. But by the 1990s and 2000s, even State Department officials in

Afghanistan, or USAID representatives in Egypt, hardly did the dirty, physical work of empire anymore. The long arm of American power allowed for most Americans to remain completely isolated from the foreigners they were in denial of ruling; there would never be any guts to splay with a bayonet. For many of us, there may not even be a bayonet. We would not know them, and therefore, as Baldwin said, could not love them, could not care so much for their deaths. Distance, distance, distance was the American way, a frigid, loveless distance, a kind of power and violence that destroyed intimacy in all its other manifestations, that destroyed empathy in all of its imperial citizens, in us, in me.

But it was darker than this, wasn't it? We all wanted to hold on to this imperial dream, because the loss of the empire meant we might someday be the ones who were ruled. It meant we would not be the strongest, it meant we would not chart our own course, it meant all the freedoms we believed ourselves divinely ordained for, all the power to "be whatever you want to be"—everything that made up the meaning of our American lives—would be gone. We couldn't stand it. We couldn't stand a world in which we might one day be the Afghans. We could not imagine it and so, from Kabul, we never left.

7.

AMERICAN DREAMS: AMERICA, IRAN, AND TURKEY

It was hardly understood that the real fear of Iranians at the time was that the United States, the most powerful country in the world, would simply not allow a political system to develop that didn't mirror its own.

—HOOMAN MAJD

ONCE, WHILE I WAS VISITING New York, I got pneumonia. Afterward, countless American friends remarked with concern, "Well, thank God you happened to be in America!"—because they had never been to Turkey, or because they knew nothing about the majority of hospitals in the United States of America.

That week, I had been staying at an apartment in Brooklyn, thinking I had the flu. When I felt dizzy one morning, I called a friend to take me to the hospital. We went to the closest one, a charity hospital set amid the projects and directly across the street from a row of magnificent brown-stones, most of them some three million dollars each. I almost passed out at the registration desk, but once I got to the emergency room, things really went downhill. A nurse yelled at me for dropping my purse next to my bed "because someone might steal it"; there was no food on offer; at night, ador-able but hapless residents stood before a group of students, saying, "Now. This patient's name is *Su-zy Han-sen*, but she's from *Turkey*. Wow." Over the first twenty-four hours, a series of doctors on shifts vacillated in their diagnosis of me; first lung cancer, and then "possibly" HIV, and then tuber-culosis, at which point I was actually quarantined for forty-eight hours, no last phone calls, no Internet. My glasses got mysteriously thrown out; fami-lies of flies lived in the public hallway showers; at night a mentally ill man stood in the middle of the hallway and screamed over and over, "*Get*. The *fuck*. Out the *way*." The patient next to me cried silently the whole time.

Thank God I happened to be in America.

If I had been in Turkey, I would have gone to a hospital as beautiful and immense as a luxury shopping mall, it would likely have cost far less money than the Brooklyn charity hospital, and my friends' mothers would have brought me homemade food and pestered the doctors for me every day. That fancy Turkish hospital was available to me, of course, only because of the power of the American dollar in Turkey. But at the height of the health care crisis, most Americans still did not know just how terrifying our hospitals were, and in a way I did thank God I had been in America when I got pneumonia, because that night in the hospital was one of the two times I viscerally understood how degraded America had become for many of its people. The other time was when I came home from Istanbul to spend several months in Mississippi.

At the time, 2012, it was an odd decision to return home to work; most foreign correspondents in Istanbul had begun covering the war in Syria, and the refugees fleeing over the Turkish border, which from the po-sition of Istanbul, and Europe, still seemed very far away. I remembered the refugees I had seen in Greece; so many of them, I knew, had for years got-ten to Greece through three major refugee routes that passed through North Africa, Syria, Iran, and Iraq, and then Turkey. There, many went to an area in Istanbul nicknamed Somali Stand-Up Street to find a smuggler who would get them to Greece. Istanbul had long been a transit hub, and I had always wanted to write about the refugees. But I had never been to Syria, and I was no expert on the Arab Spring, and I had begun to lose my belief that I was qualified to cover a region I knew little about. So when I read that a black doctor in Mississippi named Dr. Aaron Shirley was arguing that Americans should consider adopting a health care system pioneered in Iran, I went home to cover the country I thought I knew.

In the United States then, the financial crisis, to some degree, had prompted self-examination: Occupy Wall Street denounced the One Percent; the concept of gross inequality evolved from a leftist preoccupation to undeniable fact. Soon the French economist Thomas Piketty would question the very nature of capitalism and his book would become a best-seller. But the old American habits returned, too: white people hated the black president, the occupation in Afghanistan continued while the defunct one in Iraq was bearing new terrorist groups, drones detached from human emotion or responsibility continued to seek out their targets in Yemen and Pakistan. Guantánamo Bay was open. Obama's efforts to reform health care earned him the epithet "Socialist," and the American conservatives I knew had begun believing the man himself was a conspiracy against the country. Something in America wasn't working: you could feel it in the dread vibrating in newscasters' faces, and in the president's deepening, self-protective cool. But Mississippi wasn't part of this fast-changing world; in Mississippi, not much had changed at all.

The historian John Dittmer once wrote in his book about the civil rights movement that the state of Mississippi was "the standard by which this nation's commitment to social justice would be measured." He wrote that in a book about a time when words like "social justice" were used more frequently, when the United States, both at home and abroad, still aspired to fulfill the myths of its perfect modernity, when the Turks still told American visitors they loved America. John Dittmer said that Mississippi would be the standard by which Americans' commitment to social justice would be measured in a book about a bloody but hopeful time.

It was then, too, that James Baldwin debated William F. Buckley at Cambridge. The topic of the 1965 debate was: "Has the American dream been achieved at the expense of the American Negro?" In 2009, when I watched it, I wondered whether a related question couldn't still be asked: Was the American dream at the expense of the world? "From a very literal point of view," Baldwin says in the beautiful, grainy video; he is small in stature, and proud, and surrounded by admiring British boys, while William F. Buckley looks on with his nose pointed to heaven. "The harbors and the ports and the railroads of the country—the economy, especially in the South—could not conceivably be what they are if it had not been, and this is still so, for *cheap labor.*"

His voice became stronger. "I am speaking very seriously, and this is not an overstatement: *I* picked the cotton, *I* carried it to the market, *I* built the railroads under someone else's whip—*for nothing. For nothing.*"

In that spirit, did it not mean that as a white American, *I ran the plantations, and I owned the slaves, and I lashed the whip—for everything? For everything?*

Dittmer's concept of "social justice," Baldwin's beautiful accusation—these statements, questions, and assumptions seemed comparatively so innocent, language from a time swept away long ago. To go to Mississippi and to read about the civil rights movement again—to speak to people who still carried with them the language and spirit of that time, no matter how downtrodden they felt—was to realize that those violent years had actually been more progressive than our own. When I went to Mississippi, it was clear not only that the United States' standard of commitment to social justice had declined, but that the larger forces of political corruption, economic decline, and indifference had made it impossible for social justice to exist. As the author Ta-Nehisi Coates would write some years later, back then African Americans aspired to the dream, but today they know that it was built on their backs.

Dr. Aaron Shirley's belief that Americans needed to look to Iran to solve their health care crisis wasn't meant to be some heartwarming act of innovative international diplomacy. His plan—which never went very far—was, like Coates's pessimism, a middle finger to the system, an acknowledgment of hopelessness. But most remarkable to my eyes was that Dr. Shirley's idea reversed the logic of American modernization theory: here was the United States asking a so-called developing country for help, and not any third-world country, but Iran, the country that spurned America's destructive embrace with the greatest and most lasting force.

DR. SHIRLEY was a rabble-rouser, an old civil rights–era hero who for a long time was the only black pediatrician to see black patients in Mississippi, the type of activist who, in the 1960s, wasn't necessarily of the "non-violent persuasion." At that time, black people were killed and houses were bombed regularly, and policemen were the ones doing the killing and the bombing. Upon hearing that the local KKK was headed to his home to kill him, Dr. Shirley would warn the police department that each of his four children knew how to shoot and all of them were ready.

Dr. Shirley was the first black doctor to do his residency at the University of Mississippi Medical Center. For a decade, he worked at the Delta Health Center in Mound Bayou, which was one of the only hospitals in Mississippi where black people could go. He was trailed by the State Sovereignty Commission, which began spying on black people shortly after *Brown v. Board of Education*, and in 1964 he went to Atlantic City with the Mississippi Freedom Democratic Party to challenge the Democratic Party to recognize black candidates. He did things that don't end up in history books, too, such as build wells for poor black people when they didn't have clean drinking water; travel throughout rural areas to treat malnourished babies; fight for federally qualified health centers and welfare rights and Medicaid. He was, by all accounts, a take-no-shit kind of guy. "When Aaron was doing his residency, he was the only black resident, and one day a black soldier came in with a head injury," said Dr. Jack Geiger, who worked with Shirley. "He was sitting in a back room, and the doctor's attitude was 'Oh, just another drunk nigger,' you know, we'll just leave him back there. Well, Aaron heard this and walked right out and called the Pentagon. And soon enough there was a general or a colonel or whatever he was standing in the emergency room, demanding to know what was going on with his soldier. That's Aaron."

When I visited him, Dr. Shirley was working at the Jackson Medical Mall, his name emblazoned on a wall inside the building. For decades, the Mall was an actual mall, with a JCPenney and a Gayfers, but the mall and the area around it began to depreciate as whites fled integration for whiter, suburban areas such as Brandon and Madison and Pearl. Historic downtown Jackson emptied out altogether, and Capitol Street, the bustling avenue that Medgar Evers boycotted in 1962, looked shuttered and ghosty, a Lott Furniture collecting dust on its desks. Entire industrial mills, warehouses, and office buildings had been abandoned just minutes from the capitol building, and it was hard not to be embarrassed by the naked deterioration of this American city, as if seeing a guy who'd accidentally left the house without his pants on. The Mall was just five minutes from downtown and business was ailing, so Dr. Shirley and others decided to buy it and turn it into the kind of place they knew would generate business among poor black people for quite some time: a health care mall for the sick.

Dr. Shirley, then seventy-nine years old, had observed for the last two decades a dispiriting development. The millions of dollars that poured into Mississippi every year—federal funds, Kellogg grants—had disappeared into wells of political and economic dysfunction. In fact, he said, in order to remind his guests that none of these problems would necessarily be fixed by the election of a black president, Dr. Shirley hung a COLORED sign above the doorframe of the entrance to one of his office rooms, which you had to walk under on your way to his bathroom. The implication was that Obama's historic election wasn't enough to transform people's circumstances. Dr. Shirley had gray curly hair and a sad face, but he laughed when he talked about the other signs he made, including DON'T NEED NO TEA PARTY, MISSISSIPPI ALREADY HAS A KLAN and YOU CAN BE A CHRISTIAN AND A COWARD TOO and MUSLIMS DIDN'T ENSLAVE MY ANCESTORS, SO-CALLED CHRISTIANS DID.

"Look, Head Start was also once treated like a Communist conspiracy," he told me one day, "like they're doing with Obamacare. The anger against Obama reminds me of the reactions to JFK. When Kennedy was shot the white elementary and middle school children cheered. And you call yourself a Christian? It's the same attitude. They don't say it's because he's black, but you just listen to the rhetoric. Ninety percent of the whites in Mississippi, if it were Obama versus Sarah Palin, they will vote for Sarah Palin. I mean, this woman is dumb, this man is not! He's got a family, he's never been divorced! He represents all the values you cry about! And you'll vote for Gingrich!

"I'm proud of Obama," he continued. "But when he was trying to accommodate the Republicans, I became anxious and thought, *When is he going to recognize that you can't.*"

Dr. Shirley had more reason for conveying his sympathy for Islam ever since 2009, when he heard about Iran's rural health care model and realized it might be transplanted to Mississippi. He had worked outside of the system his entire life. He didn't share the assumptions of American exceptionalism that many others did; namely, that the most advanced nation in the world didn't take tips from poor countries, never mind a poorer country whose leaders regularly challenged American power. He did not think the American system, as it existed, could produce real change in people's lives.

"I've been coming here for forty years," he said one day after a trip to the Mississippi Delta, "and nothing has changed."

Mississippi was the poorest state in the nation. A Mississippi black man's life expectancy was lower than the average man's expectancy was in 1960. Sixty-nine percent of adult Mississippians were obese and a quarter of households didn't have access to decent, healthy food, so Mississippians were dying from diabetes, hypertension, congestive heart failure, asthma, and chronic obstructive pulmonary disease. It was common to hear a sick person offhandedly mention that their thirty-nine-year-old cousin just had a stroke, or their thirty-two-year-old diabetic sister just lost a toe. In the 1960s people starved; now they died from cheap, terrible food.

The South was also the epicenter of the HIV epidemic in the United States, and Mississippi had one of the highest HIV acquisition rates of all. African Americans in Mississippi were dying from AIDS at a rate 60 percent higher than the nation's average. In the Delta, which stretches north and west of Jackson like a diamond, AIDS was a full-blown but silent crisis. Waiters got fired because restaurant owners didn't want them handling food; dentists refused to serve patients with HIV. Half of HIV-positive Mississippians didn't seek or receive treatment, because the vast majority of the people didn't have health insurance. Forty percent of the people in the Delta were illiterate. Often, people didn't even understand the words the doctors were using when they treated them.

ONE APRIL MORNING, I accompanied one of Dr. Shirley's nurses, Claudia Cox, who was driving far from Jackson's empty downtown to visit a patient named Vonda Wells. "The rural people are the worst," she said. "'Come to the oak tree.' Well, hell, I'm from the city, I don't know what no oak tree is. I know magnolia. I know pine trees." Cox referred to her seven-year-old Ford Freestyle as her "office," but it had the ambience of a video arcade: the petulant *ding-ding-ding* of her unused seat belt, the whir of a phone charger stuck in the cigarette lighter, a Galaxy S that rang with the opening of Cheryl Lynn's disco hit "Got to Be Real." Cox, a forty-five-year-old divorced mother of three, juggled phone calls and patients' charts and cigarettes like some serene octopus, always catching the steering wheel just before the truck veered onto the grass. After twenty minutes, she pulled into a pebbly country driveway to suss out why Vonda Wells kept returning to the emergency room.

Ms. Wells's large figure filled the doorframe of the tiny old house. She was jovial despite the oxygen tubes running from her nose. "Is that yours?!" Cox exclaimed, pointing to the baby in Wells's arms. "That's my grandbaby!" Wells laughed and passed off the child to a teenager who disappeared behind a closed door. The two women sat down in a dark, damp living room crammed with couches.

"All right, Ms. Wells, we come out and check on everybody," Cox said in a tone that makes you want to put your head on her shoulder. "You had pneumonia, right?"

Cox didn't know oak trees, but she knew how to figure out the real causes of chronic health problems. For example: when to ask people whether they could not afford their insulin, or for some reason were not taking their insulin, or were not keeping their insulin cold, or couldn't keep their insulin cold because they didn't have a refrigerator, or couldn't keep their insulin cold because they did have a refrigerator but didn't have electricity to keep it running. Not having health insurance was a huge problem in Mississippi, but it wasn't the only one.

"So you good with doing your medicines?"

Wells made a guilty face.

"You oxygen dependent?" She was. "You know, you're not typically overweight for us southern folk . . ."

Laughter. "Oh, I'm overweight," Vonda said softly.

Wells had worked at a Jackson hospital as a certified nursing assistant for five years before she started getting sick with asthma-related illnesses. No one wanted a nurse carrying around an oxygen tank, she said, so now she was trying to work a handful of hours a week at the Four C's, a Christian community center.

"I stayed in Illinois for twenty-five years," she said. "I didn't really have asthma symptoms till I came down here . . ."

"You been in this house?" Cox said. The house was obviously old, the rug thick, the air damp. "There's something in the house that's triggering it. I bet you need to get tested." Cox made a note. "And I'm putting a little checkmark down here that you got the basic light, gas, and water . . . Your major problem is the asthma."

"And congestive heart failure."

"And congestive heart failure." Cox paused and tilted her head. "Have you been taught how to manage your congestive heart failure? Because you should have a scale." She looked around the house gamely as if she believed a scale might pop out from behind the TV.

"I need a scale?"

Cox explained why people retain fluid. She then asked whether Wells had checked her blood pressure and told her that on her chart her blood pressure had been at 212 over 100, which is stroke level. Wells didn't know that, and she looked briefly bashful, but Cox had a way of soothing embarrassment away. She asked Wells how many sodas she was drinking, and explained that juice has a lot of sodium in it, too. "Knowledge is power. Okay?" Cox said gently. " 'Cause you're forty and you're oxygen dependent. We don't want you goin' on a date with an oxygen tank!" Wells laughed again.

Cox said she would try to find a company who would come and test the house for toxins, and made an appointment for Wells to come back to a medical clinic. Wells got up to walk her to the door, the oxygen tube dragging the length of the house. Cox paused at one of the photographs on the wall.

"You got a beautiful family!" Cox said. She zeroed in on a slim, healthy-looking, smiling woman. "Now, is that Mama?"

"That's Grandma," said Ms. Wells. "She was ninety-five when she passed. I moved down here to help her out."

I saw something dark pass over Cox's face, which might have been the same as what went through my mind: *What had happened to America? Why had the previous generation lived to ninety-five, and the current one could barely breathe?*

All of the sick people I met shared a story of personal economic decline. There was Regina Huggins, a white woman in her forties who had been in the hospital twenty times in eight months, had no health insurance, and couldn't afford a primary physician. She had worked for the Presto factory in Jackson for many years, until it closed, and after she was laid off, at the Piggly Wiggly. Neither the factory nor the grocery store offered health insurance, and after a lifetime of low-paying work she had nothing to show for it but three hundred thousand dollars in medical bills. There was Mamie Marshall, a licensed beautician who had worked for Packard Electric, a subsidiary of General Motors, and also as a bus driver for the Jackson public schools, and in her last working years as a nanny. She was dying of bone cancer. "I *worked*," she said. But none of these employers—not one of America's greatest companies, nor one of her country's public school systems—had left her with the means to care for her health.

IT TOOK THE IRANIANS no less than a revolution and twenty difficult years to reform their own health care and economic disparities. Throughout the 1960s and 1970s, the Shah of Iran encouraged Iranians to become Westernized urban consumers, ignoring the concerns and plight of poor villagers living in the countryside. These policies, among many others, led to the Shah's overthrow in 1979 and the rise of the Ayatollah Khomeini, who came to power in part because of his furious defense of the lives of the poor. Around that time, in the spirit of the revolution, a group of Iranian doctors proposed a new rural health care system. Such initiatives were what made the Islamist and Islamic movements from Hezbollah to the Muslim Brotherhood to Turkey's AK Party so lasting; they provided basic human services.

The Iranians built "health houses" in thousands of villages, to be used by fifteen hundred people within no more than one hour's walking distance of the house, which was a thousand-square-foot building equipped with examination rooms and sleeping quarters. They staffed the houses with community health workers, or *behvarzan*, one man and one woman, and gave them basic medical training. The *behvarzan* were trained in nutrition, they could take blood pressure, they could keep tabs on who was pregnant and needed prenatal care, they could advise on family planning, provide immunization, and assess environmental conditions such as water quality and housing safety.

It was these "health houses" that Dr. Shirley, and his Iranian partner, the academic Dr. Mohammad Shahbazi, wanted to imitate. The *behvarzan* came from the villages they would serve. Rural Iranians wouldn't trust people they didn't know, something that struck Dr. Shirley as similar to poor black patients unlikely to trust white people from the city. The *behvarzan* got to know many of their patients from birth. Even during the most brutal years of the Iran-Iraq War, the Iranians implemented their plan, and today, seventeen thousand health houses have served twenty million Iranians. The idea of building seventeen thousand health houses seems daunting, but to Dr. Shirley, the system's great appeal was its simplicity.

When Dr. Shirley went on his tour of Iran in 2009, he noticed that some of the men did not look happy about the Americans' arrival. While inside a teahouse, one Iranian man said to Dr. Shirley's translator:

"What are the Americans doing here? Did they come back to ruin our country again?"

THE HISTORIAN TONY JUDT once told me that when he was invited to speak at American high schools about world history, the question he often asked students first was "Who was Mossadegh?" None of the students had ever heard of him. For these Americans, the name Mossadegh meant nothing, while for the entire Middle East, Judt said, it meant everything—everything about America's role in the Middle East, and in the world.

In the 1950s, Mossadegh, the democratically elected leader of Iran, nationalized the Anglo-Persian Oil Company, which at the time was the British government's largest single investment abroad. Mossadegh was able to unite his country's monarchic, Communist, and Islamic communities under the banner of independence and a nationalist vision. Mossadegh wanted to modernize Iran's legal and political systems without also Westernizing Iran. Most of the world cheered on Mossadegh's challenge to the West, especially young nations with still-fresh memories of colonial excesses, such as India, Turkey, and Egypt. The West, unsurprisingly, had a different response. The editors of *Time* magazine named Mossadegh Man of the Year in 1951, out of anger; the article characterized Mossadegh as a child who threw temper tantrums. Still, Mossadegh believed that the United States would intervene on his behalf against the British.

The United States worried they might lose the country to the Soviets. British diplomats didn't believe that Iran's communist party posed a threat, but happily manipulated the Americans' fears, and convinced the Americans to join forces and wreak a special kind of havoc on Tehran. American intelligence officers used, according to the journalist Christopher de Bellaigue, "alarmist propaganda" to "instill panic that the country was sliding towards a communist takeover." In August 1953, they bought off newspapers, employed thugs to pose as Communists, attacked mullahs and mosques, and spread rumors that Mossadegh was a Jew. In response to this phony violence, the real Communists soon rampaged through the city. A *New York Times* correspondent was nearly lynched.

In the chaos, Mossadegh was overthrown and Iran's political development was forever disrupted. In a sense, all the tensions that define the relations between the United States and Iran today are rooted in the fall of Mossadegh. An older Iranian once asked an American journalist, "Why did you Americans do that terrible thing? . . . To us, America was the great country, the perfect country, the country that helped us while other countries were exploiting us. But after that moment, no one in Iran ever trusted the United States again."

The coup preceded another historic event that would inspire young Muslims everywhere to rise up in defense of their country: the Algerian war for independence. In the academic Roy Mottahedeh's *The Mantle of the Prophet*, his book about the political evolution of a young religious Iranian man before the Iranian revolution, a group of Iranian students learn about the plight of Algerian fighters battling against the French during the Algerian war of the 1950s and '60s: hundreds had been burned alive in the Algerian desert. One student says, "The Iranians, as usual, confine themselves to weeping. If Mossadegh were still prime minister and we had freedom to act, Iran would do more than Egypt . . . We had a Rostam, a genuine lion." It was the Iranians, these young Iranians said, who "let the English and Americans take Mossadegh away. The shame is ours as much as anybody else's."

After Mossadegh, the Shah returned to power. The American ambassador recommended to the Shah to create an "undemocratic independent Iran." The Shah soon became one of the United States' closest allies. Iran was as much a modernizing ideal for the Americans as Turkey and Afghanistan had been. Modernization projects sprung up throughout the countryside, destroying local communities and draining the country of millions of dollars. As part of his "White Revolution," a massive modernization program "framed by Western ideas, experts, and aid," as the academic David Ekbladh writes, the Shah supported a development project in the Khuzestan region that would use five rivers for hydroelectric power and irrigation, with the goal of transforming indigenous agricultural practices. The regime predicted the area would become a "Garden of Eden," and for the Americans, according to Ekbladh, "one of the great symbols of postwar liberal development." Instead, the project was beset by technical problems, displaced thousands of people from their homes, and ultimately failed. Economic productivity in the region actually fell.

Between 1970 and 1979, the number of Americans in Iran jumped from eight thousand to fifty thousand. The scholar James A. Bill writes that "as time passed and the numbers grew, an increasingly high proportion of fortune hunters, financial scavengers, and the jobless and disillusioned recently returned from Southeast Asia found their way to Iran." Conservative and rural Iranians who came to Tehran for work found themselves alienated and bewildered by the Western clothes, values, and behavior celebrated in their capital city, its magazines and miniskirts. "We found ourselves wondering," one Iranian said, "is there any room for our own culture?"

At the same time, Iran became one of the United States' largest customers for weapons. The former CIA officer Kermit Roosevelt—a spy who played a large part in the overthrow of Mossadegh—now worked for the weapons dealer Northrop. Henry Kissinger promised Iran any non-nuclear weapon it wanted; the Shah once spent $10 billion on weapons in just one year. Many Iranians knew that SAVAK, the brutal secret police service, which employed as many as sixty thousand agents, as well as millions of informants, and was known for spectacular acts of torture and violence, had been trained by the CIA and Mossad. "Whoever fell into the grip of that organization," wrote the Polish journalist Ryszard Kapuściński, "disappeared without a trace, sometimes forever."

Just before the revolution in 1979, Kapuściński noted that among the Iranians' fiercest complaints were those directed at the thousands of foreign servicemen on their soil, all of them, especially Americans, operating with full diplomatic immunity. The Ayatollah Khomeini said, in one of his most famous speeches, "Our dignity has been trampled underfoot . . . If some American's servant, some American's cook, assassinates your marja in the middle of the bazaar, or runs over him, the Iranian police may not arrest him. Even if the Shah himself were to run over a dog belonging to an American, he would be prosecuted. But if an American's cook runs over the Shah, the head of state, no one will have the right to interfere with him." America and NATO had this diplomatic immunity arrangement in many countries, including Turkey, and it was deeply insulting to local people. The Shah's "Great Civilization" was for many Iranians another grand humiliation.

Living under such a dictatorship, with the secret police and an army of informants watching one's every move, Iranians found in the mosque a kind of sanctuary. The forceful and accelerated push for modernization amplified the power of the mosque. West-loving Turks feared that Turkey would become Iran under Erdoğan, but whenever I asked if they knew about the horrors of the Shah's era, they didn't believe me: "But it was modern." "It looked so much more Western." "Women didn't have to cover." All they could see, somewhat understandably, was visual evidence that a country could regress on women's rights. But Kapuściński saw this:

The Iranian who has been harassed at work, who encounters only grumpy bureaucrats looking for bribes, who is everywhere spied on by the police, comes to the mosque to find balance and calm, to recover his dignity. Here no one hurries him or calls him names. Hierarchies disappear, all are equal, all are brothers, and—because the mosque is also a place of conversation and dialogue—a man can speak his mind, grumble, and listen to what others have to say. What a relief it is, how much everyone needs it. This is why, as the dictatorship turns the screws and an ever more oppressive silence clouds the streets and workplaces, the mosque fills more and more with people and the hum of voices. Not all those who come here are fervent Muslims, not all are drawn by a sudden wave of devotion—they come because they want to breathe, because they want to feel like people.

If the Shah represented modernity to the Americans, his downfall to them was, according to the Palestinian intellectual Edward Said, a "casualty to what was looked upon as medieval fanaticism and religiosity." The Ayatollah Khomeini was just that medieval figure.

But within this paradigm, what were the Americans? During the Iranian hostage crisis of 1979 and 1980, in which fifty-two Americans were held captive at the U.S. embassy for 444 days, President Jimmy Carter pleaded with a French lawyer working for the Iranians: "You understand that these are Americans. These are innocents." The French lawyer recalled:

I said to him, yes, Mr. President, I understand that you say they are innocent. But I believe you have to understand that for the Iranians they aren't innocent. Even if personally none of them has committed an act, they are not innocent because they are diplomats who represent a country that has done a number of things in Iran . . .

But to Carter, as Said explains, "Americans were by definition innocent and in a sense outside history."

Some years after my Mississippi trips, I visited Iran as a tourist. In Tehran, I went to the SAVAK museum, which features in its exhibits the forms of torture and murder once devised and carried out between those very walls. Dummy models of Iranians are displayed: deranged-looking prisoners marching with right hands on shoulders in front of them; bloodied and scarred plastic faces of men in isolation cells; crazed-seeming figures with arms contorted behind their backs; enormously muscled prison guards administering electric shocks; naked, whipped, bloodied, wounded plastic dummies hanging from the walls. Over the loudspeakers, screams echoed through the halls. There was what appeared to be blood on the walls, and it was hot and musty inside. It went on and on, room after room of reenactments of torture, death, bloodletting: pouring hot water and sticking broken glass in the rectum, pulling out fingernails and teeth, beating people with copper whips, pinning them down on scalding bedsprings. There were helmets that magnified one's own screams, so that when an Iranian was being tortured all he heard was his own endless terror. The SAVAK museum had all the aesthetic and olfactory details of a haunted house—it smelled in fact like the inside of a rubber Halloween mask—which made the walls filled with the photos of all of its prisoners, men and women, religious and leftist, all the more powerful. A special showcase had been done for the jails of prominent Iranian dissidents; in a corner cell sat a weak but defiant-looking plastic dummy of the Ayatollah Khamenei.

The tour guides, recognizing that my friend and I were Americans, wanted us to know, judging by how many times they said it, that SAVAK had been supported by the United States, that in fact the techniques were taught to SAVAK by the Americans. (There was no mention of the current regime's ugly record of torture.) I was feeling faint, my coat and head scarf suffocating me, but I could hardly cut through the line—what if I offended the memory of the Ayatollah and drew attention to myself, the callous American, who didn't care about what we had done to the people of this country? The man leading the tour made eye contact with me with a sense of urgency.

When I told this story recently to a wealthy Turkish journalist in her seventies, a real grande dame, she said to me, smiling, with a good dose of condescension and anger: "I hate to tell you this, but your CIA taught our generals their torture techniques as well." She was referring to Turkey's 1980 coup.

To the Iranians, "modernity" had meant Americans on their soil, billions of dollars in weapons, dictatorship and poverty, the SAVAK museum.

In the region, "modernization" is, according to Said, "connected in the popular mind with foolish spending, unnecessary gadgetry and armaments, corrupt rulers, and brutal United States intervention in the affairs of small, weak countries." Yet to this day, when a journalist like myself arrives in a foreign country, modernity is the measurement through which all standards of "success" or goodness are judged, and the rejection of modernity by men such as the Iranian ayatollahs or those in al-Qaida or in the Islamic State is reviled as barbarism and backwardness, with complete disconnection from what modernization projects actually meant to that country's hapless subjects. Kapuściński seemed to have been writing about the imperial bloodlust of the Islamic State when he said almost forty years ago, of revolutionary Iran: "A nation trampled by despotism, degraded, forced into the role of an object, seeks shelter, seeks a place where it can dig itself in, wall itself off, be itself . . . This is why the gradual rebirth of old customs, belief, and symbols occurs under the lid of every dictatorship—in opposition to, against the will of the dictatorship. The old acquires a new sense, a new and provocative meaning."

IN TURKEY, ERDOĞAN'S people had mimicked this return to the old as well. "What does modern mean?" someone once asked Atatürk. "It means being a human being," he replied. Atatürk's conception of modernity and humanity, however, had meant the desecration of a culture—of religious motifs and beliefs, and people who wore the fez and the head scarf, and people who liked to pray in public. The Kemalist elite who defined the fashions and politics of the country took the expression of modernity further, celebrating a vision of secular, Western gentility. Erdoğan's own cultural revolution was to reinvigorate Ottoman themes in Turkish life: he spoke often of long-ago battles in Anatolia, some six hundred years old; he would build an Ottoman-style palace for himself decorated with life-size mannequins in Ottoman dress; his speaking events were soon accompanied by light shows and holograms depicting Mehmet the Conqueror on horseback invading Byzantium. Erdoğan even called himself the Conqueror. And in 2013, he proposed destroying tiny Gezi Park in the middle of Taksim Square in order to build a giant mall in the shape of Ottoman military barracks.

There was very little green space in Istanbul. Gezi Park was a rare sanctuary for trees. So in response to Erdoğan's decision, around fifty environmentalists in a city of fifteen million people pitched tents in Gezi to stop Erdoğan's destruction of it. The police attacked them viciously, but within a week, the activists' tiny sit-in spread to seventy cities. In Istanbul, almost every night, thousands of Turks streamed into Taksim Square and Gezi Park to celebrate what was a historic act of state defiance, the first of its kind in Turkey's recent history.

I was skeptical of Gezi at first, and after a couple of days, as usual, had gone to seek counsel from Caner. His wife had just had a baby, and that day he seemed consumed by the new demands of his life. In 2007, when I moved to Istanbul, he was the prism through which I saw Turkey. Back then the central preoccupation was whether Abdullah Gül would be allowed to become president, and whether Tayyip Erdoğan would be allowed to be in government at all. Caner had gently reminded me that both the Islamists and the secularists were equally horrible. The rising AK Party was bad, but the old elite was worse; in any case, neither cared about the poor and the dispossessed. I was sure the Gezi Park protest was merely another battle between these two powers, a Kemalist revolt against the Islamist ruler, and I thought my friend would be cynical, skeptical, unromantic about the protesters.

"So what do you think?" I said after we sat down.

"It is incredible," he replied, eyes shining. "I have never seen anything like this in my life."

"You're kidding me," I said. "Really? This isn't kids protesting supposed alcohol bans?"

"No, not at all," he said. "As it turns out, the only thing that could have brought all of us together was something as innocuous as a park."

For Rana, who by then was also married, to an American, and would soon have her own first son, it was a moment of political transformation; in future elections she would vote for a leftist party sympathetic to the Kurds. The 1980s generation, the kids who had been told to stay out of politics by parents terrified into submission by the 1980 coup, had learned from the nineties generation, who did not fear fighting the government. The Gezi Park protests were against economic disparities and police brutality, but also against a decade of Erdoğan's omnipotence, the creeping sense that he was never going away. Long ago, he promised his people real democracy. Now he was attacking teenagers with water cannons and ripping out the last trees from their concrete-covered city. The Minister of Trees had become a heartless thief.

I had been suspicious of Gezi because of the roots of my early days in Turkey, its twenty-first-century renaissance. When I arrived, the army had been eased out of politics like a senile king, intellectuals wrote in the newspapers about the Armenian genocide and the suffering of the Kurds, and women's rights had become part of the national conversation. Erdoğan had transformed the country's infrastructure and services, building highways and hospitals and putting in place universal health care. Istanbul changed dramatically; Rana, who usually moaned that she wished she lived in Manhattan, began saying, "Istanbul is where everything is happening now."

But Istanbul's era of regeneration and repair started acquiring the feeling of a crime scene. The city was being tortured: its parks peeled away, its shoreline mangled, its gardens ripped up, its hills sawed off for rich people's towers and rich people's malls, its woodlands bulldozed. The AK Party posted online sophisticated videos of entire neighborhoods, such as Okmeydanı, being replaced with new ones in fantastical urban regeneration schemes. Like a monster discovering this delicious country for the first time, the AK Party dammed the rivers, built hydroelectric and thermal power plants, and sent more men into coal mines—in part so the country would have enough electricity to eat up the forests and build hotels, and malls, and apartment buildings, and bridges, and tunnels, and airports. Nothing seemed to make Erdoğan happier than the smell of freshly laid asphalt.

Yet wasn't this what these nascent modernizing democracies were supposed to do? Westerners, comforted that the Muslims liked money just as much as they did, saw Turkey as a reassuring success story, a country experiencing growing pains endemic to progress. I, too, had been distracted by this illusion of progress. I was enraged about Wall Street greed and income inequality, even the ravaging effects of capitalism itself, and yet still I had thought, somewhere deep down, that Turkey under Erdoğan was getting better because it was imitating the West. Even when I saw the evidence of the system's ravages in America, I still saw countries like Turkey as "behind" us in some way, as if the course of maturity and democracy was to go through the same painful process we had. These ideas about my country and the world, no matter how often I challenged them, were foundational. Like many expatriates, I often reminded myself that I couldn't understand everything about Turkey because I wasn't Turkish. But the problem in seeing this foreign country clearly was not that I wasn't Turkish; it was that I was American.

The other person processing the world like me, in fact, was Erdoğan. In one way, he exploited cultural nostalgia for the Ottoman Empire as a retreat from the depredations of Kemalist modernity, but in other ways, Erdoğan was destructive capitalist progress in human form. After the mining disaster in Soma—which will be forever linked to Gezi in my mind—Erdoğan suggested that he was not responsible for the Soma tragedy, because Turkey, just like England in the nineteenth century, was industrializing, and would suffer some of the same consequences every developing nation has experienced. Erdoğan even called the Soma massacre the men's "fate," as if it were what God had wanted. Erdoğan was revealing something else: his fervent belief in the divine power of the capitalistic system he learned from the West and used for his own ends. By 2014, Erdoğan's lust for expansion would cause him to go to war, in Syria, and later in the eastern Kurdish lands of his own country. I had once unconsciously seen in Erdoğan's up-by-the-bootstraps background my own mythical American story; I had not known then what inevitably comes with that narrative: the longing and imperative for imperial power.

In 2014, I had gone to Soma in May, a time when the farm hills glow golden and the sun begins to burn white, and met a sensitive, angry young man named Rıza, at a teahouse near the black-windowed union to which he belonged. Rıza was very smart, and he had heavy-hooded brows, under which his eyes seemed to fire bullets. He had been a rescue worker the day of the mine fire, but what really enraged him were the systemic problems that afflicted workers, all of which he could outline with sophisticated scientific precision. He was even angry enough to tell an American journalist something I had never heard any Turkish man—or any man period—admit before.

"My wife stays home all day because she can't go visit friends because she has to calculate how much that will cost her," he said. "I can't even promise her a present. I don't have time to spend with my kids. And because of this, and how much the men work, domestic violence is rising, as are divorces. We're going crazy. They say Turkey is growing, but we are constantly shrinking."

He seemed to be admitting to me that the stress of their lives had been causing Turkish men to hit their wives. A liberal Turkish feminist and sociologist had once told me, at a time when a spike in domestic violence had caused many to cast blame on the AK Party's Islamic conservatism, that domestic violence was often a response to other forms of violence in the country and even in the world: wars, militarization, poverty. Rıza wanted me to understand that the labor conditions of Turkey were not just making work dangerous; they were shattering the larger society and reshaping the Turkish soul. Rıza, who had never graduated high school, had just articulated in a sentence what a thousand textbooks could not: that when an economic system humiliated its workers, when the system was, essentially, violent, it meant the humiliation and abuse of women, children, an entire society. Atatürk's new Turk had been remade into this traumatized man, forced to endure the habits of this new Turkey, Erdoğan's Turkey, which sounded a lot like what I had seen at home, in Mississippi, in America.

I had been startled at first when the miners used the word "octopus" to describe how power was enforced in Soma. At the turn of the previous century, the Big Four railroad monopoly in America, owned by the dominant oligarchs of the time, had also been called the octopus, its tentacles reaching into every aspect of American life, controlling government policy and political parties and citizens. But even American industrialists of those earlier eras eventually had been forced to cooperate with leftist movements and unions to improve working conditions for their employees, not because they were decent but because they were pragmatic. The industrial magnates had something to fear: socialism, communism, an alternative system, anything for which capitalism could be rejected. Over time, the possibility of any alternative faded, and one hundred years later, Turkish coal miners were thrust into a world subsumed by globalization. They had no protection. Neither, it would turn out, did the American workers who angrily cheered on the presidential candidate Donald Trump. Turkey and the United States, as I had discovered, often shared the same fate. That week in Soma, in 2014, I read in a book called *Turkish-U.S. Relations* that since the 1940s, as part of the Truman Doctrine and Marshall Plan, "America tried to shape and orient the Turkish labor movement in ways that would not conflict with its own benefits," and so the two longest periods of American imperial history—the Cold War and the age of neoliberalism—finally came together for me, in a coal mine, in Turkey.

A FEW OF the Iranian academics working on the health houses project came with their wives to Mississippi from Iran in 2010. They were shocked by what they saw: "This is America?" they said.

I felt the same way when I went to the Delta with Dr. Shirley and Dr. Shahbazi and another doctor named Eva Henderson-Camara. The first thing you notice about the Delta, especially when you've gone looking for images of poverty, is that you don't see any people. So much of it is bucolic and sun-dappled that at first it doesn't seem poor. When I made this observation, Claudia Cox had replied sternly, "That's because poverty in America doesn't look like what y'all think. It used to be bare feet, now it's Nikes. If I miss two months of work because I get sick, well, guess what? I'm in poverty. This is the new poverty. You don't know." The Delta was all segregated schools and unemployed men, drugs and poverty and sickness. There was no social life except for church and the juke joint. The porches of small houses sagged with the weight of old washing machines, televisions, and trash bags, as if a barricade against the world. The only place to shop for food was Walmart, Dollar General, or the Piggly Wiggly, and for some, these stores were fifty miles away. In what is one of the country's most fertile regions, many people of the Delta shopped for their groceries at the closest gas station market.

"Imagine waking up every morning and this is all you see," said Dr. Henderson-Camara, looking out the window. "And you think: Should I shoot myself now or later?"

Dr. Henderson-Camara, now in her sixties, grew up on a Delta plantation, a system that in Mississippi existed well into the 1970s. This plantation was her grandfather's, and he "treated us just like any plantation owner would." Kids worked much of the typical school year. Dr. Henderson-Camara escaped by winning a scholarship to Yale for a special program for disadvantaged students. She studied anthropology before she went to medical school and could quietly analyze the most basic of human interactions and spin them into an artful anthropological story.

When we sat down with white nurses in the Delta, she got angry.

"There's a lot of distrust," Dr. Henderson-Camara said about health services in the area, leaning forward. "We don't trust people who don't look like us. Having grown up in a very segregated community, I know this for a fact. When you walk out that door they will laugh and say 'I just told her that so she'll stop asking me questions.' But if you live in that community and sister Edna tells you something, you say, 'Now, Edna,' and she will say, 'Okay, you got me.' I have lived on a plantation and I have lived in the projects and people do not trust people who do not look like them. We are animals, dogs don't trust strange dogs, and human beings are the same."

"I don't think that's a problem here," replied one white nurse we met. "I may be way smoozed."

"I think you're smoozed."

"Do you?"

"I know you're smoozed."

"You think that people . . . are you saying . . . You're saying that basically from a racial perspective . . ."

"If you're not from the community—"

"But we are!"

"You are an outsider."

"I don't know, I have never been kicked out of a home."

"Oh, you don't get kicked out, you'll just be told a bunch of lies."

I remembered the first patient I had gone to see with Claudia Cox. He was fifty-six but looked about seventy and lived in a stale, small house with two limp dogs tied to a tree in the front yard. He was having seizures, and besides not having Medicaid and not having any refills on his prescription, the man was clutching a coffee cup in the afternoon and looked to be drunk. When Cox asked him in her smooth, warm Claudia Cox way if he had been drinking, he said no. The entire time he didn't look me in the eye—he actually didn't look at me, not once. Cox saw the man at the clinic the next day. This time when she asked him whether he'd been drinking, he said, "Aw, baby, you know . . ."

When I told Dr. Henderson-Camara about the drunk man, she nodded. "Well, a man of his generation wouldn't be looking at you out of respect."

"Because I am a younger woman," I said.

She waited patiently.

"Oh, sorry. Because I am white."

"And also because he is self-conscious," she said. "What happens sometimes during these encounters with health care professionals is that they are so self-conscious they can barely even hear."

I thought about my reporting trips in Turkey, in Egypt, in Greece, in Afghanistan, in America—my ten years abroad. I wondered how often it was that anyone told white Americans the truth.

The Egyptian writer Sonallah Ibrahim visited the United States in the 1990s. Ibrahim had viewed America as an overweening and destructive empire, but according to the scholar Mara Naaman, when he arrived at the source of world power, he was struck by the poverty and suffering he saw. Perhaps he had imagined a place of frivolous, wealthy people enjoying the fruits of their reign over the rest of the world. Surely, he could not hold all of these poor, marginalized people responsible for the suffering of his own Egyptian people. In his novel *Amrikanli*, he attempts to resolve the fact that this empire had not only exploited other nations, it had exploited its own people.

Perceiving the terrible connection between racism at home and imperialism abroad, Ibrahim saw that perhaps if the empire did decline, it would, as Baldwin had predicted long ago, first decline from within. After my time in Mississippi, I left America knowing for sure that the promise of the country had not failed with the financial crisis or September 11; it failed long ago. It failed itself, its own people, and its own ideals, in places like the Delta, in Athens and Cairo and Kabul and Tehran and Soma, in places Americans like myself had long ignored, long denied, all in preservation of that innocence that sets us apart from most everyone on earth. We cannot go abroad as Americans in the twenty-first century and not realize that the main thing that has been terrorizing us for the last sixteen years is our own ignorance—our blindness and subsequent discovery of all the people on whom the empire-that-was-not-an-empire had been constructed without our attention or concern.

"But, ma'am, I have a question for you," Ahmet, the Turkish miner who survived the Soma mine fire, had asked me. "Why didn't you come before the fire? Why didn't you think of us before?"

What I had wanted to say—but did not have the courage to say—were the reasons, Ahmet, I had not thought of so many things.

EPILOGUE

You must accept them and accept them with love. For these innocent people have no other hope. They are, in effect, still trapped in a history which they do not understand; and until they understand it, they cannot be released from it.

—JAMES BALDWIN

O N THE EVENING OF JULY 15, 2016, I was working at home when a friend from New York messaged to say she saw on Twitter that there was a military coup happening in Turkey. I immediately looked out the window, but for what, I do not know. "It's either a military coup or a massive antiterrorist operation," my Turkish friend, Aslı, said on the telephone. Army soldiers had taken over the main bridges in Istanbul, the ones that join Europe and Asia, the closeness of which I had, on my first day in Turkey nine years earlier, seen as hopeful.

Somehow I knew to go downstairs to the *tekel*, the only shop still open, to stock up on bottles of water, cans of beer, the remains of the Doritos and ketchup-flavored Ruffles, and to get cash out of the ATM. The hipsters of my neighborhood stuffed cans of Efes in their pockets; the shop owner asked everyone whether they were sure they didn't need three packs of cigarettes. On the sidewalks, many people stood still, scrolling through their phones. Some had their heads cast back, searching the sky.

Then, suddenly, as if on cue from some internal coup-recognition instinct, the Turks started walking quickly, to get inside. I did as well, though I of course had only *read* about the Turkish coups: 1960, the tanks in the streets and a prime minister executed; 1971, torture in the prisons; 1980, pure terror, a country forever transformed; 1997, the charismatic Islamist mayor of Istanbul sent to jail and turned into a national hero. Was this Erdoğan's fate? The leader born from a coup would be brought down by a coup?

Erdoğan had long warned that a coup against him was in the works, but the idea of a military coup happening in Erdoğan's Turkey, in which he seemed to control every aspect of state power, was actually so ludicrous that for a long time that evening few of us believed it was real. When I first saw on TV the handful of Turkish soldiers standing on the Bosphorus Bridge, I said, "What is this? This isn't a coup. Come on, this is Erdoğan." Just minutes later, when I saw those soldiers actually *shooting* Turkish people, I said, "Where is Erdoğan? Can someone get him back here so he can save the country?" I was terrified, and irrational. But that response captures how many of us had seen Erdoğan over the last decade: as either Satan or Superman, and rarely anything in between.

The night went on in its surreal way. A military jet bombed the Parliament building in Ankara. Taksim Square, up the street from my house, was occupied by tanks. Istanbul shook with tremendous booms that tweeters in Istanbul identified as bombs. I ran into my bathroom. It turned out, the booms were the putschists' fighter jets, flying so low and fast, they broke the speed of sound. In my neighborhood, windows shattered. But the coup failed.

The coup plotters, allegedly, were members of the Gülen movement, the one that had so tenderly inducted me into the world of Istanbul journalism in 2007, the one that wiretapped my journalist friends' phones, the ones whose schools I visited all over the world, from Kabul to Houston. By then Erdoğan had subsumed almost all of the institutions in the country; his only remaining enemy, it turned out, was the one from within. Neither Erdoğan nor the Gülenists, those who felt they couldn't control the military that once oppressed them, ever truly got over their obsession with dominating the Kemalist state. Its own violence and impenetrability had long ago created in both of them a natural and, apparently, pathological desire to capture it.

The attempted military coup of 2016 was a fracturing of Islamist power, rooted in a long history, and likely one that would emerge ever more important to understand in the years to come. It took me ten years to correct the crude categories I had once imposed on this country; that the so-called Islamists were a group of diverse longings, politics, and histories; and that the so-called secularists were not one monolithic group, either, but Alevis, Armenians, liberals, atheists, devout people, gays, Kurds, leftists, feminists, nationalists, and people who didn't care about politics or religion at all. The question now was whether in Turkey any such diversity would survive.

TURKEY BY THEN had already become a different place. By 2016, either ISIS or Kurdish militant groups had bombed Istanbul, and greater Turkey, some thirty times, including at the Istanbul airport, which I had observed on my first day as the airport of a stable country. The Turkish state had gone to war with the PKK again, and the cities of southeast Turkey looked like parts of Aleppo, blocks of buildings completely collapsed, rubble for miles. In Istanbul, raids against ISIS, or the PKK, or drug barons, seemed to occur every night, with police helicopters constantly circling the sky. Young people who were excited about Istanbul four years ago talked about relocating. "I don't want to raise my children here" was a common refrain among the half of the population who didn't vote for Erdoğan. The gaggles of foreigners walking down Istiklal Caddesi, their necks craning in delight as mine once had at Istanbul's many treasures, stopped coming.

Three million Syrian refugees now lived in Turkey. Housing projects Erdoğan had built on top of old Roma encampments, or had begun in rundown Kurdish neighborhoods, became largely occupied by families from

Damascus and Aleppo. It would have been strange ten, even five years ago, to hear men arguing in Arabic in the street, but Arabic was everywhere now, even back on shop signs in Beyoğlu, like it was a century ago, before Atatürk made the shopkeepers and schools take down that beautiful script that to him was backward in every way. It wasn't just Turkey; Athens, which I visited twice again in 2015, had become similarly deluged with refugees. Turkey and Greece, the two countries where the post-1945 world order began, had become the dumping grounds for all the broken products of that century: the war refugees and economic migrants, the terrorists and their hangers-on, the collapse of Europe and the collapse of the Middle East. The migrant and refugee phenomenon—the refusal of humans to accept the circumstances dealt to them—had begun to seem like the world-wide revolution so many had once predicted. They protested with their feet, they rebelled against borders, against passports, and against the absence of cooperation among nations, and they defied regional categories that kept them living in a disintegrating Middle East. Refugees rebelled against the superficial idea of East and West, for which Turkey had not been the bridge, I realized, but the wall that had once kept the two apart.

After the failed coup, Erdoğan's purge began. It is difficult to keep count of how many people he has purged from government, military, financial, educational, media, and corporate institutions, but estimates range around one hundred and twenty thousand. Ahmet Altan, whom I interviewed in 2007, was among the hundreds of journalists who went to jail. Members of the democratically elected Kurdish party went to jail, too. One of the last remaining opposition newspapers, *Cumhuriyet*, where one of my closest Turkish friends worked, was nearly shut down. Theater directors were detained for staging Bertolt Brecht. Thousands of teachers belonging to the same union were fired. Stories of torture, even rape, began slowly drifting from Turkish jails. Erdoğan began talking about reinstating the death penalty. The period felt like the time after the 1980 coup, when the Turkish military had gotten rid of the entire left and allowed for Islamic conservatism to fill the vacuum. I don't know what will someday fill this one.

For a while, anti-Americanism in Turkey spiked, largely because Erdoğan's newspapers wanted to whip up that old reliable nationalism to distract from the government's own mistakes. They claimed the Americans were behind the coup. My corner *bakkal* guys, İrfan and Bilal, whom I had known for seven years, even got angry at me for complaining when Erdoğan persecuted so many people. "This was a *coup*, Suzy!" they said. "Do you know what that means?" I didn't think the Americans had anything to do with the 2016 coup, but there was another reason that the Turks' suspicions weren't strange: because in the 1980s and 1990s, it was entirely plausible that the CIA had supported the Gülen movement as part of its Islamic green belt against communism. We would never know.

My *bakkal* guys and I made up quickly, though, because most Turks, like most of the rest of the world, had long grown accustomed to distinguishing between the American government and American citizens, and also because my daily apple juice, as İrfan noted sincerely, had nothing to do with politics. What was more disturbing to me, actually, was to watch America dismiss its alleged role in the military coup, as merely crazy conspiracy theories. Once again, the Americans were ignoring their own long, tangled history with a foreign country. The United States influenced Turkey for seventy years. It reorganized its military, put soldiers on its soil, and meddled in its domestic and foreign affairs. When I moved here in 2007, many Turks told me that if America would invade Iraq in the careless, groundless manner it did in 2003, then there was no reason to think Turkey wouldn't be next. This was the reality people lived in. The time had long passed when Americans should have learned to be more sensitive to the traumatized people of their former satellite countries. Sovereignty is a privilege that Americans take for granted. Much of the rest of the world still feels they must guard it with their lives.

After the coup, I even felt an unexpected sympathy for the Turkish people's nationalism. I could see how this nationalism—especially at a time when nations from West to East seemed to be crumbling apart—was the force that for some repaired the wounds of a coup in remarkable ways. Even people who hated Erdoğan despised the idea of a coup more. That November, when the sirens went off signaling the anniversary of Atatürk's death, I watched from my window. A man had stopped in the middle of the street. A woman paused on the curb. Someone got out of his car. Maybe these were people who didn't subscribe to Erdoğan's version of nationalism, but no matter; at that stage in world disorder, it was reassuring to see a moment of any nation's harmony. Even if, toward the end of the siren, a lone, young girl in full black head scarf and dress strode in between the frozen people, walking briskly as if there had been no siren at all.

MONTHS LATER, DONALD TRUMP became the president-elect of the United States, and my country, too, seemed to collapse, if only psychologically, into angry factions. (The day after the election, my Turkish Pilates teacher said, "Now you are Küçük Türkiye," or "Little Turkey.") In retrospect, the schism was a long time coming for all of us. The twentysomething life crisis that had propelled me out of New York and into Istanbul might have been much deeper than any crisis of gender, class, or profession. My crisis, like many other Americans', was about my American identity. Confusion over the meaning of one's country, and over that country's place in the world, for anyone, but especially for Americans, might be the most foundational identity crisis of all.

I knew Trump supporters, had grown up with them, had them in my family, and so I wasn't as surprised as some when he won. Afterward, my sense was that the phenomenon was more incoherent, fuzzy, irrational than any of the articles about coal country; Flint, Michigan; or the white working class ever showed. But I did believe that in at least one way Trump voters were little different from anyone else in the country. They, like all Americans, had been told a lie: that they were the best, that America was the best, that their very birthright was progress and prosperity and the envy and admiration of the world. I did not blame those voters for Trump's election, and I didn't even blame them, in all cases, for their racism. I blamed the country for Trump's election because it was a country built on the rhetoric and actions of white supremacy, by which I mean it was a country built on the rhetoric and actions of American supremacy. American supremacy, or "greatness," or "exceptionalism," had not, contrary to what many said painfully after the election, been a by-product of America's melting pot, or of America's celebration of diversity, or of its values of freedom, human rights, and democracy; it had been built on the presupposition that America was, and should be, the most powerful country on the planet. When both the most vulnerable and the most nationalistic sensed the slow draining of that power from their own hands, America began to break.

Trump also had been right about one thing: immigrants did get a free ride. They had been let into the country too easily. Immigrants did need stricter qualifications for citizenship. There was no doubt that the white European immigrants who one hundred years ago knocked on the doors of Ellis Island should have faced a higher bar for entry. They should have gotten a months-long education on the Americans' destruction of its indigenous populations, on its history of slavery, on its persecution of darker-skinned immigrants, on its invasion and occupation of Cuba and the Philippines— and later, on its vast and endless empire—and they should have been made to swear that they accepted this ugly American history as their own, that they vowed to take responsibility for it and its repercussions, and that they promised to protect nonwhite peoples as much as they protected their white selves—forever. This vow should have been the price of American citizenship. Because clearly something did go wrong in America. Americans had been bound to myth, not history. They got a free ride. We got a free ride. I got a free ride.

This Trump phenomenon has also been referred to as "white fragility," but white fragility is not just the problem of conservatives or red staters. White fragility also prevents elite white Americans from accepting—even with their meritocracy and Ivy League degrees and good intentions—that they, too, might not be exceptional, that they were the beneficiaries of a period of unprecedented national prosperity and military might, and that they, with their ignorance and even exploitation, had contributed to the anguish of foreigners and the pain of their own people. After Trump's election, the Vietnamese-American novelist Viet Thanh Nguyen wrote in *The New York Times*, "Empires rot from the inside even as emperors blame the barbarians." He could see America so much more clearly than so many Americans could.

From abroad, when I used to hear President Obama say that America is the greatest country on earth, I never felt contempt. I felt like I did as a child, not wanting to admit to my parents I knew there was no Santa Claus. When I consider giving this book to my parents—and to my figurative parents, the older Americans far more invested in American myths than I ever was—I feel a physical pain in my heart. The hurt is automatic, it is *from* me, I cannot control it. It is common to say Watergate shattered American innocence, that Vietnam shattered American innocence, that September 11 shattered American innocence, that Trump shattered American innocence. But this was all wishful thinking. American innocence never dies. That pain in my heart is my innocence. The only difference is that now I know it. If there was anything fully shattered during my years abroad, it was faith in my own objectivity, as a journalist or as a human being.

I might know, too, what Baldwin meant when he said only love could assuage America's race problem, but I can only grasp it when I think of romantic love. I did, after all, fall in love with Turkey. I fell in love with Istanbul, with Rana, with Caner, with all the Turks and *Istanbullus* who welcomed me; I fell in love with foreign men, with the cats of Cihangir, with the Anatolian roads, with even the smell of burning coal in winter. When you are in love, you feel a superhuman amount of empathy because, crucially, it is in your self-interest to do so. It wasn't until I loved like this that I could understand why only love could solve America's race problem, and by extension its imperial one: that it is not until one contemplates loving someone, caring about that person's physical and emotional well-being, wanting that person to thrive, wanting to protect that person, and most of all wanting to understand that person, that we can imagine what it would feel like if that person was hurt, if that person were hurt by others or, most important, if that person was hurt by you. Only if that person's suffering becomes your suffering—which is in a sense what love is—and only when white Americans begin to look upon another people's destruction as they would their own, will they finally feel the levels of rational and irrational rage terrifying enough to vanquish a century of their own indifference.

Who do we become if we don't become Americans? We are benevolent and ordinary and we are terrible things, too; we are missionaries and oil speculators, racists and soldiers, bureaucrats and financiers, occupiers and invaders, hope mongers and hypocrites. The American dream was to create our own destiny, but it's perhaps an ethical duty, as a human being, and as an American, to consider that our American dreams may have come at the expense of a million other destinies. To deny that is to deny the realities of millions of people, and to forever sever ourselves from humanity. I went abroad for the same reason everyone else does: to learn how to live. Whoever Americans become after this time of reckoning, it will, hopefully, not be about breaking from the past but about breaking from the habit of its disavowal. If this project of remembrance requires leaving the country, then so be it, because it is not an escape; we will find our country everywhere, among the city streets and town squares and empty fields of the world, where we may also discover that the possibility of redemption is not because of our own God-given beneficence but proof of the world's unending generosity.

NOTES

INTRODUCTION

6   *Soma's main street looked like many Turkish towns*: Quoted in Suzy Hansen, "It Had the Strange Light of Hell," *New York Times Magazine*, November 26, 2014.

12 *"King Hussein of the Hejaz Enjoys the Crane Bathroom"*: David Hapgood, *Charles R. Crane: The Man Who Bet on the People* (Bloomington, IN: Xlibris, 2001), 79.

12 *"Americans and especially American policy-makers were not well enough informed"*: Ibid., 91.

12 *"Each man will be undertaking perhaps as difficult a task as there is"*: Ibid., 92.

13 *"You do not know and cannot appreciate the anxieties that I have experienced"*: Erez Manela, *The Wilsonian Moment: Self-Determination and the International Origins of Anticolonial Nationalism* (New York: Oxford University Press, 2009), 215.

13 *"the least harmful solution"*: Quoted in Patrick Kinross, *Ataturk* (New York: William Morrow, 1969), 188.

14 *"genuinely democratic spirit"*: "Report of American Section of Inter-allied Commission on Mandates in Turkey," August 28, 1919.

14 *"knew the Fourteen Points by heart"*: Hapgood, *Charles R. Crane*, 60.

14 *"an awesome spectacle"*: "Report of American Section of Inter-allied Commission on Mandates in Turkey," August 28, 1919.

17 *"celebrity complex"*: Alison Lurie, "The Revolt of the Invisible Woman," *New York Review of Books*, May 9, 2013.

20 *"tragedy"*: James Baldwin, *Nobody Knows My Name* (New York: Random House, 1961), 12.

21 *"This is the way people react to the loss of empire"*: Ibid., 25.

23 *"headmistress of our country"*: Russell Brand, "I Always Felt Sorry for Her Children," *Guardian*, April 9, 2013.

24 *"There's an America that exists"*: Quoted in "Freedom of Speech, the Second Person, and 'Homeland,'" New York *Daily News*, October 24, 2012.

24 *"which decides what price some other country's civilian population must pay"*: Quoted in Kamila Shamsie, "The Storytellers of Empire," *Guernica*, February 1, 2012.

25 *"dependence on empire for their prosperity"*: Jackson Lears, *Rebirth of a Nation* (New York: HarperCollins, 2009), 279.

1. FIRST TIME EAST: TURKEY

37 *"I've been traveling around our country for a year'"*: Quoted in "Why America Napped," Suzy Hansen, Salon.com, October 2, 2001.

37 *"because it's being pitched to the world as righteous retaliation"*: John Edgar Wideman, "Whose War," *Harper's Magazine*, March 2002.

38 *"reality instructors"*: Clifford Geertz, "Which Way to Mecca?" *New York Review of Books*, June 12, 2003.

38 *"to arouse the West"*: Ibid.

42 *"If all Turkey's leaders come from the same Islamist background"*: Quoted in "Sex and Power in Turkey: Feminism, Islam, and the Maturing of Turkish Democracy," European Stability Initiative, June 2007.

42 *"driven out 'bag and baggage'"*: "Christians and the Turk," *New York Times*, June 21, 1896.

43 *"a community of individuals who have in common"*: Quoted in Üner Daglier, "Ziya Gokalp on Modernity and Islam: The Origins of an Uneasy Union in Contemporary Turkey," *Comparative Civilizations Review*, vol. 57 (2007): 58.

43 *"republic must be forced through"*: Quoted in Kinross, *Ataturk*, 379.

44 *"it was necessary to abolish the fez"*: Quoted in Sibel Bozdoğan, *Modernism and Nation Building* (Seattle: University of Washington Press, 2001), 56.

44 *"Turkish schoolbooks taught new generations"*: Quoted in Charles King, *Midnight at the Pera Palace: The Birth of Modern Istanbul* (New York: Norton, 2015), 189.

44 *"a racialized conception of* the history of all civilization": Ayşe Gül Altınay, *The Myth of the Military Nation* (New York: Palgrave Macmillan, 2005), 22.

45 *"a bare hillock"*: Christopher de Bellaigue, *Rebel Land: Unraveling the Riddle of History in a Turkish Town* (New York: Penguin Press, 2010), 153.

45 *"Turkish architects today abandoned domes"*: Behcet and Bedrettin, "Turk Inkilap Mimarısı," 1933; quoted in Bozdoğan, *Modernism and Nation Building*, 56.

45 *"The temples that the Egyptians"*: Quoted in Bozdoğan, ibid., 106.

46 *"appealed particularly to 'planners'"*: Ibid., 6.

46 *"the universal trajectory of progress"*: Ibid., 106.

46 *"leaving them in their underpants"*: Quoted in Hale Yilmaz, *Becoming Turkish: Nationalist Reforms and Cultural Negotiations in Early Republican Turkey* (New York: Syracuse University Press, 2013), 133.

46 *"What was the woman of fifteen years ago"*: Quoted in Bozdoğan, *Modernism and Nation Building*, 82.

46 *"What does the word 'modern' mean?"*: Quoted in Kinross, *Ataturk*, 432.

47 *"The advance in little more than a decade from the veil"*: *New York Times*, June 20, 1937; quoted in Altınay, *The Myth of the Military Nation*, 45.

49 *"No one who's even slightly Westernized"*: Orhan Pamuk, *Snow* (New York: Knopf, 2005), 203.

55 *"There is something called 'neighborhood pressure'"*: Quoted in Cüneyt Ülsever, "An Analysis of the AKP," *Hurriyet Daily News*, May 26, 2007.

57 *"They're all orphans of a civilization collapse"*: Ahmet Hamdi Tanpınar, *A Mind at Peace* (Brooklyn: Archipelago Books, 2008), 219.

57 *"Atatürk has had to force through everything"*: Quoted in Karlheinz Barck and Anthony Reynolds, "Walter Benjamin and Erich Auerbach: Fragments of a Correspondence," *Diacritics* 22, no. 3/4 (2008): 81–83.

57 *"Ours was the guilt, loss"*: Orhan Pamuk, *Istanbul: Memories and the City* (New York: Vintage, 2006), 211.

61 *"Western leaders have been scouring"*: Andrew Purvis, "The 2004 Time 100," *Time*, April 26, 2004.

68 *"did not think the novel was about Africa at all"*: Chimamanda Ngozi Adichie, *Americanah* (New York: Knopf, 2013), 190.

2. FINDING ENGIN: TURKEY

69 *In those early years, Turkish women often asked me what I thought of Turkish men*: Suzy Hansen, "There Goes the Neighborhood," *The National*, 2008.

70 *"When you see a beautiful woman in the street"*: Quoted in Orhan Pamuk, *Istanbul: Memories and the City*, 140.

70 *"scowls"*: Orhan Pamuk, *The Black Book* (New York: Farrar, Straus and Giroux, 1994), 303.

79 *"What I was really feeling, during these journeys"*: Joseph O'Neill, *Blood-Dark Track* (London: Granta, 2001), 305.

82 *"humiliation"*: Orhan Pamuk, *Other Colors* (New York: Vintage, 2007), 328.

83 *"Yes, despicable as it may sound"*: Mohsin Hamid, *The Reluctant Fundamentalist* (Orlando, FL: Harcourt, 2007), 72.

89 *"its values and steadfast adherence"*: David F. Schmitz, *Thank God They're on Our Side: The United States and Right-Wing Dictatorships* (Chapel Hill: University of North Carolina Press, 1999), 306.

90 *"But I have always been struck"*: James Baldwin, *No Name in the Street* (New York: Dial Press, 1972), 53.

90 *"All of the Western nations have been caught in a lie"*: Ibid., 85.

90 *"White Americans are probably the sickest"*: Ibid., 55.

91 *"White children, in the main"*: Ibid., 128.

91 *"Unjust societies tend to cloud the minds of those who live within them"*: Jonathan Lear, "Waiting with Coetzee," *The Raritan*, Spring 2015, 1–26.

93 *Around that time a bomb went off in the Istanbul neighborhood of Güngören*: Suzy Hansen, "Istanbul Asks: Why Gungoren?" *New York Observer*, July 31, 2008.

98 *"produced carnage"*: Drew Faust, *This Republic of Suffering* (New York: Vintage, 2008), xii.

98 *After fifteen months in Istanbul, I finally met Engin Cezzar*: Suzy Hansen, "The Importance of Elsewhere," *The National*, July 3, 2009.

104 *"people who, whatever they are pretending"*: Ibid.

104 *"Christianity has operated with an unmitigated arrogance and cruelty"*: James Baldwin, *The Fire Next Time* (New York: Dial Press, 1963), 45.

104 *"In order to deal with the untapped"*: Ibid., 39.

104 *"I feel free in Turkey"*: Quoted in Magdalena J. Zaborowska, *James Baldwin's Turkish Decade: Erotics of Exile* (Durham, NC: Duke University Press, 2009), 87.

105 *"The American power follows one everywhere"*: Ibid., 18.

105 *"imperial presence"*: Ibid., 17.

105 *"power politics and foreign aid . . . in that sort of theatre"*: Ibid., 99.

106 *"When the ship anchored"*: Quoted in Aylin Yalçın, "American Impact on Turkish Social Life (1945–1965)," *Journal of American Studies of Turkey* 15 (2002): 41–54.

106 *"Turkish children to love the white Americans and hate the Indians"*: Ibid.

3. A COLD WAR MIND: AMERICA AND THE WORLD

109 *"American ignorance is a new phenomenon"*: Quoted in Zaborowska, *James Baldwin's Turkish Decade*, 25.

110 *"empire"*: Tony Judt, "Dreams of Empire," *New York Review of Books*, November 4, 2004.

111 *"a rattling of chains, always was"*: D. H. Lawrence, *Studies in Classic American Literature* (New York: Penguin Classics, 1990), 17.

111 *"creating of more and higher wants"*: Quoted in Lears, *Rebirth of a Nation*, 32.

112 *"sincere"*: William Appleman Williams, *The Tragedy of American Diplomacy* (New York: W. W. Norton, 1972), 2.

112 *"rational man who stood at the center of an enlightened world"*: Greg Grandin, *The Empire of Necessity: Slavery, Freedom, and Deception in the New World* (New York: Metropolitan Books, 2014), 8.

114 *"world power was thrust upon"*: Williams, *The Tragedy of American Diplomacy*, 20.

115 *"like children, like schoolboys on holiday"*: Curzio Malaparte, *The Skin* (New York: New York Review of Books Classics, 2013), 194.

115 *"would blush crimson"*: Ibid., 20.

115 *"men can recover"*: Ibid., 61.

115 *"as though with enough time"*: James Baldwin, *Giovanni's Room* (New York: Vintage, 2013; orig. pub. 1956), 34.

115 *"founded on the conviction"*: Malaparte, *The Skin*, 63.

115 *"they believe that a conquered nation"*: Ibid., 15.

116 *"The source of the plague"*: Ibid., 34.

116 *"carpet of human skin"*: Ibid., 293.

116 *"It is a shameful thing to win a war"*: Ibid., 334.

116 *"a hole in human history"*: Quoted in Ran Zwigenberg, *Hiroshima: The Origins of Global Memory Culture* (Cambridge, UK: Cambridge University Press, 2014), 17.

116 *"I don't want to be told"*: Doris Lessing, *The Golden Notebook* (New York: Simon & Schuster, 1984), 452.

116 *"The eyebrows of some were burned off"*: John Hersey, *Hiroshima* (New York: Vintage, 1989), 29.

117 *"even touch on the public debate"*: Gore Vidal, "Tenacity," *The New Yorker*, February 1, 1963.

117 *"the moment when total war"*: Garry Wills, "Carter and the End of Liberalism," *New York Review of Books*, May 12, 1977.

117 *"it was naïve to imagine that serious treatment"*: John Dower, *Ways of Forgetting, Ways of Remembering* (New York: New Press, 2012), 176.

118 *"was to advance the claim that it did not exist"*: Frances Stonor Saunders, *The Cultural Cold War: The CIA and the World of Arts and Letters* (New York: New Press, 2000), 1.

119 *"a way station in humankind's attempt"*: Robert Herzstein, *Henry R. Luce, Time, and the American Crusade in Asia* (New York: Cambridge University Press, 2006), 2.

119 *"If we had to choose one word"*: Quoted in Alan Brinkley, *The Publisher* (New York: Knopf, 2010), 312.

119 *"toward the anti-Communist cause'"*: Herzstein, *Henry R. Luce*, 211.

120 *"fortified democratic values at home and abroad"*: Eric Bennett, "How Iowa Flattened Literature," *Chronicle of Higher Education*, February 10, 2014.

120 *"preoccupied by family and self"*: Eric Bennett, *Workshops of Empire: Stegner, Engle, and American Creative Writing During the Cold War* (Iowa City: University of Iowa Press, 2015), 38.

121 *"Today's creative-writing department"*: Bennett, "How Iowa Flattened Literature."

121 *"The thing to lament"*: Ibid.

121 *"the fruits of the free world"*: Quoted in Annabel Jane Wharton, *Building the Cold War* (Chicago: University of Chicago Press, 2001), 8.

121 *"not only to produce a profit"*: Ibid.

122 *"my parents attended the opening of the hotel"*: Orhan Pamuk, *The Museum of Innocence* (New York: Knopf, 2009), 101.

123 *"The United States is no longer a spatially distant entity"*: Claus Offe, *Reflections on America: Tocqueville, Weber and Adorno in the United States* (Malden, MA: Polity, 2005), 98.

123 *"an existential debt of gratitude"*: Quoted in Offe, ibid., 70.

123 *"a totalitarian structure of a medieval kind"*: Italo Calvino, *Hermit in Paris: Autobiographical Writings* (New York: Vintage, 2004), 49.

124 *"country where everything is done to prove"*: Albert Camus, *American Journals* (New York: Spear Marlowe, 1995), 43.

124 *"self-assurance and confidence"*: Octavio Paz, *Labyrinth of Solitude* (New York: Grove Press, 2009), 21.

125 *"It is impossible to hold back a giant"*: Ibid., 219.

125 *"I think the only purpose of military aid"*: Saadat Manto, *Letters to Uncle Sam*, http://www.urduacademy2012.ghazali.net/Manto_Letters_to_Uncle_Sam1.pdf.

125 *"We must embark on a bold new program"*: Harry S. Truman, "Inaugural Address: 1949," Harry S. Truman Library and Museum, https://www.trumanlibrary.org/whistlestop/50yr_archive/inaugural20jan1949.htm.

126 *"diminish other people by exaggerating"*: Michael Hunt, *Ideology and U.S. Foreign Policy* (New Haven: Yale University Press, 2009), 176.

126 *"irresistible and obviously superior path"*: Hemant Shah, *The Production of Modernization: Daniel Lerner, Mass Media, and the Passing of Traditional Society* (Philadelphia: Temple University Press, 2011), 1.

127 *"sincerely interested in improving the welfare"*: Nils Gilman, *Mandarins of the*

Future: *Modernization Theory in Cold War America* (Baltimore: Johns Hopkins University Press, 2004), 22.

128 *"like the person who measures"*: Quoted in Shah, *The Production of Modernization*, 6.

128 *"The United States is presiding"*: Quoted in Daniel Lerner, *The Passing of Traditional Society* (New York: Free Press, 1958), 43.

129 *"after the fashion of Kemal Atatürk"*: Quoted in Schmitz, *Thank God They're on Our Side*, 201.

129 *"American advisors wanted to replace"*: Nicholas Danforth, "Malleable Modernity: Rethinking the Role of Ideology in American Policy, Aid Programs, and Propaganda in Fifties Turkey," *Diplomatic History*, April 2014.

130 *"It was more than a decade"*: Ibid.

130 *"U.S. officials believed that wanting to be modern"*: Ibid.

130 *"state of noble innocence"*: Anatol Lieven, "US/USSR," *London Review of Books*, November 16, 2006.

4. BENEVOLENT INTERVENTIONS: GREECE AND TURKEY

133 *"a condition of the soul"*: Michael Wood, "Americans on the Prowl," *New York Times*, October 10, 1982.

133 *"Wasn't there a sense"*: Don DeLillo, *The Names* (New York: Vintage, 1989), 58.

133 *"I think it's only in a crisis"*: Ibid., 41.

133 *"humor of personal humiliation"*: Ibid., 7.

134 *"'All countries where the United States'"*: Ibid., 58.

136 *The streets of central Athens*: Suzy Hansen, "A Finance Minister Fit for a Greek Tragedy?" *New York Times Magazine*, May 20, 2015.

136 *For much of the last century, Greece had been run*: Suzy Hansen, "Life Amid the Ruins," *Bloomberg Businessweek*, November 2010.

138 *"The flames may die down"*: Quoted in Helena Smith, "In Athens, Middle Class Rioters Are Buying Rocks," *Guardian*, December 12, 2008.

141 *"'young' or 'immature' appears throughout"*: Gilman, *Mandarins of the Future*, 170.

143 *"national character"*: Quoted in Schmitz, *Thank God They're on Our Side*, 106.

143 *"disinclination to obey a leader"*: Ibid., 106.

143 *"savior of the country"*: Ibid., 112.

144 *"The very existence of the Greek state is today"*: Quoted in *Public Papers of the Presidents of the United States: 1947* (United States Government Printing Office, 1965), 56.

145 *"We have to stand for decency and for freedom"*: Quoted in Kati Marton, *The Polk Conspiracy: Murder and Cover-Up in the Case of CBS News Correspondent George Polk* (New York: Farrar, Straus and Giroux, 1990), 81.

146 *"American are now so numerous"*: Quoted in ibid.

146 *"American officials were given authority"*: Quoted in Robert V. Keeley, *The Colonels' Coup and the American Embassy: A Diplomat's View of the Breakdown of Democracy in Cold War Greece* (University Park, PA: Penn State University Press, 2011), xvii.

146 *"no cameras to expose the ravaged faces"*: Marton, *The Polk Conspiracy*, 93.

147 *"an omnipotent Communist Party taking orders"*: James Becket, *Barbarism in Greece* (New York: Walker, 1970), 10.

147 *"In the Cold War lexicon"*: Marton, *The Polk Conspiracy*, 143.

148 *"I have come to Guatemala to use the big stick"*: Quoted in Tim Weiner, *Legacy of Ashes* (New York: Anchor, 2008), 107.

148 *"Public opinion in the U.S."*: Quoted in Piero Gleijeses, *Shattered Hope: The Guatemalan Revolution and the United States, 1944–1954* (Princeton, NJ: Princeton University Press, 1992), 257.

148 *"a shock wave of anti-American feeling"*: Alex Von Tunzelmann, *Red Heat: Conspiracy, Murder, and the Cold War in the Caribbean* (Toronto: McClelland and Stewart, 2011), 56.

148 *"You do not want Walt Whitman"*: Quoted in Greg Grandin, *The Last Colonial Massacre: Latin America in the Cold War* (Chicago: University of Chicago Press, 2011).

149 *"capitalism"*: Von Tunzelmann, *Red Heat*, 107.

149 *"the obedient army"*: Quoted in Von Tunzelmann, ibid., 42.

149 *"Do nothing to offend the dictators"*: Quoted in Schmitz, *Thank God They're on Our Side*, 185.

149 *"Vietnam is the place"*: Quoted in Von Tunzelmann, *Red Heat*, 229.

150 *"The key question is to pass beyond the facts"*: Quoted in Gabriel García Márquez, "The CIA in Latin America," *New York Review of Books*, August 7, 1975.

151 *"The kid who owns the ball is usually captain"*: Quoted in Benn Steil, *The Battle of Bretton Woods: John Maynard Keynes, Harry Dexter White, and the Making of a New World Order* (Princeton, NJ: Princeton University Press, 2013), 9.

152 *"a controlled disintegration"*: Quoted in Yanis Varoufakis, *The Global Minotaur* (New York: Zed Books, 2013), 100.

153 *"This smells like Indonesia"*: Quoted in Neni Panourgia, *Dangerous Citizens: The Story of the Greek Left* (New York: Fordham University Press, 2009), 133.

154 *"involvement in torture went beyond simply moral support"*: Becket, *Barbarism in Greece*, xii.

156 *"unpleasantness"*: Lieven, "US/USSR."

158 *"between Turkish labor and anti-communist"*: Amy Austin Holmes, *Social Unrest and American Military Bases in Turkey and Germany Since 1945* (New York: Cambridge University Press, 2014), 56.

158 *"economic rather than political"*: Quoted in ibid., 56.

158 *whom a CIA officer once tried*: Marc Edward Hoffman, "As Big as Mount Ararat," *The Nation*, June 24, 2010.

158 *"from the disgust of other nations"*: Quoted in Charlotte Wolf, *Garrison Community: A Study of an Overseas American Military Colony* (Westport, CT: Greenwood Press, 1970), 41.

159 *"Fuck your parliament"*: Quoted in Gary Younge, "Obama's Dilemma Is America's Appetite for Power but Aversion to Risk," *Guardian*, September 7, 2014.

160 *"It was widely believed that the military"*: Maureen Freely, *Enlightenment* (New York: Overlook Press, 2008), 26.

5. MONEY AND MILITARY COUPS: THE ARAB WORLD
AND TURKEY

164 *"freedom"*: Anthony Shadid, *Night Draws Near* (New York: Henry Holt, 2005), 15.

164 *In the fall of 2011, six months after the revolution*: Suzy Hansen, "Egypt's Mean Queen," *Newsweek*, January 2012.

172 *"It makes me turn your question round and round"*: Nawal El Saadawi, *The Nawal El Saadawi Reader* (London: Zed Books, 1997), 117.

172 *"to attempt to evangelize the lands of the Bible"*: Ussama Makdisi, *Faith Misplaced: The Broken Promise of U.S.-Arab Relations* (New York: PublicAffairs, 2010), 19.

173 *"openly blaspheme or insult"*: Ibid., 29.

173 *"I cannot tell you"*: Ibid., 39.

173 *"literate, scientific"*: Ibid., 65.

173 *"Sarruf and Nimr extolled"*: Ibid., 70.

174 *"Roosevelt should act"*: Ibid., 84.

174 *"Here was the man of the Fourteen Points"*: Muhammad Haykal, quoted in Manela, *The Wilson Moment*, 149.

175 *"To place the brunt of the burden"*: Quoted in Makdisi, *Faith Misplaced*, 178.

176 *"The Americans were something completely new and strange"*: Abdelrahman Munif, *Cities of Salt* (New York: Vintage, 1989), 44.

176 *"Why did they have to live like this"*: Ibid., 595.

176 *"insufficiently Westernized to produce a narrative"*: John Updike, "Satan's Work and Silted Cisterns," *The New Yorker*, 1988.

177 *"ruthless and efficient"*: Hazem Kandil, *Soldiers, Spies, and Statesmen: Egypt's Road to Revolt* (New York: Verso, 2014), 23.

178 *"Nasser may have fallen"*: Makdisi, *Faith Misplaced*, 299.

178 *"I almost died of disgrace"*: Quoted in Kandil, *Soldiers, Spies, and Statesmen*, 152.

178 *"a perpetually dependent market"*: Kandil, ibid., 161.

178 *"Phillips, Toshiba, Gillette"*: Sonallah Ibrahim, *The Committee* (Syracuse, NY: Syracuse University Press, 2001), 18.

179 *"While the words used for God and love"*: Ibid., 18.

181 *"Merak etmeyin"*: Quoted in Mehmet Ali Birand, *The Generals' Coup: An Inside Story of 12 September 1980* (London: Brassey's, 1987), 172.

181 *"Should we not hang them?"*: Quoted in Stephen Kinzer, "Kenan Evren, 97, Dies; After Coup, Led Turkey with Iron Hand," *New York Times*, May 9, 2015.

182 *"The policy was not necessarily to kill you in jail"*: Ibid.

182 *"Your boys have finally done it!"*: Quoted in Birand, *The Generals' Coup*, 185.

182 *"We admire the way in which order"*: Quoted in "From the Editors," Middle East Research and Information Project (MERIP), Summer 2016.

182 *"more subtle, more cunning and terrifyingly effective"*: Quoted in "Mr. Allende Follows Outlines of Speech," *New York Times*, December 5, 1972.

183 *"We lived in a country totally isolated from the world"*: Quoted in Claire Sadar, "I Only Remember Fear," Muftah.org, September 11, 2015.

185 *"the collective well-being of the nation"*: Kandil, *Soldiers, Spies, and Statesmen*, 212, quoting Timothy Mitchell in "Dreamland: The Neoliberalism of Your Desires," MERIP 279, Summer 2016.

186 *"Simply because we are forced to say yes"*: Galal Amin, *Egypt in the Era of Hosni Mubarak* (Cairo: American University in Cairo Press, 2011), 169.

186 *"Since the rejection of the West"*: Salim Yaqub, *Containing Arab Nationalism: The Eisenhower Doctrine and the Middle East* (Chapel Hill: University of North Carolina Press, 2004), 9.

186 *"Bin Laden rejected the secular"*: Makdisi, *Faith Misplaced*, 340.

186 *"The one thing that everybody in the prison"*: Quoted in David Kirkpatrick, "U.S. Citizen, Once Held in Egypt's Crackdown, Becomes Voice for Inmates," *New York Times*, August 28, 2015.

188 *"Baghdad University in the 1980s"*: Tariq Ali, "The New World Disorder," *London Review of Books* (April 9, 2015): 19–22.

188 *"The Arabs were once a great civilization"*: David Riesman, introduction to Daniel Lerner, *The Passing of Traditional Society*, 13.

6. LITTLE AMERICAS: AFGHANISTAN, PAKISTAN, AND TURKEY

191 *"reverse the momentum and gain time"*: Quoted in Helene Cooper, "U.S. Eyes New Target: Heartland of Taliban," *New York Times*, February 26, 2010.

193 *"do the things we thought the Americans"*: Qais Akbar Omar, "Where Is My Ghost Money?" *New York Times*, May 4, 2013.

202 *"Afghan people's right to freedom"*: Shamsie, "The Storytellers of Empire."

202 *"public floggings and hangings"*: Ibid.

202 *"By the mid-eighties"*: Kamila Shamsie, "Pop Idols," *Granta* 112, September 2010.

203 *"Please explain"*: Shamsie, "The Storytellers of Empire."

203 *In 2009, General McChrystal had promised*: Suzy Hansen, "The Nowhere War," *Bookforum*, June 2014.

204 *"carried out raids against a phantom enemy"*: Anand Gopal, *No Good Men Among the Living* (New York: Henry Holt, 2014), 110.

204 *"As the soldiers approached a home"*: Ibid., 220.

204 *"All ISAF personnel must show respect for local cultures"*: Quoted in Vanessa Gezari, *The Tender Soldier: A True Story of War and Sacrifice* (Simon & Schuster, 2014), 24.

204 *"What we need is cultural intelligence"*: Ibid.

205 *"If you could have found a way to project"*: Ibid., 198.

209 *"aimed at propagating a strict religious fundamentalism"*: Banu Eligür, *The Mobilization of Political Islam in Turkey* (New York: Cambridge University Press, 2010), 113.

209 *"improvement of our relations"*: Ibid., 116.

209 *"an inextricable part"*: Ibid., 116.

209 *"Both 'red imperialism' and 'capitalist imperialism'"*: Julia Alexandra Oprea, "State-Led Islamization: The Turkish-Islamic Synthesis," *Studia Universitatis "Petru Maior,"* issue 1, 2014, 131–39.

209 *"useful tool for creating citizens"*: Eligür, *The Mobilization of Political Islam in Turkey*, 93.

210 *"tactically opened up a social and political space"*: Ibid., 24.

210 *"His dream was to make Turkey another America"*: Sedat Laçiner, "Turgut Ozal Period in Turkish Foreign Policy," *USAK (Uluslararası Stratejik Araştırmalar Kurumu)* 2 (2009): 153–205.

212 *"Of course Uncle Sam isn't sending you"*: United States Department of Defense, *A Pocket Guide to Turkey* (June 11, 1953), 3.

213 *"All I knew was that I was stuck"*: George Orwell, "Shooting an Elephant," *George Orwell: An Age Like This, 1920–1940* (Boston: David R. Godine, 2000), 236.

7. AMERICAN DREAMS: AMERICA, IRAN, AND TURKEY

217 *"the standard by which this nation's commitment"*: John Dittmer, *Local People: The Struggle for Civil Rights in Mississippi* (Champaign: University of Illinois Press, 1995), 425.

217 *"Has the American dream been achieved"*: James Baldwin, "The American Dream and the American Negro," *New York Times*, March 7, 1965.

219 *Dr. Shirley was a rabble-rouser*: Suzy Hansen, "Hope in the Wreckage," *New York Times Magazine*, July 2012.

226 *"instill panic that the country was sliding towards a communist takeover"*: Christopher de Bellaigue, *Patriot of Persia* (New York: Harper, 2012), 221.

226 *"Why did you Americans do that terrible thing?"*: Quoted in Stephen Kinzer, *All the Shah's Men: An American Coup and the Root of Middle East Terror* (Hoboken, NJ: Wiley & Sons, 2008), xxv.

227 *"undemocratic independent Iran"*: Quoted in de Bellaigue, *Patriot of Persia*, 254.

227 *"one of the great symbols of postwar liberal development"*: David Ekbladh, *The Great American Mission: Modernization and the Construction of an American World Order* (Princeton, NJ: Princeton University Press, 2011), 231.

227 *"as time passed and the numbers grew"*: Quoted in Michael Axworthy, *Revolutionary Iran: A History of the Islamic Republic* (New York: Oxford University Press, 2013), 80.

227 *"We found ourselves wondering"*: Quoted in ibid., 81.

228 *"Whoever fell into the grip of that organization"*: Ryszard Kapuściński, *Shah of Shahs* (New York: Knopf, 2014), 46.

229 *"The Iranian who has been harassed at work"*: Ibid., 76.

229 *"casualty to what was looked upon as medieval fanaticism and religiosity"*: Edward Said, *Covering Islam: How the Media and the Experts Determine How We See the Rest of the World* (New York: Vintage, 1997), ii.

229 *"You understand that these are Americans"*: Quoted in ibid., xv.

231 *"connected in the popular mind with foolish spending"*: Ibid., 30.

231 *"A nation trampled by despotism"*: Kapuściński, *Shah of Shahs*, 113.

233 *But Istanbul's era of regeneration and repair*: Suzy Hansen, "Diary: Istanbul," *London Review of Books*, May 2015.

235 *"America tried to shape and orient the Turkish labor movement"*: Ralph H. Salmi

and Gonca Bayraktar Durgun, *Turkish-U.S. Relations: Perspectives from Ankara* (Boca Raton, FL: BrownWalker Press, 2005), 82.

EPILOGUE

243 *What was more disturbing to me*: Suzy Hansen, "Corruptions of Empire," *The Baffler* no. 33, 2016.
245 *"Empires rot from the inside"*: Viet Thanh Nguyen, "The End of Empire," *New York Times*, November 9, 2016.

ACKNOWLEDGMENTS

This book could not have been written without the advice, love, and support of others. As a journalist and an American abroad, I have been privileged to meet so many incredible people—they invited me into their lives, gave me their time, and answered my endless questions. Their wisdom has been a gift. I am also indebted to hundreds of writers who informed this book.

A special thanks to the Institute of Current World Affairs, and particularly Steve Butler, for choosing me for the incomparably generous and thrilling ICWA fellowship, even though I couldn't pronounce the word "Erdoğan." It changed my life forever, and you will always have my gratitude.

Over the years, so many editors have nurtured my articles and much of this book into fruition: Chris Lehmann, Lidija Haas, Lindsey Gilbert, Hugo Lindgren, Sheelah Kolhatkar, Christian Lorentzen, Sarah Goldstein, Jonathan Shainin, Tom McGeveran, Josh Benson, Taylor Antrim, Rebecca Dana, Emily Biuso, Allen Freeman, Chloe Schama, and Rachel Morris. I am especially grateful to Dean Robinson, Bill Wasik, and Jake Silverstein, and to Cynthia Cotts and the heroic *New York Times* magazine fact-checking staff, who save us all from ourselves.

My agent, Amanda Urban, took a chance on an unformed idea and offered me guidance, friendship, and love—Binky, it is a privilege to know you. I am also lucky to have the best editor in the world, Eric Chinski, who seemed to know exactly what this book was, even before I did. He made every word of it better, and the last few years a total pleasure.

Thank you, too, to the wonderful people at FSG: Jonathan Galassi; Jeff Seroy and Sarita Varma; the very patient Laird Gallagher; Rob Sternitzky and Debra Helfand, for handling the manuscript with care; and Richard Oriolo, for his beautiful design. Thank you to Julie Tate for her eleventh-hour fact-checking.

My reporting abroad would not have been possible, period, without Caner, Arif Afzalzada, Iason Athanasiadis, Olga Alexopoulou, and Mandi Fahmy.

My brilliant and loving friends read this manuscript carefully and improved it immeasurably: Pankaj Mishra, Mary Mount, Jessica Alexander, Hillary Frey, Sarah Topol, Olga Alexopoulou, Alex Travelli, Jenna Krajeski, Aslı, Rana, Nichole Sobecki, Gloria Fisk, Caroline Finkel, Tobias Garnett, and Izzy Finkel, whose critique was so comprehensive, it practically came in book-length form. Dawn MacKeen, Sarah Goldstein, Catherine Steindler, Yasmine Seale, and Lidija Haas also went above and beyond. To Meg Sylvester, Sheelah Kolhatkar, Mark Lotto, Lydia Polgreen, Anna Louie Sussman, the *New York Observer* crew, Laura Miller, Stephanie Zacharek, Charley Taylor, Maria Russo, Amy Reiter, and my favorite Jersey girl, Meghan Johnson Womack—with whom I have been having a conversation for twenty-five years—I am forever grateful to you all.

My years in Turkey have been a dream only because of so many Istanbullular. The Aydıntaşbaş family—Aslı, Defne, Figen, Mert, and Garo—welcomed me before I even arrived and embraced me with love. Aslı, thank you for teaching me everything about Turkish politics and for your unwavering friendship. I also learned immensely from Gül Tuysuz, Özsel Beleli, Zehra Altaylı, Zeynel Gül, Özge Kelekçi, Naciye Çitil, Fatoş Minaz, the brilliant Kristin Fabbe, and countless others. For fun and friendship: Maddy and Ansel, Sabrina Tavernise, Nichole Sobecki, Kathryn Cook, Patrick Legant, Lynsey Addario, Jed Boyar and Gloria Fisk, Bicey and Izzy. Elif Batuman, Jenna Krajeski, and Sarah Topol have been the most loyal and entertaining of late-night companions, as has Olga, who taught me all things Greek. To Marc, my favorite debate partner, and to Sibel, for her shrewd analysis of all things. To Caner, who still answers my thousand questions. To Rana, who still makes Istanbul magical. And to the beautiful people of Turkey: thank you for sharing with me your wondrous country.

Jessica Alexander and Hillary Frey—your friendship, love, and humor have been the great comforts of my life. Thank you both for being there, every day, in that ever reassuring little corner on my computer screen. I love you.

Peter Kaplan taught me how to exhaust every angle of an idea for hours, and then—just when I thought I had come up with something new to say—to look at it slightly sideways. It was in a messy office in New York that I learned how to think. His words of encouragement were like fairy dust. I miss him every day.

Pankaj Mishra and Mary Mount listened patiently to me every time I came out of Istanbul, eager to tell them of my very American realizations about it. I wanted to write a book about Turkey; Mary said, "Your book is about America." Pankaj, our conversations, and your endless book recommendations, were my entry into a world of ideas, and indeed into the rest of the world. Thank you both for your faith and generosity.

To my father, who braved the roads of Cappadocia and who loves to argue with me; to my brother, who told me to write every day and to notice the trees; and to my mother, who took me to the library, bought me the college books, and cheered me on with curiosity and humor—you never asked for my ten-year absence, but it is all of you who made this life possible.

INDEX

A NOTE ABOUT THE AUTHOR

Suzy Hansen is a contributing writer for *The New York Times Magazine* and has written for many other publications. In 2007, she was awarded a fellowship from the Institute of Current World Affairs to do research in Turkey. She lives in Istanbul. *Notes on a Foreign Country* is her first book.